POLITICS UNDER THE
LATER STUARTS

STUDIES IN MODERN HISTORY

General editors: John Morrill and David Cannadine

This series, intended primarily for students, will tackle significant historical issues in concise volumes which are both stimulating and scholarly. The authors combine a broad approach, explaining the current state of our knowledge in the area, with their own research and judgements; and the topics chosen range widely in subject, period and place.

Titles already published

POLITICS UNDER THE LATER STUARTS

Party Conflict in a Divided Society

1660–1715

Tim Harris

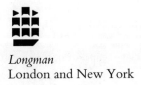

Longman
London and New York

Longman Group UK Limited
Longman House, Burnt Mill,
Harlow, Essex CM20 2JE, England
and Associated Companies throughout the world.

*Published in the United States of America
by Longman Publishing, New York*

© Longman Group UK Limited 1993

First published 1993

ISBN 0 582 04081 7 CSD
ISBN 0 582 04082 5 PPR

British Library Cataloguing in Publication Data
A catalogue record for this book is
available from the British Library

Library of Congress Cataloging in Publication Data
Harris, Tim, 1958–
    Politics under the later Stuarts : party conflict in a divided
society, 1660–1715 / Tim Harris.
      p.   cm. -- (Studies in modern history)
    Includes bibliographical references and index.
    ISBN 0–582–04081–7. -- ISBN 0–582–04082–5 (pbk.)
      1. Great Britian--Politics and government--1660–1714.
  2. Political parties--Great Britain--History--17th century.
  3. Political parties--Great Britain--History--18th century.
  I. Title.   II. Series: Studies in modern history (Longman (Firm))
DA435.H243 1993
324.241'00941--dc20   92–13841
                                                                              CIP

Set 7B in 10/11pt Bembo
Produced by Longman Singapore Publishers (Pte) Ltd.
Printed in Singapore

Contents

Contents

Preface

My decision to write this book stemmed largely from the frustrations I felt as a teacher about the lack of a short, analytical book on the origins and nature of party politics in England covering the period 1660–1715 as a whole. Admittedly there are several excellent monographs, but these by their nature are rather specialised, and it has always required an extensive amount of reading for a student, coming fresh to this period, to acquire a basic grasp of the intricacies of English politics in the first age of party. In addition, insights generated by my own research have led me to question some of the received wisdom found in textbooks covering this period. In short, I felt there was a need for a book synthesising the latest research in a relatively brief and coherent manner which could serve as a way of introducing new students to the many exciting issues of late-Stuart politics, but one which at the same time would be sufficiently grounded in original research so as to have something new to say to scholars in the field.

The process of researching and writing this book soon made it clear to me why no-one has ever published such a book in the past. The topic of party politics in late-Stuart England is an extremely complicated one, and it is impossible to do justice to all the complexities, over such a wide timespan, and keep the book straightforward and brief enough to be accessible to a non-specialist audience. Inevitably I have had to make compromises, and some areas could not be explored as fully as I would have liked. Very early on it became clear that it would not be possible to write a truly British history. The development of parties in Scotland, which was a self-governing Kingdom until the Union of 1707, was a very different affair, and to have tried to cover that topic as well would have meant diluting the depth of the analysis more than I would have wished. Although Scotland does make an appearance in the text where appropriate, what I offer is largely an Anglo-centric history, concentrating on the institutions of English (and Welsh) politics. In writing this book, I have tried not to take too much knowledge for granted, and I have felt it necessary to spend time on many things which will be quite familiar to experts. On the other hand, this is certainly not a textbook; chronological narrative has been kept to a minimum, with the emphasis being on analysis, and wherever possible I have drawn extensively on my own research, so that the book contains not only new material but also a number of novel insights. My aim has been to raise questions and to suggest ways of thinking about party politics in this period, and if I manage to stimulate fresh interest in this period amongst students and scholars, then the book will have served its purpose.

There is a danger that the debate about the nature of party politics in late-Stuart England can get hung up over the definition of terms. This can be unproductive. Different historians might essentially agree in their understanding of political conflict in this period, but whereas some might be prepared to describe what was happening as 'party conflict', others might so define party as to argue that it is inappropriate to talk about party politics at this time. Definitions are, of course, important, but understanding what was going on is more so; it would be unfortunate if the debate came to focus on the validity of the labels used to describe what was happening, rather than on the interpretation of the history. I do offer my own definition of party in the introduction, and we should clearly expect a political party to evince some degree of ideological and organisational coherence. Yet our criteria should not be too unrealistic. Even in modern Britain, we may question how ideologically coherent the two great parties are; divisions can be detected over fairly fundamental issues of principle in both the Labour and Conservative parties. Many parties in modern democracies are monolithic neither in organisation nor in policy – the examples of France, Italy and the United States spring to mind, yet no-one would deny that parties exist today in these countries.

In writing a book of this nature one inevitably accumulates a large number of debts. Perhaps the greatest lies to the scholars who have already worked in this field; I have drawn heavily on their work in places, and although I give formal acknowledgement in both the footnotes and the bibliography, they deserve to be thanked again here. I should also like to thank the Master and Fellows of Emmanuel College, Cambridge – my former College – who made me so welcome on my various research trips back to England, lunching and dining me, giving me a place to stay (when needed), and even allowing me the occasional game of bowls to recoup my spirits. I am also indebted to the President and Fellows of Wolfson College, Oxford, who elected me to a Charter Fellowship when I was on sabbatical leave from Brown during the spring semester of 1990. Much of the research for this book was undertaken whilst I was at Wolfson; I hope the end result is a sufficient testimony to how much I enjoyed my stay there. I am also extremely grateful to the staffs of the various libraries and repositories where research for this book was undertaken. I cannot mention all of them here (again, some form of acknowledgement is given in the footnotes), but I should offer some special thanks to the staff of the Bodleian Library, Oxford, the University Library, Cambridge, the British Library, London, and the Rockefeller Library, Brown University. I am particularly indebted to Eveline Cruickshanks and David Hayton, of the History of Parliament Trust (and everyone else in their office), who allowed me access to the data they are collecting for the volume of the History of Parliament covering the years 1690-1715. I should also like to thank Brown University for the intellectual and financial support they gave me whilst writing the book, and in particular the Watson Institute for International Studies, which provided grants towards the cost of my trips back to England.

A number of scholars spent a great deal of time reading over drafts of the book. I am especially grateful to Mark Goldie and John Morrill, who read everything I wrote very closely, and gave me much valuable, critical feedback. David Hayton read several draft chapters and not only provided many helpful references and insights, but also saved me from a number of errors. I must also thank my publishers for their time, patience, and moral support, and John Morrill and David Cannadine, who are the general editors for the series in which the book appears. Some of the themes of this book were presented at colloquia or seminars on both sides of the Atlantic – at Brown, Harvard, Worcester (Massachusetts), Yale, and Cambridge (England) – and I gained tremendously from the comments and remarks offered by the various audiences there. Steve Pincus – who as a fellow researcher in late-Stuart history seems to have been following me around the world these last few years – has been a constant source of stimulus, and we have had many lively discussions about problems of interpretation and sources (including additional manuscript reference numbers) in Cambridge, London, Oxford, the other Cambridge, Providence and – would you believe – San José. I have also learned a lot from conversations with Jeremy Black, Eveline Cruickshanks, Rebecca Epstein, Andrew Hanham, Stuart Handley, Mark Kishlansky, Mark Knights, Becky More and Bill Speck.

A number of students at Brown have given me much critical feedback on this book. In particular, I should like to thank those graduate students who were forced to do research seminars on party politics in late-Stuart England: Todd Galitz, Susannah Ottaway, Shambie Singer, Ingrid Tague and Dan Tapiero. All of them read with care and scepticism all the draft chapters of this book. Jonathan Dreyfous served as my undergraduate research assistant for one semester, and helped me work on pamphlet sources for chapter six, whilst Dan Tapiero spent another semester helping me piece together material for chapter seven. I have always prided myself that I train my students to develop a critical and independent way of thinking, to challenge everything that they are told, and I tell them that if they end up disagreeing with me (and can provide a compelling intellectual justification for that disagreement), then that is the greatest compliment I can receive. There were times when I wished these particular students had not learnt that lesson quite so well; they proved an especially difficult group to please, but their criticisms certainly sharpened my own thinking about many of the issues I explore, and undoubtedly this book is much better for their input.

I owe a special debt to my family. My wife and children – Beth, Victoria and James – had to put up with me during the writing and researching of this book; even if they never saw me, they knew I was up in the attic somewhere scribbling away at various drafts. My parents – Ron and Audrey – on the other hand, had to put me and the rest of us up on our trips back to England; it is so convenient that they bought a house half-way between Heathrow and Gatwick airports, right on the M25. In return for their support and love over the years – and also the provision of the airport taxi service – I dedicate this book to them.

Abbreviations

BIHR	*Bulletin of the Institute of Historical Research*
BL	British Library
Bodl. Lib.	Bodleian Library
Burnet, *History*	*Bishop Burnet's History of His Own Time: From The Restoration of Charles II to the Treaty of Peace at Utrecht, in the Reign of Queen Anne* (1838)
CHJ	*Cambridge Historical Journal*
CJ	*Journals of the House of Commons*
CLRO	Corporation of London Record Office
CSPD	*Calendar of State Papers, Domestic*
CSPVen	*Calendar of State Papers, Venetian*
EHR	*English Historical Review*
Evelyn, *Diary*	*The Diary of John Evelyn*, E. S. De Beer (ed.) (Oxford, 1952)
GLRO	Greater London Record Office
Grey, *Debates*	Anchitell Grey, *Debates of the House of Commons, from the year 1667 to the year 1694* (10 vols, 1763)
HJ	*Historical Journal*
HLQ	*Huntington Library Quarterly*
HLRO	House of Lords Record Office
HMC	*Historical Manuscripts Commission*
JBS	*Journal of British Studies*
JEccH	*Journal of Ecclesiastical History*
LJ	*Journals of the House of Lords*
Pepys, *Diary*	*The Diary of Samuel Pepys*, Robert Latham and William Matthews (eds) (11 vols, 1970–83)
POAS	*Poems on Affairs of State*, G. de Forest Lord et al. (ed.) (7 vols, New Haven, 1963–75)

Abbreviations

PP	*Past and Present*
PRO	Public Record Office
State Trials	*A Complete Collection of State Trials*, T. B. Howell (ed.) (13 vols, 1816–26)
TRHS	*Transactions of the Royal Historical Society*
VCH	*Victoria County History*

Note: All works cited were published in London unless otherwise stated. In quoting from primary sources I have retained the original spelling, although I have extended contemporary contractions and occasionally supplied punctuation necessary to the sense of the passage. Dates are given in the Old Style, but with the year regarded as beginning on 1 January. I am extremely grateful to the Trustees of the History of Parliament for giving me permission to use and cite unpublished material to which they hold the copyright.

For Ron and Audrey

CHAPTER ONE

Introduction

The later-Stuart period saw the emergence of party politics in England. From the late 1660s contemporaries began to talk of the existence of rival Court and Country groupings in Parliament, whilst as early as February 1673 the MP, Sir Thomas Meres, could make a distinction between 'this side of the house, and that side'.[1] By the mid-1670s it became common to accuse one's political opponents of belonging to a party, and to talk of a basic split between the Court and the Country. The terms 'Whig' and 'Tory' were first employed as party labels during the Exclusion Crisis of 1679-81, becoming common usage from 1681.[2] This crisis had arisen following the revelations made in the late summer and autumn of 1678 of a Popish Plot to kill the King, Charles II, which brought heightened anxieties about the security of the Protestant religion at a time when the heir to the throne – Charles's brother, James, Duke of York – was himself a Catholic. Two rival groups with distinct platforms now emerged: the 'Whigs', as they were soon christened, who sought to get Parliament to pass an Act excluding the Duke of York from the succession, and the 'Tories', who opposed this policy and defended the hereditary succession to the Crown. Although James was eventually 'excluded' from the throne by the Glorious Revolution of 1688-9, conflict between Whigs and Tories continued to be a central feature of political life, and reached a new intensity in the early eighteenth century under Queen Anne, before party passions gradually began to cool following the Hanoverian Succession of 1714.

Despite the importance of the theme, there is no study which traces the growth and nature of party politics in England between the reigns of Charles II and Queen Anne. The closest we have is J.H. Plumb's account of the growth of political stability in England bet-ween 1675 and 1725, based on his Ford Lectures of 1965, an important book in its day, which has much to say in passing about the instability caused by party strife during this period, although mainly for the period after the Glorious Revolution.[3] One of the rare books to explore the history of party politics from its inception until the Hanoverian Succession is Sir Keith Feiling's study of the first Tory party published in 1924, although needless to say this is now rather old and covers only half of the story.[4] In fact, with the exception of text-books and some works of political biography and intellectual history, few studies of later-Stuart politics cover the years 1660-1714 in their entirety; instead, most accounts focus on the period either before or after the Glorious Revolution, with the result that our understanding of the development of party has become truncated, cut in half by the events of 1688-9. Most of the scholarship concentrates on the years from the Glorious Revolution to the Hanoverian Succession. Thus we have some excellent specialised monographs on politics under William III and Anne,[5] early eighteenth-century elections,[6] and Church–State re-lations,[7] as well as a more general survey[8] and a collection of sources with an extended commentary on the partisan divisions within English society during the years 1694–1716,[9] though even here our understanding of party conflict is continually being expanded and refined by the latest research. In contrast, the only modern study we have specifically on party politics before the Glorious Revolution is J. R. Jones's study of the first Whigs, published as long ago as 1961![10] In the last few years, however, there has been a resurgence of scholarly interest in the Restoration era, and a number of new monographs and articles have appeared offering a fundamental revision to our understanding of politics under Charles II and James II, and inviting a fresh examination of the development of party strife during this time.

A modern, thematic analysis of the first age of party in England is desperately needed for a number of reasons. At a basic level, there is a need for an up-to-date synthesis of the existing scholarly literature, consolidating the findings of specialised research undertaken in the past few years, and presenting them in a format which will be more accessible to a wider audience. Furthermore, the range and depth of recent research has been such that there now exist a number of unresolved historiographical controversies and differences of interpretation – particularly for the period prior to the Glorious Revolution, but even, to a lesser degree, for the period thereafter – which require resolution. These specific historiographical debates will be considered

Introduction

in their appropriate places in the chapters that follow. The most serious deficiency with the current state of scholarship, however, concerns the fact that so few studies have attempted to span the Glorious Revolution. As a result, our perspective on party politics under the later Stuarts has been seriously hampered. The historiography of the respective halves of the period has developed so independently, that not only do we have no clear understanding of how we get from the world of the 1680s to that of the early eighteenth century, but it is even the case that some of the conventional wisdom about party under Charles II is difficult to reconcile with what is known about party under William and Anne.

This last point can be illustrated in a number of ways. Let us start with the question of the genesis of party itself. Historians with their roots in the Restoration have traditionally located the origins of party either in the emergence of the Court–Country divide in the 1670s or, more commonly, in the clash between Whigs and Tories during the Exclusion Crisis. J. R. Jones, for example, believes that both the first Whigs and the first Tories were 'unmistakably parties', and has written of the 'rage of party' between 1679 and 1681, although he does concede that it would be wrong, as yet, to talk of the existence of a two-party system.[11] Scholars who do not venture before 1688, by contrast, tend to see the period after the Glorious Revolution as the first age of party. For B. W. Hill, 'the beginnings of the party system of modern Britain coincided with the emergence of Parliament as a permanent institution' from 1689.[12] At the same time, however, the years immediately following the Glorious Revolution are normally seen as witnessing a temporary blurring of the old party distinctions, so that during the early 1690s we find Country Whigs and Country Tories combining in opposition to a mixed administration. If the Exclusion Crisis is an illegitimate point from which to date the first age of party, why, then, is 1689 any better? There are some who would maintain that although the first Whigs of the Exclusion Crisis might qualify as a party, the first Tories certainly do not, since it was not until after 1689 that they developed any identity independent of the Court.[13] Yet how can the validity of such an argument be tested unless we have a history of both parties which spans the Glorious Revolution?

The divergence between pre- and post-1688 scholarship has also created tensions in our understanding of the significance of religion in the political struggles of this era. Until very recently, Restoration historians tended to stress the secular nature of politics after 1660. Jones believes that the Restoration era saw 'the demotion of religion from its previously dominant position' as a source of political tension, which

3

he attributes to 'a spread of religious indifferentism'. Although there were a handful of older Whigs who were motivated by a genuine zeal for religious reform, 'few of the younger Whigs', he tells us, 'were absorbed by religious questions'.[14] Plumb has characterised 'the question of Dissent' as one of those 'difficult' but nevertheless 'minor problems' facing successive governments after 1660.[15] It is true that 'fear of popery' played an important part in generating party conflict towards the end of Charles II's reign, but the concern here, it is normally suggested, was more political than it was religious, since 'popery' was associated with a particular style of government: the royal absolutism practised by Louis XIV in France.[16] Most accounts of early eighteenth-century party, by contrast, stress the central importance of religious issues, and especially 'the question of Dissent', as a source of partisan strife under Queen Anne. Thus Geoffrey Holmes, the leading scholar of Anne's reign, has argued that 'the status of religious minorities, the future of the religious establishment and the very health of religion itself' were 'among the most obtrusive and emotive issues confronting the lay politicians and the electorate' and 'the cause of bitter divisions between Tories and Whigs'.[17]

There are a number of interesting questions concerning change over time which cannot be adequately explained by a historiography cut in half by the events of 1688-9. For example, it is normally thought that in Charles II's reign the Whigs were a Country party, whilst the Tories were the party of the Court; by Anne's reign these roles seem to have been reversed, with the Whigs now emerging as a Court party, and the Tories as champions of the Country platform. Likewise, the first Whigs are normally thought to have been the party of the people; by the time of the Sacheverell affair of 1710, however, 'the mob' appears to be on the side of the Tories. Existing accounts explain these transformations in terms of developments that happened in the reign of William III, during which time the Whigs gradually abandoned their erstwhile Country stance and lost their former popular appeal. Without a longer perspective, however, it is impossible to tell how much this alleged transformation involved a shift in party principles, or the extent to which the Whigs and Tories of the end of Anne's reign were the recognisable heirs of those groups which had come into existence during the Exclusion Crisis. In fact, recent research has shown that, contrary to received wisdom, the Tories did have a considerable popular following during the reign of Charles II.[18] Does this mean that previous attempts to explain the supposed shift in popular political allegiances after 1689 have been misguided?

In short, a book on party politics in England between the Restoration and the Hanoverian succession will not only rectify a serious lacuna in the existing historiography, but also facilitate the resolution of a number of historical issues which can only be satisfactorily explored through an analysis which covers the later-Stuart period as a whole. Before embarking on the substantive analysis, however, it is necessary to begin by defining our terms and saying something about the conceptual approach to be taken in this study.

Our first responsibility is to clarify what we mean by the term party. It is important to avoid anachronistic definitions. Later-Stuart parties were not like their modern-day counterparts, with highly-developed central organisations, paid-up membership, party conferences and detailed manifestoes. The key determinant of party in the seventeenth and eighteenth centuries, so far as contemporaries were concerned, was not organisational structure, but political allegiance. As the author of *The Detector Detected* (1743) put it: 'A Party is, when a great Number of Men join together in Professing a Principle, or Set of Principles, which they take to be for the Publick Good, and therefore endeavour to have them established and universally professed among their own countrymen'.[19] Unity based on 'professed principles' distinguished parties from 'factions', which were groups of men united purely for the advancement of their own political self-interest, and from 'connections', which were groups of men united first and foremost by family and patronage ties. This is not to say that party politicians were unconcerned with promoting their own political self-interest, or that family and patronage ties were unimportant to party formation; it is merely to state that party was something more than mere faction or connection. Such 'joining together' inevitably required some degree of organisation, to co-ordinate tactics and ensure unity of action. Yet party organisation developed gradually over time in order to help cement a common political identity that had already been formed. Things could not have been otherwise; it is not as if a group of people suddenly decided to form a political organisation, and then sat around trying to work out what principles they agreed on. In short, organisation, although important, was nevertheless a secondary development; rather than stressing organisational structure, it is better to see party during this period primarily in terms of political identity.

Parties can be distinguished from pressure groups in the sense that they seek to achieve their aims through the pursuit of political power for themselves, whereas the latter merely seek to persuade those in power to agree to implement their objectives. Hence our analysis of party must look extensively at political struggles in Parliament. Yet it should also be stressed that for a group to constitute a party its shared political principles have to be publicly professed, with the aim of cultivating public support for its cause. Thus our examination cannot restrict itself to the goings-on at Westminster, but must also investigate the various media through which party principles were expressed (pamphlets, newspapers, sermons, and so forth), as well as the political sympathies of the nation at large.[20]

As indicated by the title, this book covers the years 1660–1715. The intention is not to suggest that the whole of this period was an age of party strife, nor that parties were born in 1660, nor even that once they had come into being parties remained essentially the same creatures until the terminal dates set by this study. What needs to be stressed is that the emergence of party politics was not an event but a *process*, which took several decades to work itself out. Although it might be possible to talk about the existence of Whig and Tory parties during the Exclusion Crisis, these two groups were not yet as cohesive and well-organised as they were to become under Anne. Likewise, the subsequent history of party under the later Stuarts is impossible to understand without considering developments that took place during the 1660s and 1670s, even though this study would argue that parties as such did not really come into being until after the Popish Plot. In addition to exploring the nature of party conflict, therefore, this book will examine the process of party formation. And since parties were defined first and foremost by shared attachment to certain professed principles, it is necessary to begin by investigating the ideological roots of the partisan divide, a search which takes us back not to 1689, nor to 1679, nor even to the mid-1670s, but to 1660, and the restoration of the monarchy.

The claim that we need to start as early as 1660 is contentious, and needs some justification. Until recently, most historians would have endorsed the view that the political tensions that emerged under Charles II were the result of 'essentially new (post-1660) developments and changes' which created 'new situations and new sets of problems for the restored monarch and his ministers'.[21] The roots of party strife are normally traced to the concerns about popery and arbitrary government which began to appear in the 1660s and 1670s in response to the religious leanings and political practices of the Court. Although the importance of these new developments and situations should not be denied, many of the political tensions we see in the later-Stuart period were related to issues and problems which derived from the political and religious struggles of the 1640s and 1650s, and had been left unresolved by the Restoration. Although most people welcomed the return of monarchy in 1660, there was little consensus over what sort of monarchy should be restored. There were disagreements over how much power the King should have, with some wanting Charles II restored to all the powers his father had enjoyed, and others wanting a monarchy severely constrained by Parliament. There were also disagreements over the desired religious settlement: hard-line Anglicans wanted the restoration of the old Church of the bishops and the Prayer Book, with no toleration for those who refused to conform; Presbyterians and moderate Anglicans favoured keeping certain reforms that would enable most people to be comprehended within a national Church; whilst separatists wanted to be granted liberty of conscience.

Given the wide range of expectations different groups had of the Restoration, it was inevitable that whatever settlement was worked out, some were bound to be left dissatisfied. The constitutional settlement restored the monarchy to its position on the eve of the Civil War, avoiding any stringent limitations, but keeping most of the reforms passed in the early months of the Long Parliament in 1640–1, which had been designed to prevent a repeat of the experiment with personal rule of the 1630s. Nevertheless, there remained much room for argument over precisely what the constitutional position of the Crown was, leaving a potential for conflict between those who wanted the monarchy to develop in a more autocratic direction and those who stressed the Parliamentary nature of the English monarchy. In religion, the High Anglican vision won out; neither comprehension nor toleration was achieved, and a fierce penal code was established with harsh penalties for those who failed to conform to the re-established Church, causing much bitterness and creating one of the most serious and enduring sources of political tension, namely the conflict between the Church and Dissent.

Contemporaries often traced the emergence of party tensions back to the Restoration. For example, in 1675 the leading Country spokesman and future Whig, the Earl of Shaftesbury, in his famous attack on the policies being pursued by the government under the Earl of Danby's administration, complained of 'a Project of several Years standing . . . to make a distinct Party from the rest of the Nation of the High Episcopal Man, and the Old Cavalier', which he dated back to at least 1661.[22] The Tory Francis North, writing during the Exclusion Crisis, thought that England's troubles could be blamed on republicans, Presbyterians and sectarians, who had been 'Restless under the Monarchy' and 'under Episcopacy, from the first Resetlement of it upon their legall foundation'.[23] Likewise, the Tory publicist Edmund Bohun, writing in 1682, traced the beginnings of the Whig plot against the Church and State 'from the Time his Majesty set his Foot upon the English shores at his Return'.[24] Throughout our period, the rhetoric of party strife reflected a preoccupation with Civil War issues, with Whigs being compared with the Parliamentarians, Puritans and republicans of the 1640s and 1650s, and the Tories with the Cavalier supporters of Charles I. In this context it is interesting to note that we can find country people in Somerset using the term 'Tory' as a synonym for 'Cavalier' as early as 1655, long before it came into common usage in England as a party label.[25]

Recognising the importance of the Civil War legacy forces us to revise our opinion about the predominantly secular nature of politics after 1660. Political conflict in Restoration England developed along two major axes: the constitutional, involving questions about the relative balance of power between Crown and Parliament, the extent of the royal prerogative, and the potential for corruption by the Court; and the religious, centring around the issue of the Church and Dissent. Neither axis should be treated in isolation, since the process of party formation in later-Stuart England is the story of the interaction of both constitutional and religious sources of conflict. Of the two, however, primacy of place belonged to religious factors in the determination of party identity, with the Whigs being the party sympathetic towards Dissent and the Tories the champions of High Anglican intolerance. The language which contemporaries used to describe the partisan conflicts of their day reflected the priority of religious considerations. Thus 'Whig' had initially meant a Scottish Presbyterian rebel, 'Tory' an Irish Catholic. In the late 1670s and 1680s, however, before these new labels became common, Whigs were more frequently described as 'fanaticks', 'covenanters', and 'the Presbyterian party', whilst the Tories were styled 'the Church party', 'the episcopal party', 'tantivies', and 'high flown church men'.[26] Daniel Defoe, writing at the turn of the century, noted that although the 'two contending Parties' had over the years frequently changed their names, 'as Cavalier and Roundhead, Royalists and Rebels, Malignants and Phanaticks, Tories and Whigs, yet the Division has always been barely the Church and the Dissenter, and there it continues to this Day'.[27] Even as late as Anne's reign, by which time the terms Whig and Tory had become the predominant usage, it was still common to use the vocabulary of Church politics, and to talk in terms of distinctions between 'the High Church Party' or 'the Church of England Party', and 'the Low-Church Party' (as the Whigs were now being called).[28]

The addition of the religious dimension to the traditional constitutional frame of reference not only allows for a more subtle interpretation of Restoration politics, but it also forces a reconsideration of the relationship between Tory–Whig and Court–Country tensions. It is true that during the last ten years of Charles II's reign High Anglicans tended to champion the cause of strong monarchy in England, whilst the fiercest opponents of the Court tended to be those who were most hostile to the intolerance of the High Anglican establishment. Yet to assume that prior to the Glorious Revolution the Tory interest was inevitably associated with the Court, and the Whig with the Country opposition, would be misleading. Because at times both Charles II and James II showed themselves to be better friends to Dissent than did their Parliaments, we can on occasion find the High Anglican interest aligning against the Court in order to defend the Church and the Dissenting interest rallying behind the Crown in the hope of securing relief from religious persecution. Likewise it would be wrong to assume that the split between the Whigs and the Tories during the Restoration era corresponded to a straightforward clash between champions of Parliamentary constitutionalism and of royal absolutism. Cavaliers and High Anglicans saw the Restoration as marking the return to constitutional propriety after the tyrannies and constitutional irregularities committed by the Parliamentarian and republican regimes during the 1640s and 1650s, and looked to the rule of law to protect their vision of the proper order in both Church and State. In short, we can often find the Church party, or the first Tories as they were to become, acting independently of the Court under Charles II (and especially under James II); indeed, we can even identify a potential for what might be called a Country-Tory position prior to the Glorious Revolution.

Historians have tended to downplay the importance of the issue of Dissent in Restoration politics because Nonconformists were only a tiny minority of the population. A religious census of 1676, commissioned by the Earl of Danby but executed by Bishop Compton of London, found that Nonconformists comprised just under 5 per cent of the population. This figure was certainly a gross underestimate. The task of compiling the data about Nonconformists was left to local parish incumbents, but an ambiguity in the wording of the instructions sent out in the province of Canterbury left it unclear whether they were being asked to make a return of those who failed to take the sacrament or those who had completely withdrawn from the services of the Church of England. As a result, for some areas the returns enumerate only those who had totally separated themselves from the Church of England, such as Quakers and Baptists, omitting such groups as occasional conformists, Presbyterians and Independents, who divided their allegiances between conventicles and the established Church. How one interpreted the instructions could make a huge difference to the numbers reported, as indicated by the few returns where the incumbents specifically addressed the ambiguity in the instructions. The vicar of St Lawrence in Thanet, for example, reported that of 1,200 inhabitants over the age of sixteen, only fifty people 'wholly absent themselves from the church' (about 4 per cent) but that 'there are not two hundred that receive the holy sacrament once in a year' (which would put the total number of those who were not communicating Anglicans at 83 per cent). Similarly the minister of Stoke by Clare, in the diocese of Norwich, found that of 295 parishioners who were of age to receive, 276 'either obstinately refuse or wholly neglect and absent themselves from the communion of the lord's supper' (94 per cent), although no more than twenty (7 per cent) 'either obstinately refuse or wholly neglect themselves from the communion of the church during the time of divine service'.[29] Not all who failed to take the sacrament, of course, did so out of religious scruple; many can probably be counted as lax Anglicans. However, we do know that the practices of occasional conformity and occasional nonconformity were fairly widespread, which means that the dividing line between Dissenters and Anglicans was not always easy to draw. In December 1681 the Bishop of Salisbury reported the existence in his cathedral city of 'a Samaritan Conventicle of persons Pretending themselves friends of our Church, partakers of the publick Service and Sacraments and afterwards resorting to an exercise of a presbiterian'.[30] There was even a problem with clerical non- or partial conformity. A sizeable number of those clergy who had served under the Commonwealth or Protectorate regimes conformed after 1662 – about half the churches and chapels in the dioceses of Canterbury and Winchester in 1663 were served by Commonwealth conformists – and many of them held on to old Puritan practices. We hear frequent reports of clergy who refused to wear the surplice, allowed people to receive the sacrament standing, dispensed with the sign of the cross in baptism, or who in general had a rather relaxed attitude towards the stricter rules of conformity.[31] In 1682 the Archbishop of Canterbury, William Sancroft, received a complaint that a minister of Lyme, Dorset, was 'half Nonconformist, for every Sunday, after he hath preached in the afternoon he goes home, layes aside his Gown, putts on a jump Coat, causeth a bell to be tolled, upon which the Dissenters come to Church, to whom he prayes ex tempore, repeats all his Sermon in a canting language, and this he calls bringing them to Church'.[32] Furthermore, it must be remembered that Nonconformists often had conformist relatives, friends and neighbours, who sympathised with their plight. A recent study of Huntingdonshire, Cambridgeshire and Bedfordshire, where Dissent was fairly widespread geographically and sociologically, has concluded that 'almost every early modern family, whatever their social rank, must have known a Dissenter'.[33] Our impression of the religious balance in this society would be very different if, instead of trying to establish how many people were out-and-out Nonconformists, we asked how many were out-and-out Anglicans. The sources do not permit us to answer such a question, of course, but it is certain that those who were totally committed to the Church of England as re-established after the Restoration were far from being the preponderant majority of the population as suggested by the findings of the Compton Census.

The Compton Census is equally unreliable as a guide to the geographical distribution of Dissent, since the practice of incumbents with regard to reporting occasional conformists was not uniform. Supplementing the evidence of the Compton Census with data about the number of licences taken out under the provisions of the Declaration of Indulgence of 1672 we find that Dissent was strongest in the southeast (especially London and Middlesex) and in the west country (particularly Devon and Somerset).[34] Having said that, it is clear that Dissenters were to be found in most parts of the country, and that there could be strong concentrations of certain Nonconformist groups in parts of the north, the west midlands and Wales.[35] Contemporaries were convinced that Dissent was primarily an urban phenomenon. Two ecclesiasts as different as Samuel Parker, James II's Bishop of Oxford, or Gilbert Burnet, who became Bishop of Salisbury after the Glorious Revolution, agreed that the bulk of Nonconformists was concentrated in the cities and the corporations.[36] Daniel Defoe, himself a Nonconformist, thought that 'the Dissenters in England, generally speaking, are the Men of Trade and Industry'.[37] Local historians have confirmed that some urban areas housed considerable concentrations of Nonconformists. According to one recent estimate, some 15–20 per cent of the population of London in the early eighteenth century were Dissenters; the figure was undoubtedly higher for the Restoration period. Over one third of the population of Lewes (Sussex) were Nonconformists, whilst in Coventry (in the west midlands) Dissenters formed somewhere between 25 per cent and 40 per cent of the population.[38] There was also a significant Dissenting presence in Norwich, Bristol and many of the west country towns.[39] Where Dissent did flourish in the countryside, it was often in areas of rural industry, such as the cloth-producing region of Wiltshire.[40]

Yet we should not exaggerate the urban or industrial nature of Dissent. Early seventeenth-century historians have taught us that Puritanism attracted a significant following amongst certain sections of the nobility and gentry, and there is evidence to suggest that many members of the rural elite remained attached to the same type of Puritan tradition after the Restoration, perhaps not being out-and-out Dissenters themselves, but nevertheless being critical of the Anglican establishment and occasionally attending or supporting Nonconformist conventicles.[41] Indeed, the development of party tensions in the Restoration cannot properly be understood without appreciating that a significant number of the gentry who served in Parliament as MPs and who ruled the localities in their capacity as JPs retained some sympathy towards Dissent. Some of the rural poor could also be attracted to Dissent, as the work of Margaret Spufford on Cambridgeshire has shown.[42] In Huntingdonshire, Cambridgeshire and Bedfordshire Dissenters were drawn from all sections of society: not just from the professional, manufacturing, trading and labouring classes of the towns, but also from gentlemen, yeomen, husbandmen and labourers in the countryside.[43] It is significant that when the Quaker William Penn suggested that the Dissenters were 'a chief part of the trading people of the nation', he explicitly included farmers in this category in addition to the trading classes of the towns.[44]

More work needs to be done on the sociology of Dissent in Restoration England. At the present state of research we can perhaps agree with the contemporary witness who in 1667 observed that Nonconformists were 'spread through city and country; they make no small part of all ranks and all sorts of men. They are not excluded from the nobility, among the gentry they are not a few; but none are more important than the trading part of the people'.[45] There are reasons to suspect, however, that the social composition of the Nonconformist population changed over time. By Anne's reign the older Puritan tradition amongst the rural landed elite seems to have declined, as some of the old Dissenting families converted to Anglicanism (the Harleys of Herefordshire being an important case in point), so that by the early eighteenth century Dissent may have been a more distinctly urban phenomenon.

Roman Catholics comprised a tiny minority of the population: a mere 1.2 per cent according to one recent estimate.[46] The figure is suprisingly small given the intense terror of popery shared by most English people in the later-Stuart period, and has led historians to conclude that popery was feared not so much as a domestic religious threat, but as a political threat, associated with the popish leanings of the royal Court under Charles II and James II and the challenge posed to Protestant security in Europe by Catholic France under Louis XIV.[47]However, certain qualifications need to be made to this view. Roman Catholics were not evenly distributed across the country, but tended to be concentrated in pockets. In particular, they were strong in the north (especially Lancashire), and parts of the west midlands and Welsh borderlands (especially Herefordshire and Monmouthshire), and in such areas concerns about popery often were a direct result of local religious tensions between Protestants and Catholics.[48] Furthermore, anxieties about popery also fed into the domestic religious tensions between Anglicans and Dissenters. Nonconformists frequently complained about what they saw as being relics of popery within the Church of England, condemning certain Anglican rituals (such as kneeling for the sacrament) and forms of Church government – even the bishops themselves – as being popish. Many Anglicans, on the other hand, saw the threat posed to the established Church by the Dissenters as tantamount to popery; whatever their precise theological differences, both the Pope and the Protestant Nonconformists had the same ultimate end, they believed, namely to destroy the Church of England.[49] The intensity of people's fear of popery at this time can only be understood once we realise that the struggle for the proper settlement in the Church was invariably articulated within the rhetoric of anti-popery.

Our earlier definition suggested that parties, as distinct from factions or connections, deliberately seek to cultivate support for their position amongst the nation at large, and that party principles have to be publicly professed. A major concern of this book, therefore, will be a consideration of how far down into society party divisions permeated. During this period it was not just the political elite at the centre who became polarised along Whig–Tory lines; party rivalry can also be detected at the local level, in the shires and corporations, amongst the electorate, and even amongst the 'crowd', at the level of street politics. Of course, not all communities were torn by party strife, and not all that were experienced the same intensity of partisan rivalry at all times. In most places local issues interacted with national ones to give a distinctive dimension to party identity on the ground level. Yet it is clear that no study of party can afford to limit itself to the goings-on at Westminster, but must endeavour to set its findings in a broader social context. The specific ways in which the political conflicts of the later-Stuart period affected those below the level of the elite will be explored as appropriate in the various chapters of this book, whilst chapter seven looks in detail at the divided society under William and Anne. What is offered here are some more general reflections on the workings of politics in this society, to provide the context for the analysis which is to come.

It goes without saying that England was a hierarchically structured society, with immense differentials in wealth, power and education, where the potential for political participation and influence varied considerably according to status. The ruling elite was a small group, comprising the monarch and his or her advisers and ministers at Court, the lords, bishops and MPs who sat in Parliament, and the judges, lord lieutenants and JPs who were responsible for keeping law and order throughout the realm. The monarch determined all questions of policy and selected all ministers of state, and until 1689 also had undisputed control over the armed forces. Judges and JPs were royal appointees, and both the judicial and magisterial benches could be – and frequently were – purged by the Crown to alter their political complexion. The monarch could not legislate or raise taxation without Parliament's consent, and the Crown's chronic shortage of money was probably the most constraining factor on its potential for political autonomy. Yet the Crown had the right to veto legislation, and before the Glorious Revolution it is probably true to say that the King had the power to suspend or dispense with Parliamentary statute by his royal prerogative (although this was a point of some controversy).

Prior to the Glorious Revolution, Parliament had no independent existence, since the King had the right to determine its sitting, prorogation and dissolution; the 1641 Triennial Act which had provided that Parliamentary sessions should be held at least once every three years was repealed in 1664. Under Charles II and James II Parliamentary sessions were extremely irregular; the Cavalier Parliament of 1661–1679 met for a total of sixty-three months over sixteen sessions, the first of which lasted eight months, the shortest (in late 1673) only a week, although typically in the 1670s sessions lasted for about two months or less. By contrast three Parliaments met in rapid succession between 1679 and 1681 – the first lasted just over two months in 1679, the second a little over three in 1680–1, and the third, held at Oxford in March 1681, barely a week. Parliaments became more regular after the Glorious Revolution, with sessions being held every year, and the Triennial Act of 1694 restricted the life of a Parliament to a maximum of three years. Yet the Crown could – and often did – terminate the life of a Parliament earlier, if it so desired.[50] Within Parliament, we should not assume that the representative chamber, the House of Commons, was dominant. Historians are increasingly coming to realise that the House of Lords was vitally important throughout this period.[51] Indeed, many of the early party leaders sat in the upper chamber. The Earl of Shaftesbury, the Duke of Buckingham, the Marquis of Halifax, and the Earl of Danby, were all key actors in the Court–Country and subsequent Tory–Whig conflicts under Charles II. Under William and Anne the Whigs were led by the Junto lords – Baron Somers, Baron Wharton, Charles Montagu (Lord Halifax) and Edward Russell (Earl of Orford) – whilst the prominent Tory leaders were the Earls of Rochester and Nottingham. Robert Harley, when he came to head a Tory administration after 1710, soon found himself promoted to the upper chamber as the Earl of Oxford, whereas his chief rival for power within the party at the end of Anne's reign was another member of the Lords, Viscount Bolingbroke. Promotion to the peerage was in the gift of the Crown, and tampering with the composition of the upper house was one way in which the royal administration might seek to facilitate the passage of its business through the Parliament. To cite the most notorious example, which caused a great outcry at the time, the Earl of Oxford created a dozen new peers at the end of December 1711, in order to defeat the opposition to his peace proposals from the Lords.[52] Put like this, it might seem that there is a strong case for seeing England under the later Stuarts as essentially a political oligarchy, headed by a personal monarch.

It would be wrong, however, to conclude that this was a closed political system, sharply polarised between the rulers and the ruled, the political and the sub-political nation, with little chance for political participation – except at election time for those who possessed the franchise – for the vast majority of the population. The political elite did not operate in isolation at the centre; they had to govern people, they had to implement their policies in the localities, and what they might attempt to do would be tempered by an awareness of what it was possible to achieve and what the people would accept. As an ultimate sanction, the people had the ability to call their rulers to account through rebellion, a not insignificant consideration during the later-Stuart period. England had experienced 'a Great Rebellion' in the 1640s and 1650s, which saw the overthrow of the traditional ruling elite; there were various alleged plots against the monarchy in the 1660s and 1670s; extremist Whigs plotted against the government in the early 1680s and launched a rebellion in the west country led by the Duke of Monmouth in 1685; many of James II's subjects in effect rebelled against him by deserting to William of Orange in 1688; there were Jacobite plots and intrigues in the 1690s and a serious Jacobite rebellion in 1715. Short of rebellion, a variety of opportunities existed

15

for political participation in this society. People of all social backgrounds could make their feelings known through petitions, demonstrations and riots, which became increasingly common forms of political expression in this period. No monarch could feel that his or her position was strong enough safely to ignore public opinion; the one who did, James II, soon discovered the cost.

Nor should we assume that those who sat in Parliament, once elected, had total independence of action. MPs were also delegates of their local communities, and were supposed to represent not just their own interests but also the interests of their constituents; for many of them there was the fear of not being re-elected if they failed to do what their electorates demanded from them. From the time of the Exclusion Crisis we see the beginnings of the practice of constituents issuing instructions to their newly elected representatives, telling them how they expected them to behave in Parliament. Many MPs also served as JPs in the shires or borough corporations, responsible for the implementation of governmental policies in their localities, and their attitudes towards national issues could often be influenced by their perception of what impact they would have on the provinces. For example, some Anglican MPs, with little sympathy for Dissent, nevertheless opposed the implementation of harsh measures against Nonconformists, because they were aware of the problems this would create at the local level.[53]

Those responsible for political decision-making at the centre, therefore, could not help but be influenced, at least to some degree, by the mood or opinions of those outside the political elite. If we turn our attention to how policy decisions were actually implemented, then we discover that the influence of ordinary people was greater still. Because England in the early modern period lacked a large, professional bureaucracy, effective government depended on the willingness of unpaid people in the localities to act as agents of central institutions. Let us take the system of law-enforcement as an example. Without denying the importance in the power hierarchy of professional Assize Court judges or the unprofessional JPs who ran the Quarter Sessions, they could not have performed their tasks effectively without the co-operation of a wide-range of people of lesser social status – husbandmen, yeomen, and lesser gentry in the countryside, merchants, petty traders and artisans in the towns – who served as constables, militiamen, sheriffs, undersheriffs, bailiffs, coroners and jurors.[54] The potential for involvement in local government was particularly high in London; for the first half of the seventeenth century it has been estimated that in the City itself as many as one in ten held annually some form of office, be it at parish, precinct or ward level, whilst in the borough of South-wark, south of the river, the corresponding figure was one in eleven.[55] Although jurors, constables, and churchwardens were responsible for presenting offences or offenders before the courts, most typically legal proceedings were initiated either by the person offended against, or by witnesses to the offence, which meant that even those excluded from the level of local officeholders could be drawn into the process of law-enforcement. The fact that under the 1670 Conventicle Act informers were given a statutory entitlement to a proportion of the fines levied on conventiclers testifies to the government's awareness of its dependence on the people to initiate prosecutions, even in an area as politi-cally sensitive as the persecution of Dissent.[56]

In short, a wide range of people at the local level – not just the middling sort, but occasionally even more humble types – were drawn into involvement in the processes of government, with the result that 'the rulers', for the effective implementation of their rule, were to a surprising degree dependent upon the support of those whom histo-rians normally think of as 'the ruled'. Without the support of the local-agents of law-enforcement, government could be virtually par-alysed. Charles I had lost control of the streets of the capital in 1640-2, when constables and militia men refused to suppress the crowds that demonstrated in support of the Parliamentary cause.[57] Likewise James II ran into difficulty because so many of those responsible for enforc-ing his policies in the localities – from gentry and bishops down to constables and churchwardens – refused to co-operate with what he was trying to do.

Those with the right to vote could have a significant impact on affairs at the centre at election time. After the enfranchisement of Durham and Newark in Charles II's reign, there were 52 county and 217 borough constituencies in England and Wales, returning a total of 513 MPs. Most English constituencies returned two members, which meant that the electors had two votes; the Welsh constituencies, and five English boroughs, returned just one member, whilst London, by contrast, returned four. In the counties the franchise was invested in the forty-shilling freeholder, although for electoral purposes copyhold land was usually regarded as of equivalent status. This qualification was not particularly restrictive, and some counties boasted huge electorates; in Yorkshire, for example, some 8,000 could vote. Moreover, after 1664 the clergy, in return for giving up their right to tax themselves in Convocation, were given the right to vote in Parliamentary elections, provided they met the franchise qualification. The borough franchises, however, varied considerably. There were forty-one boroughs where the franchise was restricted to the proprietors of burgage property; a further nineteen where only the members of the corporation could vote; another hundred where only freemen could participate in Parliamentary elections; whilst the MPs for the Universities of Oxford and Cambridge were returned by the MAs. In the remaining fifty-five constituencies the franchise was restricted to certain types of residents, be they householders, local taxpayers (the scot and lot franchise), pot-wallopers (i.e. those not in the receipt of alms or charity), or even, as at Preston, all adult male residents, including those only staying over-night. The situation was further confused by the fact that there was much uncertainty in many areas as to the nature of the franchise, with the result that the size of the electorate not only varied considerably from borough to borough, but also within the same borough from election to election. In the populous borough of Westminster, where the franchise was invested in the inhabitant householders, the electorate numbered some 25,000 in 1679. This contrasts with the tiny burgage borough of Aldborough in Yorkshire, where there were just nine voters in the period 1660–78. In the borough of Shaftesbury (Wiltshire), where the franchise was invested in those paying scot and lot for much of this period, there were 332 voters in 1679; in 1685, when the right to vote was restricted to members of the corporation, the electorate numbered only twelve.[58] On the whole, the franchise was fairly broad; indeed, it has been estimated that by the early eighteenth century almost one in four adult males had the right to vote, a figure that was higher than it had ever been in the past and which was not to be exceeded until the passing of the Second Reform Act of 1867. In many constituencies, the franchise extended quite far down the social scale, and could even include the rural poor and the labouring classes in the towns.[59]

The opportunity to exercise the right to vote was also greater under the later Stuarts than it had been before or was to be again for quite some time. The older practice of Parliamentary selection, whereby local elites sought to avoid a competition at the polls by agreeing on the choice of the two men who were to serve their community, became increasingly difficult to sustain as society became more politically polarised, with the result that contested elections steadily increased in frequency as the Stuart century progressed.[60] Admittedly, prior to the Glorious Revolution elections were somewhat irregular. After the two General Elections of 1660 and 1661, there was not to be another until 1679, although it should be said that many constituencies experienced by-elections during the long life of the Cavalier Parliament (1661–79). Between 1679 and 1715, however, there were a total of sixteen

General Elections, an average of one every two and a quarter years. It would be wrong to assume, of course, that those with the right to vote had a totally free and independent choice at election time. A variety of techniques were used to influence the outcome of election results, from 'treating' through to bribery, intimidation, and fraud. (These are discussed in detail in chapter seven.) Landlords often put pressure on their tenants to vote in a particular way, magistrates used their local influence for electoral advantage, whilst returning officers could use their control over the poll (they determined when to adjourn the poll and who was eligible to vote) in order to secure a favourable outcome. Influence was most in evidence in the borough constituencies. There were a number of 'pocket boroughs' where a particular family controlled enough local property that it could usually guarantee the return of their preferred candidates. Thus the Russells controlled Tavistock (where the franchise was invested in the freemen), the Howards Castle Rising (burgage tenure) and the Turgises Gatton (scot and lot).[61] There were some venal boroughs, such as Weobley in Herefordshire, where candidates were often able to bribe their way into the Commons. In other places the government interest was so strong, such as at Portsmouth, where there were the naval dockyards, that government candidates could normally expect to be returned. The Crown, with extensive sources of patronage at its disposal, had considerable potential for influencing the outcomes of elections, and at times – such as during the 1680s – could even try more blatant techniques such as interfering with electoral franchises. But it would be equally wrong to suggest that voters had little impact on electoral choices. The electorates in the open boroughs and counties were extremely difficult to control, and in these constituencies at least decisions at the polls were likely to reflect the preferences of the electorate. On the whole, electoral swings at General Elections appear to have corresponded to swings in public opinion, and the government of the day, despite the resources at its disposal, sometimes found it very difficult to secure the electoral outcome it desired.

A final question to consider is how politically aware most people were at this time. We should certainly be wary of attributing too high a degree of political consciousness to the masses; on the other hand, it would be wrong to think that we are dealing with a politically naive or ill-informed public. There were many ways in which people could be politicised, one of the most important of which – though rarely mentioned by scholars – was the experience of being governed. Many of the government's decisions had a direct impact on the lives of ordinary people: whether to persecute Dissenters, go to war, raise taxes, and so on. A central initiative to enforce the penal laws, to take one example, would affect not only Nonconformists, but also a whole variety of local officials responsible for law-enforcement, as well as those who worked for Nonconformists, who might lose their employment if their employer were to be sent to prison or subjected to heavy fines.

The media – pamphlets, newspapers and sermons – also played an important role in generating a political awareness. At the Restoration some attempt was made to control the dissemination of political opinions. The Licensing Act of 1662 established official censorship of the press through the agency of the Stationers' Company, though its control was never complete, and inevitably a certain amount of unlicensed literature continued to be printed. The lapsing of the Licensing Act in 1679 led to an explosion of political pamphleteering during the Exclusion Crisis, and although this Act was renewed in 1685 it finally expired in 1695, allowing the great outpouring from the press in the second half of William's reign and under Queen Anne. Even without a Licensing Act it was still possible to regulate the press through the common law of seditious libel, which the government sought to do, somewhat unsuccessfully at first, during the Exclusion Crisis, and even to a certain degree after 1695. On the whole, however, administrations found it better to counter an opposition press with their own pro-government propaganda, a tactic which could be very successful, but which inevitably had the effect of increasing the intensity of public political debate.

We may question what impact printed propaganda had when much of the population was illiterate. David Cressy, using the test of the ability to sign one's name, has estimated that in the middle of the seventeenth century only about 30 per cent of adult males were literate, a figure which rose to about 45 per cent by 1714. Female literacy rates increased from about 10 per cent to 25 per cent over the same period. Such figures, however, grossly underestimate the extent of literacy, since in this society more people could read than write. One scholar has recently suggested that those able to read might have been as much as one and a half times the proportion able to sign, which, if true, would raise our figure of adult male literacy of 45 per cent in 1714 to over 65 per cent. It also seems evident that the sign test disproportionately underestimates the number of female readers; women tended not to learn how to write, but were not necessarily any worse at reading than men. Moreover, crude national estimates conceal wide geographical and socio-economic variations in literacy rates. Urban areas tended to be more highly literate than rural – as many as 80 per cent of adult males in mid-seventeenth century London could sign their names – whilst the middling sort in both town and countryside were much more likely to be able to read and write than poor labourers and husbandmen.[62]

Yet one did not need to be literate to have access to political information. Those who could not read could gather about one who could, and hear read aloud extracts from newspapers and tracts, or else could learn about politics through sermons or discussions with friends. The newly fashionable coffee-houses often provided a range of literature for their clientele, and became places where all sorts of people could go to read about and discuss public affairs. We also have examples of very humble types discussing politics in taverns or at street corners.[63] Political propaganda was disseminated very widely in this society. A declaration issued by Charles II in April 1681 explaining why he had dissolved the last two Exclusion Parliaments was ordered to be read in all churches and chapels throughout the country, as well as being published in printed form and reproduced in newspapers. The Whig response, according to John Dryden, was circulated through the conventicles and the Whig coffee-houses, and copies of the tract were also sent out 'in Post Letters, to infect the Populace of every County'.[64]

These introductory remarks provide the context for the analysis of party which is to follow. The book is arranged in a broad chronological framework – with different chapters covering the Restoration, Court–Country tensions during the 1660s and 1670s, the Exclusion Crisis, the Glorious Revolution, and the reigns of William and Anne – so that the process of party formation over time can be highlighted. However, each chapter takes a thematic and analytical approach, rather than opting for a straightforward narrative. The section of the book covering the period from the Glorious Revolution to the Hanoverian Succession – the period when political parties reached their fullest level of maturity under the later Stuarts – is divided into three chapters, and takes a more structural approach, as being the best way to explore in depth the nature and workings of the two-party system at this time. Because political allegiance was the crucial determinant of party identity at this time, much time is spent exploring the ideological nature of the party divide, as well as looking at the actual workings of politics in Parliament and the developing structures of party organisation. Throughout an attempt is made to set party strife in its broadest possible context, looking not just at the political elite, but also those 'out-of-doors', and integrating an analysis of high politics with both local and popular politics.

REFERENCES

1   Basil Duke Henning (ed.), *The House of Commons, 1660–1690* (The History of Parliament Trust, 3 vols, 1983), **I**, p. 29.

2   Robert Willman, 'The Origins of "Whig" and "Tory" in English Political Language', *HJ*, **17** (1974), pp. 247–64.

3   J. H. Plumb, *The Growth of Political Stability in England 1675–1725* (1967).

4   Keith Feiling, *A History of the Tory Party, 1640–1714* (Oxford, 1924).

5   Henry Horwitz, *Parliament, Policy and Politics in the Reign of William III* (Manchester, 1977); Geoffrey Holmes, *British Politics in the Age of Anne* (1967, revised edn 1987); J. P. Kenyon, *Revolution Principles: The Politics of Party 1689–1720* (Cambridge, 1977).

6   W. A. Speck, *Tory and Whig: The Struggle in the Constituencies, 1701–1715* (1970).

7   G. V. Bennett, *The Tory Crisis in Church and State, 1688–1730: The Career of Francis Atterbury, Bishop of Rochester* (Oxford, 1975)

8   B. W. Hill, *The Growth of Parliamentary Parties, 1689–1742* (1976).

9   Geoffrey Holmes and W. A. Speck, *The Divided Society: Parties and Politics in England 1694–1716* (1967).

10 J. R. Jones, *The First Whigs: The Politics of the Exclusion Crisis, 1678–83* (Oxford, 1961).

11 J. R. Jones, *Country and Court: England, 1658–1714* (1978), p. 198; J. R. Jones, 'Parties and Parliament', in J. R. Jones (ed.), *The Restored Monarchy 1660–1688* (1979), pp. 58–9.

12 Hill, *Growth of Parliamentary Parties*, p. 15.

13 Hill, *Growth of Parliamentary Parties*, pp. 21, 65–6; J. C. D. Clark, 'A General Theory of Party, Opposition and Government, 1688–1832', *HJ*, **23** (1980), p. 296.

14 J. R. Jones, 'Introduction: Main Trends in Restoration England', in his *Restored Monarchy*, p. 7; Jones, *First Whigs*, pp. 10, 12.

15 Plumb, *Growth of Political Stability*, p. 26.

16 J. R. Jones, *The Revolution of 1688 in England* (1972), pp. 75–9. Cf. John Miller, *Popery and Politics in England, 1660–1688* (Cambridge, 1973), ch. 4; K. H. D. Haley, '"No Popery" in the Reign of Charles II', in J. S. Bromley and E. H. Kossman (eds), *Britain and the Netherlands*, **V** (The Hague, 1975), pp. 102–19; Michael G. Finlayson, *Historians, Puritanism and the English Revolution: The Religious Factor in English Politics Before and After the Interregnum* (Toronto, 1983), ch. 5.

17 Holmes, *British Politics*, p. xx.

18 Tim Harris, *London Crowds in the Reign of Charles II: Propaganda and Politics from the Restoration until the Exclusion Crisis* (Cambridge, 1987).

19 Cited in John Brewer, *Party Ideology and Popular Politics at the Accession of George III* (Cambridge, 1976), p. 72.

20 Cf. the definitions offered in Frank O'Gorman, *The Emergence of the*

British Two-Party System 1760–1832 (1982), p. viii, footnote 1; Jones, 'Parties and Parliament', p. 58.

21   J. R. Jones, *Charles II: Royal Politician* (1987), p. 1.

22   [Earl of Shaftesbury], *A Letter from a Person of Quality to His Friend in the Country* (1675), p. 1.

23   BL, Add MS 32,518, fols 144–52.

24   Edmund Bohun, *An Address to the Free-Men and the Free-Holders of the Nation* (1682), p. 23.

25   David Underdown, *Revel, Riot and Rebellion: Popular Politics and Culture in England 1603–1660* (Oxford, 1985), p. 289.

26   Narcissus Luttrell, *A Brief Historical Relation of State Affairs from September 1678 to April 1714* (6 vols, 1857), **I**, pp. 124, 198–9; Mark Goldie, 'Danby, the Bishops and the Whigs', in Tim Harris, Paul Seaward and Mark Goldie (eds), *The Politics of Religion in Restoration England* (Oxford, 1990), p. 79.

27   [Daniel Defoe], *A New Test of the Church of England's Loyalty* (1702), p. 4.

28   Holmes, *British Politics*, p. 17.

29   Anne Whiteman (ed.), with the assistance of Mary Clapinson, *The Compton Census of 1676: A Critical Edition* (1986), pp. xxxvii–xxxix, lxxvii.

30   Bodl. Lib., MS Tanner 36, fol. 196.

31   I. M. Green, *The Re-establishment of the Church of England 1660–1663* (Oxford, 1978), pp. 69–71, 149, 171–3; Richard Kidder, *Life*, Amy E. Robinson (ed.)(1924), p. 19; William Urwick, *Nonconformity in Hertfordshire* (1884), *passim*; Alan Macfarlane, *The Family Life of Ralph Josselin: A Seventeenth-Century Clergyman* (Cambridge, 1970), pp. 27–30; Samuel Crispe, *A Sermon Preach'd at the Primary Visitation of the . . . Bishop of Norwich* (1686), pp. 13–14.

32   Bodl. Lib., MS Tanner 35, fol. 39.

33   William Stevenson, 'The Economic and Social Status of Protestant Sectarians in Huntingdonshire, Cambridgeshire and Bedfordshire (1660–1725)', unpub. Cambridge PhD thesis (1990), p. 344.

34   Andrew Browning (ed.), *English Historical Documents, 1660–1714* (1953), p. 415; G. Lyon Turner (ed.), *Original Records of Early Nonconformity under Persecution and Indulgence* (3 vols, 1911–14), **III**, pp. 736–7.

35   Michael R. Watts, *The Dissenters: From the Reformation to the French Revolution* (Oxford, 1978), pp. 267–85.

36   Samuel Parker, *A Discourse of Ecclesiastical Politie* (1670), p. xlix; [Gilbert Burnet], *The Ill Effects of Animosities among Protestants in England Detected* (1688), p. 19.

37   [Daniel Defoe], *The Dissenters' Answer to the High-Church Challenge* (1704), p. 48.

38   Gary S. De Krey, *A Fractured Society: The Politics of London in the First Age of Party, 1688–1715* (Oxford, 1985), p. 75; Harris, *London Crowds*, p. 66; Colin Brent, 'Lewes Dissenters outside the Law, 1663–86', *Sussex Archeological Collection*, **123** (1985), pp. 195–214; J. J. Hurwich,

'"A Fanatick Town": The Political Influence of Dissenters in Coventry, 1660–1720', *Midland History*, **4** (1977), p. 17.

39   John T. Evans, *Seventeenth-Century Norwich: Politics, Religion and Government, 1620–1690* (Oxford, 1979); Nicholas Rogers, *Whigs and Cities: Popular Politics in the Age of Walpole and Pitt* (Oxford, 1990), chs 8, 9; Jonathan Barry, 'The Politics of Religion in Restoration Bristol', in Harris et al. (eds), *Politics of Religion*, pp. 163–89; John M. Triffitt, 'Politics and the Urban Community: Parliamentary Boroughs in the South West of England 1710–1730', unpub. Oxford DPhil thesis (1985), ch. 3.

40   D. A. Spaeth, 'Parsons and Parishioners: Lay-Clerical Conflict and Popular Piety in Wiltshire Villages, 1660–1740', unpub. Brown University PhD thesis (1985), ch. 7.

41   Newton Key, 'Comprehension and the Breakdown of Consensus in Restoration Herefordshire', in Harris et al. (eds), *Politics of Religion*, pp. 191–215; Philip Jenkins, *The Making of a Ruling Class: The Glamorgan Gentry 1640–1790* (Cambridge, 1983), p. 122; Andrew Coleby, *Central Government and the Localities: Hampshire 1649–1689* (Cambridge, 1987), pp. 139, 147–8; P. J. Norrey, 'The Restoration Regime in Action: The Relationship between Central and Local Government in Dorset, Somerset and Wiltshire', *HJ*, **31** (1988), pp. 803–8.

42   Margaret Spufford, *Contrasting Communities: English Villagers in the Sixteenth and Seventeenth Centuries* (Cambridge, 1974), pp. 300–6.

43   Stevenson, 'Economic and Social Status of Protestant Sectarians'.

44   William Penn, *Considerations Moving to a Toleration, and Liberty of Conscience* (1685), p. 4.

45   Cited in Urwick, *Nonconformity in Hertfordshire*, p. 178.

46   Miller, *Popery and Politics*, p. 11.

47   Haley, 'No Popery'; Paul Seaward, *The Restoration 1660–1688* (1991), pp. 62–9.

48   Miller, *Popery and Politics*, pp. 12–13; Philip Jenkins, 'Anti-popery on the Welsh Marches in the Seventeenth Century', *HJ*, **23** (1980), pp. 275–93; Newton E. Key, 'Politics beyond Parliament: Unity and Party in the Herefordshire Region during the Restoration Period', unpub. Cornell PhD thesis (1989); Jan M. Albers, 'Seeds of Contention: Society, Politics and the Church of England in Lancashire, 1689–1790', unpub. Yale PhD thesis (1988), ch. 10; P. J. Challinor, 'Restoration and Exclusion in the County of Cheshire', *Bulletin of the John Rylands University Library*, **64** (1982), p. 385.

49   Harris, *London Crowds*, pp. 32–4, 73–4, 128, 139–44.

50   Jones, *Country and Court*, pp. 24–5.

51   Clyve Jones (ed.), *A Pillar of the Constitution: The House of Lords in British Politics, 1640–1784* (1989).

52   Holmes, *British Politics*, pp. 397–8.

53   Seaward, *The Restoration*, pp. 56–7.

54   Cynthia Herrup, 'The Counties and the Country: Some Thoughts on Seventeenth-Century Historiography', in Geoff Eley and William Hunt

(eds), *Reviving the English Revolution: Reflections and Elaborations on the Work of Christopher Hill* (1988), pp. 289–304.

55   Valerie Pearl, 'Social Policy in Early Modern London', in Hugh Lloyd-Jones, Valerie Pearl and Blair Worden (eds), *History and Imagination: Essays in Honour of H. R. Trevor-Roper* (1981), p. 116; Jeremy Boulton, *Neighbourhood and Society: A London Suburb in the Seventeenth Century* (Cambridge, 1987), p. 267.

56   *Statutes of the Realm,* **V**, pp. 648–51.

57   K. J. Lindley, 'Riot Prevention and Control in Early Stuart London', *TRHS*, 5th series, **33** (1983), pp.123–4.

58   These figures are taken from the constituency reports in Henning, *House of Commons.*

59   Geoffrey Holmes, *The Electorate and the National Will in the First Age of Party* (Lancaster, 1976), p. 23; Speck, *Tory and Whig*, pp. 15–17; Frank O'Gorman, *Voters, Patrons, and Parties: The Unreformed Electoral System of Hanoverian England 1734–1832* (Oxford, 1989), ch. 4; J. H. Plumb, 'The Growth of the Electorate in England from 1600–1715', *PP*, **45** (1969), pp. 90–116.

60   Mark A. Kishlansky, *Parliamentary Selection: Social and Political Change in Early Modern England* (Cambridge, 1986).

61   Jones, *Country and Court*, p. 36.

62   David Cressy, *Literacy and the Social Order: Reading and Writing in Tudor and Stuart England* (Cambridge, 1980), esp. ch. 6 and pp. 176–7; Keith Thomas, 'The Meaning of Literacy in Early Modern England', in Gerd Baumann (ed.), *The Written Word: Literacy in Transition* (Oxford, 1986), pp. 100–3; Barry Reay, 'The Context and Meaning of Popular Literacy: Some Evidence From Nineteenth-Century Rural England', *PP*, **131** (1991), pp. 112–14.

63   Harris, *London Crowds*, pp. 28–9.

64   [John Dryden], *His Majesties Declaration Defended* (1681), p. 5.

CHAPTER TWO

The Restoration

The Restoration of monarchy in the spring of 1660 is normally seen as being genuinely popular. The King's return, as one contemporary put it, was greeted with the 'acclamations of all the people', and met with 'the greatest and most unanimous satisfaction that ever was perceiv'd in England'.[1] Contemporaries were well aware, however, that this apparent unanimity in favour of restoring the King did not represent a genuine consensus. The High Anglican cleric, George Hickes, looking back on the Restoration in a sermon of 1684, commented that 'then were strange things to be seen, Republicans with Royalists, Churchmen with Church-robbers, Rebels and Traytors with Loyal Subjects, Papists with Protestants, Episcopalians with Anti-Episcopalians, all agreed to bring in the King, or let him be brought in'.[2] Clarendon thought that the Restoration was produced 'by a union of contradictions, by a concurrence of causes' which 'never desired the same effects'.[3]

It is a major theme of this book that the roots of party strife in England can be traced back to 1660, and the problems which the Restoration left unsolved. It will be the argument of this chapter that the Restoration was, indeed, a deeply contradictory affair, the product of an already divided society. The Restoration failed to heal these divisions, and the development of party conflict occurred as a result of the working out of these contradictions after a settlement which proved unsatisfactory to most of the different political groupings of 1660. I shall start by looking at the desire for the Restoration, and shall argue that the return of Charles II was genuinely popular. Republicanism did not die overnight, but after 1660 the republicans were a small minority, and the main political conflicts in Restoration England did not centre around tensions between those who supported the restoration of monarchy in 1660 and those who remained consistently opposed to it. Yet different people looked to the Restoration for very different reasons. When we consider, in turn, the different political and religious solutions desired by the various groups who supported the return of the Stuart monarchy, it was inevitable that the Restoration was not going to satisfy all groups.

THE DESIRE FOR THE RESTORATION

There has been some debate concerning how extensive support for the monarchy was in 1660. Godfrey Davies thought that 'one of the few safe generalisations about the Restoration' was 'that it happened because the vast majority of Englishmen wanted it to happen'.[4] Such a view has recently been endorsed by Ronald Hutton who concludes that 'the unpopularity of the republican regimes must survive any revisionary study', and that the people, especially in London, played a significant part in bringing about the restoration of monarchy.[5] Christopher Hill, in contrast, has asserted that 'Charles was restored not by popular clamour but by the men of property', and believes there is plenty of evidence to suggest that support for the Good Old Cause, especially amongst the lower orders, was a long time dying, whilst Richard Greaves has detected the existence of 'a strong undercurrent of deep-rooted hostility to monarchy in general and to the Stuarts in particular' at the time of the Restoration.[6]

The key actor in bringing about the downfall of the Republic was General George Monck (later to be made the Duke of Albemarle), who was commander of the army in Scotland. It was his decision at the beginning of 1660 to march south for London, and bring to an end the rule by the Rump Parliament (the remnant of the Long Parliament which had first been called in 1640, purged by Colonel Pride in 1648, and illegally dissolved by Cromwell in 1653), which paved the way for the restoration of monarchy. In February Monck forced the Rump Parliament to readmit those MPs who had been secluded at the time of Pride's Purge; once filled, it agreed to dissolve itself and issue writs for new elections. The new Parliament, known as the Convention because it was not summoned by the King, proved (as most people knew it would) to be dominated by gentry who were overwhelmingly sympathetic to the re-establishment of the monarchy. The Restoration settlement was then worked out by the propertied classes who sat in this and the subsequent Parliament (the Cavalier Parliament of 1661–79). In a sense, therefore, it is correct to say that the Restoration was brought about by men of property; one might even suggest that it was precipitated by a successful military invasion.

It would be wrong, however, to suggest that the people played no part. Those who had the vote had the ability to let their feelings be known in the elections to the Convention. The republicans fared extremely badly, whilst those who were known to be sympathetic to the restoration of the monarchy tended to be successful. In the City of London, from up to forty candidates nominated, the four most clearly royalist were chosen without dispute, 'which was never before known'. Despite the Rump's ordinance disqualifying from election those who had fought for Charles I and their sons, unless they had 'manifested their good affection to this Parliament', fifty-two such men were returned. If we look at those members of the Convention whose families are known to have been either Royalist or anti-Royalist supporters during the Civil War (a little over half the membership), some 158 came from Royalist families and 150 from Parliamentarian. The royalist reaction was even more noticeable in the elections to the Cavalier Parliament in the spring of 1661. Just under half the members returned were Cavaliers, in the sense of men who had been in arms for the King during the Civil War, or their sons, or those who had been engaged in conspiracy in the 1650s, and the vast majority of those returned were men with clear royalist or episcopalian sympathies. Admittedly the government was given a fright by the London election – one of the earliest to be held – where two Presbyterians and two Independents were returned on an anti-episcopalian platform, but in most areas, Presbyterians, Independents and 'fanatics' found it difficult to win or hold onto seats. And although the government did interfere in some constituencies in order to secure the return of favoured candidates, most of the results seem to reflect a genuine drift in public opinion in favour of men with royalist and episcopalian views.[7]

Moreover, there is little reason to doubt that the train of events set in motion by Monck's action was in tune with the mood of the nation at large. By late 1659 it was already apparent that the Republic was facing a deep crisis of support. Neither the Rump nor the army, who were struggling for political ascendancy after the fall of Richard Cromwell's Protectorate in April 1659, showed that they could run the country effectively, and both regimes were much disliked, in part because of their unconstitutional basis, in part because they appeared to promote the interests of radical sectarians. Public resentment was fuelled by economic discontent: a trade crisis had been brought on as a result of the war with Spain, there was a shortage of bullion, grain prices were on the increase, and unemployment was high. In London, from about November 1659, we see the emergence of a concerted campaign by tradesmen, artisans, labourers and apprentices, against rule by the Rump and the army. There were petitions, demonstrations, riots, and even a threatened tax strike, with the demand being explicitly for a full or free Parliament.[8] Similar declarations in favour of a full or free Parliament were made in many counties or corporations in different parts of England, and many of them were presented to Monck as he marched south from Scotland.[9] Although a number of these provincial declarations came from local elites, there is much evidence to suggest that their views were widely shared in their communities. In Exeter in mid-January there were disorders lasting three days, when the apprentices and other young men of the City locked the gates, setting up guards of up to 100 at each, disarmed the local Baptists and Independents, and 'lowdly exprest their Desires for a Free Parliament'.[10] The apprentices of Bristol early the next month pursued a similar strategy, securing the City, in order to keep out soldiers who had been sent to collect a recently levied tax, disarming known supporters of the Commonwealth, and declaring in favour of a free Parliament.[11]

The action Monck took against the Rump was clearly welcome to many people. When he forced the Rump to readmit the secluded members, there were extensive celebrations in London and many other places, as crowds gathered at bonfires to 'burn the Rump', shouting for a free Parliament and for King Charles.[12] Likewise, the Convention's decision to restore the King triggered jubilant celebrations throughout much of the country. When Charles was publicly proclaimed King in the City of London on 8 May, the crowds cheered so loudly that they drowned out Bow bells.[13] In Worcester, the news was greeted with 'Bonfires made at night throughout the City', as huge crowds gathered 'with high rejoicings and acclamations for the prosperity of the King'.[14] And when Charles finally entered the capital on 29 May (his birthday), there were further celebrations throughout the realm.[15]

It is true that some of this agitation, as Hill has suggested, was encouraged 'from above'. A petition by the London apprentices of November 1659 was apparently framed 'with the help of better heade peces', whilst some of the bonfires in the capital celebrating the fall of the Rump in February had the backing of the well-to-do, who put up money 'to buy faggotts and beere'.[16] The Bristol unrest of February had allegedly been 'underhand hatched and fomented' by the apprentices' masters. The fact that their published declaration of 9 February, which sought to demonstrate the unconstitutional nature of the Rump and the illegality of the present taxes, contained numerous references to specific Parliamentary statutes, and even a Latin quotation, does suggest that this document could not have been all their own work.[17] The elaborate and widespread celebrations for the return of monarchy in May often had the backing of wealthy local patrons. But to dismiss the extensive public fervour against the Republic and in favour of the monarchy as evidence of manipulated mobs strains credibility. In the first place, there must have been at least some convergence of interest between the 'meaner' and the 'better' sort (to use the language of contemporaries) for this alleged manipulation to have proven so easy. Secondly, not all the agitation of 1659–60 was led from above, not every bonfire was sponsored by a wealthy patron, and we should not assume that ordinary people were incapable of co-ordinating their efforts for themselves. In London, for example, we find apprentices meeting in a house in Cannon Street in late November, early December 1659 to co-ordinate their petitioning campaign.[18] Sometimes elite patronage came only after the initiative had been taken by the lower orders. For example, one account of the disturbances in Exeter in January admits that 'the Tumult . . . began first with the wilder and meaner Sort of People', but claims that it 'was encouraged by Persons of a better Rank, who inflamed them to cry out and shout for a Free Parliament'. Even then it appears that what happened was that 'a Knight, and a few others of note . . . got upon a Tombstone in the Church-yard, and declared the same thing' as the 'meaner sort' had, and the rest of the account suggests that the initiative in disarming the republicans and securing the gates of the City was taken by 'the multitude'. Moreover, it was these disorders which seem to have prompted the Devon gentry, already assembled at Exeter for the quarter sessions, to draw up an address to the Rump asking for the readmittance of those members secluded in 1648.[19] In such circumstances, we are entitled to wonder who was leading whom.

Not everyone welcomed the monarch's return. Some of those who had served the Republic as politicians, writers, or as members of the armed forces remained opposed to the restoration of monarchy. So too did some of the more radical sectarian ministers. There is evidence of opposition to the campaign for a free Parliament in several parts of the country, especially from the urban corporations. In Leicester and Bristol, for example, the city fathers disassociated themselves from the local campaigns against the Rump. In London radicals claimed they had been able to collect 'many thousand' subscriptions to their declaration in defence of the Rump and in condemnation of the demand for a free Parliament.[20] General John Lambert's last minute attempt to save the Republic with his abortive military rising of April 1660 attracted enough support, from both soldiers and civilians, to suggest that a sizeable minority of people in the provinces remained attached to the Good Old Cause.[21]

In addition, there are many isolated examples of individuals or groups of people expressing their hostility to the restoration of monarchy. At the end of May 1660, for example, a Leicester man got into trouble for throwing a 'stone or a clott' against a picture of the King's Arms which he saw displayed on someone's house.[22] Four Kidderminster witches, who were arrested in mid-May, claimed that 'if they had not been taken the King should never have come into England, and though he doth come yet he shall not live long, but shall die as ill a death as they'.[23] A detailed examination of court records for the early months of the Restoration reveals many examples of people speaking hostile words against the monarchy. Yet the significance of this evidence is particularly hard to assess. Not all court records survive for this period, and moreover not everyone who thought ill of the Restoration would have faced prosecution for their beliefs, so our sources might seriously underestimate the degree of disaffection to the new regime. On the other hand, the cases which did come to court are often as revealing about the political sympathies of those who made the accusations as they are of those who stood accused. An interesting example is that of John Wilson, a deputy excise collector in the north, who declared that the King was a rogue who should be hanged. He was rebuked by a local woman, who warned him, 'how dare you speake such words Against the Lords Anoynted', which provoked Wilson into asking 'did you Anoynt him, did you take up your coates and pisse upon his head to Anoynt him'. It is hardly surprising that the woman took offence and reported his words to the authorities.[24] The fact that one Thomas Blacklocke got into trouble in May 1660 for a lengthy diatribe against Charles II spoken in a drinking establishment in Southwark perhaps tells us something about the feelings this man would let come to the surface when under the influence of alcohol; it also tells us something about the royalist sympathies of the three women and two men, all from humble backgrounds, who came forward to give information against Blacklocke.[25]

On balance it is probably fair to conclude that, although some evidence of continued support for the Republic can be found, most people – of all social classes – did come to welcome the return of monarchy in 1660. Committed Royalists were naturally jubilant: this group includes not only Cavaliers and Anglicans, who had sided with the Crown during the Civil War, but many former Parliamentarians and Presbyterians, who had fought against the Crown but had opposed the regicide. There were others who became disillusioned with the Republic as a result of the political and economic turmoils of the late 1650s, and who looked to the restoration of monarchy as the only way to cure the nation's ills. And as the return of Charles II began to appear inevitable, most former servants and supporters of the Republic, though with varying degrees of enthusiasm, decided to make their peace with the Restoration, and sought to get the best out of it that they could. Even Algernon Sidney, a man regarded by contemporaries as 'stiff to all republican principles', attempted to conform, and briefly held out some hopes for continued employment under the new regime.[26] Likewise most of the religious sects decided to acquiesce in the Restoration. When Thomas Venner and a handful of his fellow Fifth Monarchists attempted a rising in favour of the Good Old Cause in January 1661, Independent, Baptist and Quaker congregations were quick to repudiate his actions, and pledge their loyalty to the government.[27]

Yet Charles was popular in 1660 because he was able to appear as all things to all people. The most pressing problem he faced at his return was not how to cope with the dying-embers of republicanism, but rather how to satisfy the different groups who for varying reasons had come to support the Restoration. Charles's own plans for compromise were laid out in his Declaration of Breda of April 1660, in which he expressed his hope that his return would help heal 'those wounds which have so many years together been kept bleeding'. In order to achieve this, he promised to grant 'a free and general pardon' to all supporters of the Republic who returned 'to the loyalty and obedience of good subjects (excepting only such persons as shall hereafter be excepted by Parliament)' and a 'liberty to tender consciences', so that 'no man shall be disquieted or called in question for differences of opinion in matters of religion which do not disturb the peace of the Kingdom'. Although he was insistent that his possession of the throne was a 'right which God and nature hath made our due', he also said that it was his desire 'that all our subjects may enjoy what by law is theirs, by a full and entire administration of justice throughout the land'. Working out the details of the re-settlement of his and his subjects' 'just rights' was to be left to the determination of a free Parliament. In this way he hoped that 'all notes of discord, separation and difference of parties' might be 'utterly abolished among all our sub-jects'.[28] When the Convention and Cavalier Parliaments set about the task of reaching a political and religious settlement, however, it soon became clear that healing old wounds and abolishing all notes of discord was going to be virtually impossible.

THE POLITICAL SETTLEMENT

Many Presbyterians and old Puritans wanted a conditional restoration, with statutory limitations placed on the powers of the Crown. Numbered amongst this group were Presbyterian peers such as the Earls of Manchester, Bedford, Anglesey and Northumberland, and commoners such as Sir Gilbert Gerard, Sir Harbottle Grimston, Sir Denzil Holles and Sir Anthony Ashley Cooper (the future Earl of Shaftesbury). There was some disagreement over what those limitations should be. The more rigid Presbyterians, nicknamed the Presbyterian Knot, wanted to revive the terms of the Isle of Wight Treaty of 1648 (to which Charles I had partially agreed before Pride's Purge), and argued that Parliament should have control over the militia and the right of appointment to all major offices of state. Others would have accepted milder measures, such as a statutory confirmation of fundamental constitutional documents like Magna Carta and the Petition of Right. It should be stressed, however, that some Presbyterians were such strong supporters of a restoration of the King, that they were opposed to the attempt to impose conditions, fearing it would unduly delay bringing back Charles II. Conditions seem to have had little support in the nation at large. The City of London opposed the 'unreasonable termes' of the Presbyterians, advising the Council of State in March 1660 that 'the more considerable you will make him [the King] at home and abroad', the more able he would be 'to protect his people'.[29] At the Surrey election to the Convention Parliament the general cry was 'No Rumpers, No Presbiterians that will put bad conditions on the King'.[30] Enjoying a brief period of political ascendancy in the final days of the Long Parliament, between the readmission of the secluded members on 21 February and its final dissolution on 16 March, the supporters of limitations lost the initiative in the Convention – in part because of their poor performance in the polls, and in part because of their own internal divisions – and in the end the King was brought back without any conditions attached.[31]

The constitutional settlement eventually worked out in the Convention and Cavalier Parliaments essentially restored the monarchy as it had been in 1641. All the reforming legislation that had been passed in the early months of the Long Parliament and which had received the royal assent was left on the statute books: ship money remained illegal, the prerogative courts of Star Chamber and High Commission were not revived, the Crown's feudal rights were not restored (wardship, knighthood fines), and even the 1641 Triennial Act remained (temporarily) in place. There had been a wide degree of consensus in the Long Parliament over the need for such legislation, and such reforms had been supported by Edward Hyde, who as Earl of Clarendon was to be the chief architect of the Restoration settlement. The constitutional consensus in the Long Parliament had broken down only when John Pym and others began to put forward more radical demands in late 1641 and early 1642 to limit the Crown's independence of action, and this platform was abandoned at the Restoration. Two Militia Acts of 1661 and 1662 restored sole control of the militia to the Crown, in rejection of Parliament's Militia Ordinance of March 1642. There was no challenge to the King's right to choose his own ministers, such as had been made in the Nineteen Propositions of June 1642. And the Act excluding the bishops from the House of Lords, passed with the King's assent in February 1642, was undone. It was a settlement that left the Crown very powerful. The monarch was free to determine both foreign and domestic policy, to appoint all officers of state, and although obliged to consult with Parliament, he had the power of vetoing legislation and of dispensing individuals from the provisions of Parliamentary statutes: indeed, as we shall see, it was even arguable that he had the power to suspend Parliamentary statutes. The major constraint on the Crown was financial. Although in compensation for the loss of his feudal dues the King was to receive the new excise tax, established by the Parliamentarians in 1643, and in addition the income from a tax on fire places established in 1662, the revenues of the restored monarchy initially fell far short of those needed to meet the expenses of government. Faced with the added burden of old debts and new foreign policy commitments, the Crown became heavily dependent upon Parliament for extra grants of money during the 1660s and 1670s. However, the inadequacies of the financial settlement of the Restoration were the result of miscalculation rather than a deliberate attempt to limit the Crown through the power of the purse. The Crown's financial situation improved considerably in the 1680s, due to the more efficient collection of the excise and hearth tax and an increase in revenue from customs during a decade of commercial prosperity; with the further assistance of subsidies from the French King, Louis XIV, Charles II was able to become both economically and politically independent of Parliament during the last years of his reign.[32]

There were a number of ultra-Royalists who wanted the restoration of a monarchy stronger than that envisaged by Clarendon. Some would have liked to see a return to the monarchy of the 1630s, with the full resumption of its old feudal and prerogative rights. John Bowring suggested that the government should follow Charles I's policies of the 1630s, and exploit all the ancient rights and dues of the Crown in order to amass a 'body of private treasure', which the King could use to make himself 'as absolute as the Grand Signior' [i.e. King of France]. Burnet informs us that at the time of Clarendon's fall in 1667 a number of members of the House of Commons – amongst them Clifford, Osborne (later the Earl of Danby) and Seymour – informed the King 'that upon his restoration they intended both to have raised his authority, and to have increased his revenue; but that the earl of Clarendon had discouraged it'. It is difficult to know what to make of this remark; even if we can trust the Whiggish Burnet, we would have to be sceptical of remarks made by men who were manoeuvring for royal favour after the downfall of the King's leading minister. Nevertheless, there were certainly a number of men close to the Crown in the early 1660s, and especially in the circle of James, Duke of York, who would have liked to have seen a strengthening of royal authority at the Restoration, amongst them the Earl of Peterborough, Charles Berkeley and Henry Bennet (later the Earl of Arlington, and leading minister of the Cabal). Bennet appears to have seen the French style of government as the model to emulate, whilst Clarendon was concerned about the 'ill principles' which Charles II himself had learnt during his years in France. Early in 1664 Pepys noted that those about the King were advising him that the privileges of Parliament did not count for anything, and that 'his will is all and ought to be so'.[33]

Not only was there disagreement over what sort of monarchy should be restored, there was also plenty of room for argument as to what type of monarchy had actually been restored by the Convention and Cavalier Parliaments. When it decided to invite back the King, the Convention announced that 'according to the antient and fundamental Laws of this Kingdom, the Government is, and ought to be, by King, Lords and Commons'.[34] The language seems to imply a mixed monarchy, with the King being one of the three estates, a co-ordinate power who shared his sovereignty with the two Houses of Parliament. There were good grounds for believing that this was the true form of government according to ancient and fundamental laws; in his *Answer to the Nineteen Propositions* in June 1642, Charles I had denied that the English monarchy was absolute and maintained that 'in this kingdom the laws are jointly made by a King, by a house of peers, and by a House of Commons chosen by the people'. The Act for the Preservation of the King in 1661 further endorsed the principle of co-ordination in the area of law-making.[35] Moreover, there could be no escaping the fact that the English people had restored Parliament before they restored their King, and that Charles II was recalled by a freely-elected representative institution.

Anglican divines, however, tended to stress the providential nature of the Restoration, and sought to revive the view that monarchy was by divine right. William Walwyn, in a thanksgiving sermon 'For His Majesties Happy Return' preached at the parish of East Coker, Somerset, on 24 May, compared Kings to Gods, saying that even God called Princes and magistrates Gods, whilst in another sermon from that time Gilbert Sheldon, soon to be Bishop of London and later Archbishop of Canterbury, claimed that Kings were 'God's Deputies'.[36] John Paradise, in a sermon given at Westbury in Wiltshire, on 30 January 1661 (the anniversary of the regicide), set out 'to vindicate the Royal Prerogative of Kings, wherewith they are invested by a Divine Charter'. Such a view Charles did much to encourage; for example, he immediately revived the practice of touching for the King's Evil.[37] For many, the championship of divine right led to the conclusion that the English monarchy was absolute. As Francis Gregory put it in a sermon preached at Oxford on 27 May 1660, Kings were 'God's Vice-gerents' and were 'accountable to none but God'.[38]

Nevertheless, it would be misleading to suggest that absolutist views triumphed at the Restoration. Most Anglicans and Cavaliers concurred in seeing the return of the King as marking a return to the rule of law and constitutional propriety after the illegal activities of the Civil War and Interregnum. One Anglican Royalist tract complained how the Protector had trampled under foot all laws from Magna Carta to the Petition of Right.[39] Sheldon himself saw the Restoration as bringing back not just kingly government, but also 'our Laws [and] Liberties'.[40] In his coronation sermon of 23 April 1661, George Morley, at that time Bishop of Worcester and dean of the chapel royal, maintained that the English monarchy was 'Political' and 'not Despotical', and that the King governed his subjects not 'as a Master doth his Servants, arbitrarily according to his own will and pleasure', but 'as a Father doth his Children, by Equal and Just Lawes, made with their own consent to them'.[41] In a speech delivered in the House of Lords on 10

May 1661, Lord Chancellor Clarendon rejoiced that 'we have our King again, and our Laws again, and Parliaments again', and urged the necessity of making provisions to ensure 'that neither King, nor Laws, nor Parliament may be so used again'. He was typical of many Cavalier Anglicans in believing that the observance of the law would guarantee both the subjects' security and obedience to the government.[42] Roger L'Estrange, licenser of the press and a key government propagandist during Charles II's reign, put it thus in 1662: 'let a Prince therefore stick to his antient Laws, and he may be sure his People will stick to him'.[43]

This royalist legalism is something which needs to be stressed if we are to understand the subsequent emergence of the Tory platform; Toryism, as will become clear later in this book, owed as much to conservative legal-constitutionalism as it did to absolutism. Yet in 1660 Cavalier–Anglican legalism worked in an ultra-conservative direction, serving to exalt the authority of the Crown over that of Parliament. Parliaments – as had been shown during the 1640s and 1650s – could threaten the rule of law and the constitution. Those attached to the Court were quick to deny that the Crown shared legal sovereignty with Parliament.[44] As Sir Robert Hyde, Lord Chief Justice of King's Bench, put it at the trials of the regicides in October 1660: 'the king is above the two houses. They must propose their laws to him. The laws are made by him, and not by them, by their consenting, but they are his laws'.[45] It is difficult to see how the Cavalier–Anglican defence of legal monarchy placed any practical restraints on the Crown. L'Estrange claimed that the King was limited by law, but only 'conscientiously', for in observing the law, 'he does but keep his own word'; the King certainly did not forfeit his right if he violated the law, and the law forbade rebellion.[46] Various statutes passed at the Restoration required subjects to swear oaths denying the admissibility of resistance to the Crown under any pretext whatsoever. The Crown's prerogatives were held to be rooted in the laws of the land, and could not be restrained even by Parliament. Indeed, many felt that the early legislation of the Long Parliament had amounted to an attack on the old constitution, which Charles I had only assented to under pressure, and therefore needed to be undone. There was some discussion about reviving the prerogative courts of Star Chamber and the Council of the North, although this came to nothing. Yet in 1664 the Triennial Act of 1641 was repealed, on the grounds that the Act had overthrown the fundamental laws by which England was governed: ''tis not in the power of a parliament to pass such a law, nor to root out the foundations of that authority under which they sit'. The repeal of the Triennial

Act enabled Charles II to rule without Parliament for four years in the 1680s.[47]

In addition to disputes about what type of monarchy should be restored in 1660, there were also tensions caused by the question of what types of people should return to power with the King. Cavaliers, who had stood by the King during the difficult times of the 1640s and 1650s, naturally expected to enjoy all the fruits of royal favour as a reward for their loyalty. Charles and Clarendon, however, recognised the political need to accommodate former enemies of the Crown who had backed the Restoration, as a way of securing their allegiance to the new regime. The first major achievement of the Convention was the Act of Indemnity and Oblivion, which pardoned all but a handful of those who had been involved in the regicide. There were many, however, who were alarmed at the moderation shown to those who had been associated with the republican regimes. Burnet recalled how 'the cavaliers were highly dissatisfied, and made great complaints of it'; in the Cavalier Parliament an attempt was even made to set the Indemnity aside, although Charles and Clarendon insisted on adhering strictly to it. Particularly galling for Cavaliers was to see prominent Parliamentarians and old-Cromwellians continue to receive honours and offices under the restored monarchy, whilst they themselves were passed by. It became a common jest that 'the king had passed an act of oblivion for his friends, and of indemnity for his enemies'. The charge of royal ingratitude was not entirely fair; as Ronald Hutton has shown, Cavaliers did in fact do better than any other group in the competition for places in the administration and for titles. But it was felt that many of the better jobs eluded them, and for many the fact that any of the Crown's old enemies were rewarded was bad enough. In the early years of the Restoration Anglican Royalists made several efforts to expel ex-Presbyterians and ex-Cromwellians from the administration, though without any success. The land settlement was also the source of much bitterness. The Crown and the Church managed to regain their estates which had been confiscated during the 1640s and 1650s, as too did many Royalists, to the obvious resentment of the Commonwealth purchasers. On the other hand, nothing was done to help recover lands which Royalists were regarded as having 'voluntarily' sold, even though such sales were often forced upon them in order to pay fines levied by the Long Parliament or during the Protectorate for their loyalty to the Crown. There was some justification to the complaint that the land settlement had perpetuated the results of the Civil War by impoverishing the Cavaliers and enriching their enemies.[48]

At the local level, an attempt was made to return to consensus government by the traditional landed elites. In this respect, the Restoration can be seen to mark the triumph of the gentry, although this did not mean that the counties were to be governed by homogeneous blocs of Cavaliers. Men of dubious loyalty were removed from the commissions of the peace, but there was no systematic purge of shire magistrates. As a result, those who served as JPs in the early years of the Restoration included men not just from Royalist backgrounds, but also many of Parliamentarian stock, and even some pragmatic Cromwellian administrators who were prepared to serve Charles II with equal commitment. In Cheshire, for example, of the twenty-seven men who sat on the bench at Quarter Sessions in the early 1660s, twelve came from Royalist families and fifteen from Parliamentarian, of whom nine had acted some time between 1649 and 1660.[49] There was a sound political and pragmatic logic behind such a policy; it would have been unwise to have alienated a potentially powerful group of gentry by removing them from office, and besides, it would not have been easy to find enough qualified men to serve as replacements if the purges had been more extensive. Yet if the assumption was that through compromise consensus politics could be restored, it turned out to be mistaken. In many areas JPs proved to be divided over how to enforce government policy – especially religious policy – with the result that as political divisions began to develop at the centre, they also found a reflection in the localities. Only in the corporations did the Cavalier desire for revenge receive some satisfaction. Under the Corporation Act, passed by the Cavalier Parliament in 1661, all municipal office-holders were required to take the Anglican sacrament, renounce the Presbyterian Covenant, and swear an oath of non-resistance to the King. The fact that the commissioners appointed to enforce the Act were staunch Royalists and episcopalians from the landed classes essentially enabled the Anglican gentry to police the boroughs to their own satisfaction. Although the intensity of the purges varied from region to region, large numbers of corporation members who were unable to meet the provisions of the Act were removed from office, and in many areas the commissioners replaced the evicted burgesses with members from their own ranks. Even so, the victory was short-lived; the powers of the commissioners lapsed in March 1663, and over the next few years many of those evicted were able to creep quietly back into office.[50]

RELIGIOUS TENSIONS

The discussion of the Corporation Act leads us naturally on to what was the most contentious issue at the time of the Restoration, namely religion. Separatist groups acquiesced in the Restoration because the King had promised them liberty of conscience in his Declaration from Breda. At the beginning of the reign, the Independent ministers of London presented an address to Charles thanking him for his declaration promising liberty of conscience, and assuring him they were peaceful and loyal.[51] The Quakers in particular, who had suffered persecution even under the Protectorate, had reason to believe that the new regime would be more favourable than the old. At the beginning of June 1660, Charles II assured the Quaker Richard Hubberthorne 'that you shall none of you suffer for your Opinions or Religion, so long as you Live peaceably and you have the word of a King for it'.[52] The Presbyterians and the old Puritans wanted the re-establishment of a comprehensive national Church, which maintained some of the reforms of the early 1640s, although most (except for the more rigid Presbyterians) were prepared to compromise on the issue of episcopacy. The moderate Presbyterians would have been happy with the settlement along the lines of the Worcester House Declaration of 25 October 1660. This stated that no bishop should ordain or censure without the advice and assistance of presbyters, and also promised an effectual reformation of the liturgy, with objectional forms made optional (which would have allowed Puritan ministers to dispense with kneeling at the sacrament, the use of the cross in baptism, bowing at the name of Jesus, and the wearing of the surplice).[53] The Presbyterians, however, did not want toleration; the Lancashire Puritan, Adam Martindale, who was later to suffer for his Nonconformity, was typical of many when he stated that he 'utterly abhorred' the idea.[54] The High Anglicans, in contrast, wanted a return to the Church of England of the Thirty-Nine Articles and Prayer Book under the government of bishops, as it had existed before the attacks of the Long Parliament, and were opposed to both comprehension and toleration.

The religious settlement eventually worked out by the Cavalier Parliament was a victory for the High Anglicans; neither comprehension nor toleration was conceded, and instead a fierce code was established penalising those who failed to conform to the re-established Church. The Act of Uniformity of 1662 required all ministers and teachers to testify their 'unfeigned assent and consent to all and every thing contained and prescribed in and by . . . the Book and Com-

mon Prayer' by St Bartholomew's Day (24 August), or face depriva-
tion.[55] By this measure alone nearly 1,000 ministers were forced to
give up their livings, including Presbyterians and moderate Puritans
who would have preferred to have remained part of a national
Church; the total number of clergy, lecturers and fellows who were
deprived of their posts in England and Wales between 1660–2 during
the process of re-establishing the old Church was more than double
that figure, at over 2,000.[56] In 1662 the Quaker Act was passed,
which provided stiff penalties for those who attended separatist conventicles or who refused to swear the oath of allegiance. Under the
Conventicle Act of 1664 anyone who attended a Nonconformist
meeting was to face fines of £5 (or three months' imprisonment) for
the first offence, £10 (or six months') for the second, and £100 (or
transportation) for the third. This Act also confirmed that the Elizabethan statute of 1593 against separatists and recusants (35 Eliz. c.1) was
still in force; anyone convicted under this Act was required to conform within three months or else abjure the realm, forfeiting one's
goods and lands during one's life to the Crown, with failure to abjure
being judged a capital offence. The first Conventicle Act lapsed in
1668, but was replaced by a second in 1670, which laid down lesser
fines for those who merely attended Nonconformist meetings, reserving the stiffer penalties for the preachers and for those who allowed
their houses to be used for illicit religious meetings. This Act was
particularly resented because it allowed conventiclers to be tried sum-
marily before one JP, subverting the normal common law procedure
of trial by jury, and also because it set up a system of financial incentives for those who came forward with information about conventicles, thereby encouraging people to inform on their Nonconformist
neighbours. Nonconformists were driven out of the towns not only by
the Corporation Act, but also by the Five Mile Act of 1665, which
prohibited any ejected minister from residing within five miles of his
old parish or any corporate town.

The failure to achieve liberty of conscience is readily explicable,
since there was little sympathy for the sects either in Parliament or in
the country at large at the time of the Restoration. Most of the anti-
Republican agitation of 1659–60 had been of an explicitly anti-secta-
rian nature, and it soon became clear that the separatists were not
going to be allowed to worship peacefully. Baptist and Quaker meetings were broken up by angry crowds in various parts of the country
in the spring and summer of 1660. For example, in June and July
Baptists at Fairford in Gloucester were abused as they went to their
meetings 'by the rude boyes and other people', who also smashed the

windows of their meeting-place. In Lincolnshire, Baptists complained of having 'been much abused' and even 'stoned' on their way to meetings, and if they were heard 'praying to the Lord in our own Families' at home, crowds would come and disturb them 'by uncivil beating at our doors, and sounding of horns'.[57] In Wales, the local authorities were quick to take action against notorious sectarians, and by midsummer 1660 Welsh gaols were crowded with Baptists and Quakers.[58] An examination of the debates on ecclesiastical matters in the Cavalier Parliament reveals that measures against the sects received enthusiastic support from the vast majority of the members, including Presbyterian MPs. William Prynne and Sir Ralph Ashton, for example, played a prominent part in the promotion of the 1662 Quaker Act.

It is more difficult to penetrate why plans for a more comprehensive Church settlement also failed. Some have sought to lay the blame on the King's advisors, others on the Laudian clergy, although the current historiographical orthodoxy is to see the Restoration Church settlement as a triumph for the militant Anglicanism of the gentry, both in the counties and in Parliament.[59] In fact, the religious settlement should not be seen as a victory for any one group, since the government, the clergy, the gentry, as well as the laity in general, were bitterly divided over what type of Church settlement was desirable. Without recognising this important fact, the subsequent nature and development of partisan strife in England would not be intelligible.

In recent years historians have come to recognise that there was spontaneous pressure to reconstruct the Church as it had been before the Civil War, even before the eventual religious settlement was worked out. In many areas, militant Anglicans took the line that since the rule of law had returned with the King, they were free to contest for their rights which they felt were theirs by law. As early as 28 May 1660 – that is, the day before the King's triumphant return to his capital – the Commons was hearing reports of 'several Riots . . . and forcible Entries' caused by incumbents seeking to repossess the livings which they felt had been illegally taken from them during the civil wars and Interregnum, and over the next few months a number of cases were brought before the courts to evict intruders, until an Act was passed in September which formally restored ejected ministers to their livings. Richard Baxter thought 'many hundred worthy Ministers' had been displaced before mid-July; by the end of the year, some 695 incumbents had been ejected.[60] The return to the rule of law was also taken to mean a return to the old Church of bishops and the Prayer Book. During June and July 1660 large numbers of gentry from various counties subscribed to addresses in favour of episcopacy and the liturgy, asking for 'the restitution of Religion . . . according to the undoubted laws of this kingdom'.[61]

Without waiting to see what settlement would be achieved, Anglicans in many areas immediately began a restoration of the traditional church service. According to one contemporary, 'those who were Episcopalians' started to read the Common Prayer 'at his Majesty's first return or before'.[62] In a nationwide sample of churchwardens accounts for some 306 parishes, Ronald Hutton discovered that nearly half of these had bought the pre-war Prayer Book within eighteen months of the Restoration, most doing so within the first year. Some of the more conservative parishes (especially in rural areas) did not need to purchase new Prayer Books, since they had managed to keep their old ones. London was the slowest – here most churches were not using the Prayer Book by the next spring.[63] Hutton also found that in the eighteen months following the Worcester House Declaration – and in defiance of it – indictments were brought against ministers for not using the Prayer Book in some eighteen counties across the country. Typically, the initiative was taken by the local landed elite. According to White Kennett, 'the Justices of the Peace, Nobility and Gentry, had insisted that the Laws returned with the King, and that the Common-Prayer was by Law establish'd, and that therefore those Parochial Ministers who would not use the Common Prayer were liable to be prosecuted for offending against the Statutes made in that Behalf'. The decision to indict Adam Martindale at the winter assizes of 1661 for refusing to read the Book of Common Prayer was apparently the design of the gentry who served on the grand jury, the foreman of which was determined to make the charge stick, even though Martindale claimed that his failure to read it was due to the fact that his parish did not yet have a Prayer Book he could read. The disproportionate number of prosecutions for failing to read the Common Prayer Book that occurred in Nottinghamshire was due in no small part to the zeal of local JP, Peniston Whalley. At the April Quarter Sessions of 1661 he instructed the grand jury that, notwithstanding the Worcester House Declaration or the Declaration of Breda, they were 'to present all ministers . . . that do not constantly upon every Sunday or other opportunity of religious worship, read the Liturgy of the Church established by law'.[64]

Yet the desire for the restoration of the old Church was not a concern peculiar to the landed elite, but appears to have had much support amongst the population at large. Many who welcomed the return of monarchy did so in the belief that it meant not just deliverance from the sects, but from Puritanism in general, including Presbyterianism. According to Anthony Wood, the people of England went 'perfectly mad' at the Restoration, because 'they were freed from the chaines of darkness and confusion which the presbyterians and phanaticks had brought upon them'. The extensive use of maypoles – which had been prohibited by the Long Parliament – in the public celebrations at the restoration of Charles II should be read as a symbolic rejection of the Puritan past. Numerous maypoles were erected in Oxford in May 1660, 'set up on purpose', Wood tells us, 'to vex the Presbyterians and Independents'.[65] We can also find evidence of ordinary parishioners petitioning for the return of the old ministers or for the use of the Prayer Book service.[66] The return of the bishops appears to have been genuinely welcomed by many groups. For example, when John Cosin, Bishop of Durham, entered his diocese in the summer of 1661, he was greeted by enthusiastic crowds not just of gentry and clergy, but also of ordinary people.[67] In March 1661 some apprentices and other youths of London addressed the King to thank him for his 'zeal in maintaining our happiness, and the wholesome discipline of the Church as it was in our glorious Martyr's days, under bishops and doctors'.[68]

However, the strength of this militant Anglican reaction should not be exaggerated. There was much support for a comprehensive Church settlement, not just from Presbyterians, but also from moderate Anglicans. Much of the anti-republican agitation of 1659–60, especially in London, had been Presbyterian in nature. In November 1659, one petition from the London apprentices expressed a preference for the religion established by 'our three last Princes, with some amendment in Discipline'.[69] Monck himself seems to have favoured a 'moderate Presbyterian' settlement in the Church, even though he conceded that 'prelacy must be brought in'.[70] There were good reasons for thinking that such a compromise could be worked out. During the Interregnum various groups of clergymen had drawn closer together in an attempt to meet the challenge of the sects, and some Anglicans and Presbyterians had begun to work towards a model of Church government which would have allowed for limited episcopacy working in alliance with presbyters.[71]

It is true that in the Cavalier Parliament militant Anglicans carried all before them, and that the key measures for re-establishing the Church along the old lines were introduced by the gentry in the Commons. Yet MPs were more divided than is usually recognised. Thus the measures which affected Presbyterians met powerful opposition in the House of Commons, and were successful only after extremely close votes. If we look at the records of persecution for the 1660s, we find that the gentry were divided over the desirability of taking action against Nonconformists. In Dorset, Somerset and Wiltshire, for example, whilst some JPs were particularly severe, others were rather lenient, and some were even prepared to protect Nonconformists from the officers of the law. A similar situation existed in Hampshire, where the campaign against Dissent was led by a minority of persecuting magistrates. During the 1660s, most of those prosecuted for Nonconformity were in fact Baptists, Quakers and Fifth Monarchists; the gentry as a whole seem to have been reluctant to take action against the more moderate Dissenters.[72]

The role of the clergy in shaping the eventual religious settlement is equally complex. R. S. Bosher's view that intolerant Anglicanism inevitably triumphed because the Laudian party amongst the clergy were able to recapture control of the ecclesiastical establishment after 1660 has to be modified in the light of the researches of Ian Green. When Charles II re-established the episcopal bench he tried to ensure that no one party predominated, whilst his early clerical appointments included a combination of Anglicans and Commonwealth divines. The King's agents urged the use of 'moderation . . . in the pulpit' and did their best to discourage 'Ranting Royalists', with the result that in their sermons, the clergy often took a neutral, even eirenic stance on the religious question.[73] Nevertheless, it would be wrong to suggest that the role of the High Church clergy was insignificant. Those who had felt strongly enough to suffer ejections from their livings in the 1650s, and who found refuge in the homes of sympathetic gentry and nobility, did much to keep alive a deep commitment to episcopalian Anglicanism amongst a small clique of men who were themselves to play a prominent part on the re-establishment of the Church of England after 1660. And whatever the overall nature of Charles's ecclesiastical preferments in the early months of the Restoration, the activists who came to have most influence within the Church were militant High Anglicans, the most important figure being Gilbert Sheldon, created Bishop of London in 1660, and promoted to Archbishop of Canterbury in 1663.[74]

Similar divisions can be detected at the level of central government. Both Bosher and Green believed that the Earl of Clarendon was all along committed to the restoration of the traditional Church of England, though his sensitivity to political considerations led him at times to oppose too drastic action against Puritans. Such a view is probably too harsh; recent studies suggest that the Lord Chancellor was sincere in his eirenic intentions, and see him as working for a compromise which would keep the Presbyterians within the Church. Nevertheless, the laws penalising Dissent would never have been passed without the backing they received from courtiers, officials and royal spokesmen in Parliament – from men such as Lord Fanshaw, Sir Job Charlton, Sir John Bramston and Sir Heneage Finch, and a number of other prominent Anglican Royalists. The problem was that the government, like everyone else, was divided on the religious question. In short, the Church settlement was a victory for a faction. One thing that seems clear is that the eventual Church settlement did not work out in the way that the King would have wished. Although Charles II was committed to the re-establishment of episcopacy and disliked Presbyterianism, he was not averse to making concessions to Puritans. Most significantly, he wanted religious toleration for those who would live peaceably under the restored monarchy – not least because of his own sympathies for Catholicism.[75]

CONCLUSION

Political conflict under the later Stuarts was to be fought out along two major axes – the constitutional and the religious. Disagreements over the relative powers of Crown and Parliament, and tensions between Church and Dissent, were to feed in to the bitter party struggle which emerged between Whigs and Tories at the end of Charles II's reign, a struggle which was to divide not just the elite but the whole of society. The roots of this conflict can be traced back to the Restoration. If there existed a broad consensus on the need for the re-establishment of monarchy by the spring of 1660, there was consensus on little else. There was wide-ranging disagreement on the desired constitutional settlement, spanning the spectrum from those who, at one extreme, wanted the restored monarch's powers to be severely limited, to those at the other who wanted a restoration of the monarchy of the 1630s. The eventual settlement, which marked a return to the position of 1641, left the Crown in a fairly strong but nevertheless ambiguous position. Thus there was plenty of room for dispute as to whether the King was absolute, or shared his sovereignty with the two Houses of Parliament, and over the extent to which he was bound, and could be constrained, by the law. The bitterest tensions, however, existed in the religious sphere. Both Presbyterians and Anglicans worked actively for the restoration of monarchy, whilst most separatists eventually came to accept its inevitability, but each of these groups expected different, and mutually incompatible, things from a restored Charles II. In the end, the High Anglicans won the day; neither the Presbyterians won the comprehensive Church settlement they so much desired, nor the separatists their liberty of conscience, with the inevitable result that both felt betrayed by the Restoration. Moreover, these tensions existed not just at the level of the political elite, or amongst the gentry, but also amongst the mass of the population; England was already a divided society in 1660.

In order to understand the subsequent emergence of party strife, it is important to recognise that no single group emerged as clear victors at this time. The Anglican-Royalist gentry achieved most of what they wanted in constitutional and religious terms, but they were not able to monopolise political control of the new regime as they had hoped, and they felt bitterly disappointed that they were not adequately rewarded for their loyalty to the Crown in the 1640s and 1650s. The Presbyterian-Royalists had greatest cause to feel cheated, but neither they nor the ex-Cromwellians lost out completely, but maintained enough of a toe-hold in the government to give them hopes of reshaping the regime more in accordance with their wishes. The King had recaptured his Crown, with many of its powers intact (including control over the militia, which had been the legal issue which had sparked the Civil War). Yet he had not been able to procure the religious settlement he desired, and it was as yet unclear how much of an independent role he would be able to carve out for himself in politics. In short, it is difficult to see what the Restoration actually settled, beyond the fact that the English state was to be headed by a monarchy. Not only were the tensions between Crown and Parliament or Church and Dissent unresolved, but the fact that no-one could feel that they had come out on top meant that all the key protagonists had everything to contend for. In such a situation, it was inevitable that political and religious strife would develop. In addition, there emerged new concerns in the 1660s and 1670s that Charles II and his followers at Court favoured an autocratic system of government and were too sympathetic to Roman Catholicism. The ways in which new fears about the growth of popery and arbitrary government combined with the old constitutional and religious tensions left unresolved at the Restoration to lead to the emergence of partisan strife in England will be explored in the next chapter.

REFERENCES

1. James Buck, *St. Paul's Thanksgiving: Set forth in a Sermon Preached before the Right Honorable House of Peers* (1660), p. 3.
2. George Hickes, *A Sermon Preached at the Cathedral Church of Worcester, on the 29th May, 1684* (1684), p. 20.
3. Cited in B. H. G. Wormald, *Clarendon. Politics, History and Religion* (Cambridge, 1951), p. 238.
4. Godfrey Davies, *The Restoration of Charles II, 1658–60* (San Marino, 1955), p. 355.
5. Ronald Hutton, *The Restoration: A Political and Religious History of England and Wales, 1658–1667* (Oxford, 1985), p. 119.
6. Christopher Hill, *Some Intellectual Consequences of the English Revolution* (1980), pp. 10–11, 15; Christopher Hill, *The World Turned Upside Down: Radical Ideas during the English Revolution* (Harmondsworth, 1975), p. 354; Richard L. Greaves, *Deliver Us from Evil: The Radical Underground in Britain, 1660–1663* (Oxford, 1986), p. 21.
7. Godfrey Davies, 'The General Election of 1660', *HLQ*, **15** (1951–2), pp. 211–35; Louise Fargo Brown, 'The Religious Factors in the Convention Parliament', *EHR*, **22** (1907), pp. 51–63; *CSPD, 1660–1*, pp. 536–9; Henning (ed.), *The House of Commons 1660–1690*, **I**, pp. 31–2, 311–12; Hutton, *Restoration*, pp. 111–13, 152–3.
8. Harris, *London Crowds in the Reign of Charles II: Propaganda and Politics from the Restoration until the Exclusion Crisis*, pp. 40–9.
9. Thomas Rugg, *Diurnal, 1659–61*, Willam L. Sachse (ed.) (Camden Society, 1961), pp. 31–2, 40–2; Clive Holmes, *Seventeenth-Century Lincolnshire* (Lincoln, 1980), p. 218; James M. Rosenheim, *The Townshends of Raynham: Nobility in Transition in Restoration and Early Hanoverian England* (Middletown, Connecticut, 1989), p. 21; Evans, *Seventeenth-Century Norwich: Politics, Religion and Government, 1620–1690*, p. 223.
10. *A Letter from Exeter Advertising the State of Affairs There* [1660]; *Mercurius Politicus*, no. 603, 12–19 Jan. 1660, p. 1035; *Ibid.*, no. 604, 19–26 Jan. 1660, p. 1049; White Kennett, *A Register and Chronicle Ecclesiastical and Civil* (1728), pp. 20, 32; Hutton, *Restoration*, p. 89.
11. *A Letter of the Apprentices of the City of Bristol, To the Apprentices of the Honourable City of London* (1660); *Mercurius Politicus*, no. 606, 2–9 Feb. 1660, p. 1084; *Ibid.*, no. 607, 9–16 Feb. 1660, p. 1108; Kennett, *Register*, p. 50; Rugg, *Diurnal*, p. 42.
12. Lucy Hutchinson, *Memoirs of the Life of Colonel Hutchinson*, C. H. Firth (ed.) (2 vols, 1885), **II**, p. 241; *CSPVen, 1659–61*, p. 119; Rugg, *Diurnal*, pp. 39, 44; Hutton, *Restoration*, pp. 94, 97; Harris, *London Crowds*, pp. 49–50; Davies, *Restoration*, pp. 283–4, 290–1.
13. Rugg, *Diurnal*, pp. 79–80; *Mercurius Publicus*, **I**, no. 19, 3–10 May 1600, pp. 300–2.
14. Henry Townshend, *Diary*, J. W. Willis Bund (ed.) (2 vols, 1920), **I**, p. 39.

15. Harris, *London Crowds*, pp. 38–9; Underdown, *Revel, Riot and Rebellion: Popular Politics and Culture in Enland 1603–1660*, ch. 10; Hutton, *Restoration*, pp. 125–6; Philip Styles, 'The City of Worcester during the Civil Wars, 1640–60', in his *Studies in Seventeenth-Century West Midlands History* (Kineton, 1978), p. 255.

16. Rugg, *Diurnal*, pp. 9, 39.

17. *Mercurius Politicus*, no. 606, 2–9 Feb. 1660, p. 1084; Kennett, *Register*, p. 50; *Letter of the Apprentices of . . . Bristol.*

18. Bodl. Lib., MS Clarendon 67, fol. 119.

19. *A Letter from Exeter; Mercurius Politicus*, no. 603, 12–19 Jan. 1660, p. 1035; *Ibid.*, no. 604, 19–26 Jan. 1660, p. 1049; Kennett, *Register*, pp. 20, 32.

20. *A Declaration of Many Thousand Well-Affected Persons, Inhabitants in and about the Cities of London and Westminster* (1660); Rugg, *Diurnal*, p. 39.

21. Hutton, *Restoration*, pp. 115–16.

22. *Records of the Borough of Leicester . . . 1603–88*, Helen Stocks (ed.), with W. H. Stevenson (Cambridge, 1923), p. 465.

23. Townshend, *Diary*, **I**, p. 40.

24. PRO, SP 29/47, no. 76.

25. HLRO, Main Papers, House of Lords, 28 May 1660.

26. Jonathan Scott, *Algernon Sidney and the English Republic, 1623–1677* (Cambridge, 1988), p. 143.

27. [George Fox], *A Declaration from the Harmless and Innocent People of God called Quakers* (1661); *The Humble Apology of Some Commonly Called Anabaptists* (1661); *A Renunciation and Declaration of the Ministers of Congregational Churches* (1661).

28. J. P. Kenyon, *The Stuart Constitution 1603–1688* (Cambridge, 1966), doc. 97, pp. 357–8.

29. Bodl. Lib., MS Tanner 49, fol. 2.

30. Henning, *House of Commons*, **I**, p. 407.

31. Douglas R. Lacey, *Dissent and Parliamentary Politics in England, 1661–1689* (New Brunswick, 1969), ch. 1; Jones, *Charles II: Royal Politician*, p. 40; Hutton, *Restoration*, pp. 105–18; Kennett, *Register*, p. 90.

32. C. D. Chandaman, *The English Public Revenue, 1660–1688* (Oxford, 1975).

33. Paul Seaward, *The Cavalier Parliament and the Reconstruction of the Old Regime, 1661–1667* (Cambridge, 1989), pp. 22–3, 42–3; Burnet, *History*, p. 169; Pepys, *Diary*, **V**, p. 60; Steven Pincus, 'Protestantism and Patriotism: Ideology and the Making of English Foreign Policy 1650–1665', unpub. Harvard PhD thesis (1990), pp. 394–5.

34. *CJ*, **VIII**, p. 8.

35. *His Majesties Answer to the Nineteen Propositions* (1642); C. C. Weston and J. R. Greenberg, *Subjects and Sovereigns: The Grand Controversy over Legal Sovereignty in Stuart England* (Cambridge, 1981), pp. 149–51.

36. William Walwyn, *God Save the King, Or A Sermon of Thanksgiving For His Majesties Happy Return to the Throne* (1660), pp. 12–13; Gilbert Sheldon, *David's Deliverance and Thanksgiving. A Sermon Preached before the King at Whitehall upon June 28. 1660* (1660), p. 3.

37. John Paradise, *Hadadrimmon, Sive Threnodia Anglican ob Regicidium. A Sermon on David's Humiliation For Cutting Off the Royal Robe* (1661), epistle dedicatory.

38. Francis Gregory, *David's Returne from His Banishment. Set Forth in a Thanksgiving Sermon of the Returne of His Sacred Majesty Charles the II* (Oxford, 1660), p. 12.

39. *Certain Considerations: Being the Legitimate Issue of a True English Heart* (1660), p. 4.

40. Sheldon, *David's Deliverance*, p. 32.

41. George Morley, *A Sermon Preached at the Magnificent Coronation of . . . Charles the II^d* (1661), p. 36.

42. *LJ*, **XI**, pp. 242–3, 248, 275–6; Seaward, *Cavalier Parliament*, pp. 17–18.

43. Roger L'Estrange, *A Memento: Directed To all Those that Truly Reverence the Memory of King Charles the Martyr . . . The First Part* (1662), p. 154

44. Weston and Greenberg, *Subjects and Sovereigns*, ch. 6.

45. *State Trials*, **V**, col. 1030.

46. L'Estrange, *Memento*, p. 119.

47. Seaward, *Cavalier Parliament*, pp. 21, 47, 131–5.

48. Burnet, *History*, pp. 108–12; Hutton, *Restoration*, pp. 132–8, 142, 162–6; Seaward, *Cavalier Parliament*, ch. 8.

49. John Morrill, *Cheshire 1630–1660: County Government and Society during the English Revolution* (Oxford, 1974), p. 327.

50. Norrey, 'The Restoration Regime in Action: The Relationship between Central and Local Government in Dorset, Somerset and Wiltshire', pp. 804–12; Coleby, *Central Government and the Localities: Hampshire 1649–1689*, pp. 90–6; Hutton, *Restoration*, 158–61.

51. PRO, SP 29/1, no. 36.

52. *An Account of Severall things that passed between his Sacred Majesty and Richard Hubberthorne Quaker* (1660), p. 7.

53. *LJ*, **XI**, pp. 179–82; *The Humble and Grateful Acknowledgment of Many Ministers of the Gospel* (1660); Hutton, *Restoration*, p. 146; R. S. Bosher, *The Making of the Restoration Settlement: The Influence of the Laudians, 1649–1662* (1951), pp. 188–90; Lacey, *Dissent and Parliamentary Politics in England, 1661–1689*, p. 13.

54. Adam Martindale, *Life*, R. Parkinson (ed.) (Chetham Society, 1845), p. 139.

55. Kenyon, *Stuart Constitution*, doc. 103, pp. 378–82.

56. A. G. Matthews, *Calamy Revised* (Oxford, 1934), pp. xiii–xiv; Watts, *The Dissenters: From the Reformation to the French Revolution*, p. 219.

57. H[enry] J[essey], *The Lord's Loud Call to England* (1660), pp. 4, 15–16; Watts, *Dissenters*, p. 215.

58. Geraint H. Jenkins, *The Foundations of Modern Wales: Wales 1642–1780* (Oxford, 1987), p. 135.

59. Green, *The Re-establishment of the Church of England 1660–1663*.

60. *CJ*, **VIII**, p. 47; *Reliquiae Baxterianae: Or, Mr Richard Baxter's Narrative of the Most Memorable Passages of his Life and Times*, Matthew Sylvester (ed.) (1696), p. 241; Matthews, *Calamy Revised*, pp. xii- xiii; Bosher,

Making of the Restoration Settlement, pp. 164–5; Watts, *Dissenters*, p. 217; Jones, *Charles II*, p. 48; George Morley, *The Bishop of Winchester's Vindication of Himself* (1683), p. 489.

61. Bosher, *Making of the Restoration Settlement*, p. 156; Jones, *Charles II*, p. 51. The quote is taken from the address of the nobility and gentry of Northamptonshire, 20 June 1660.

62. Anthony Wood, *Life and Times*, Andrew Clark (ed.) (5 vols, Oxford, 1891–1900) **I**, pp. 313, 319; Bosher, *Making of the Restoration Settlement*, p. 163.

63. Hutton, *Restoration*, pp. 172, 332 (note 124).

64. Kennett, *Register*, p. 374; Martindale, *Life*, p. 159; Bosher, *Making of the Restoration Settlement*, pp. 200–4; Green, *Re-establishment*, ch. 9; Stephen K. Roberts, *Recovery and Restoration in an English County: Devon Local Administration 1646–1670* (Exeter, 1985), pp. 69–70.

65. Wood, *Life and Times*, **I**, pp. 314, 317; Underdown, *Revel, Riot and Rebellion*, pp. 274–5.

66. PRO, SP 29/12, no. 114; Rugg, *Diurnal*, p. 154.

67. BL, Harleian MS 3784, fols 27, 31; Hutton, *Restoration*, p. 174.

68. *CSPD, 1670, Addenda 1660–1670*, p. 658.

69. *The Remonstrance of the Apprentices in and about London* (1659).

70. Joan Thirsk (ed.), *The Restoration* (1976), p. 41.

71. Hutton, *Restoration*, p. 143.

72. Norrey, 'Restoration Regime', pp. 805–6; Coleby, *Hampshire*, pp. 139, 147–8; A. J. Fletcher, 'The Enforcement of the Conventicle Acts 1664–1679', in W. J. Sheils (ed.), *Studies in Church History. 21. Persecution and Toleration* (Oxford, 1984), pp. 235–46; Jenkins, *Making of a Ruling Class*, p. 121; Seaward, *Cavalier Parliament*, p. 193; Challinor, 'Restoration and Exclusion'.

73. Green, *Re-establishment*; Bodl. Lib., MS Clarendon 71, fols 230, 233.

74. Seaward, *Cavalier Parliament*, pp. 62–7; Paul Seaward, 'Gilbert Sheldon, the London Vestries, and the Defence of the Church', in Harris et al. (eds.), *The Politics of Religion in Restoration England*, pp. 49–73.

75. Seaward, *Cavalier Parliament*, pp. 27–31, 96–8, 162–95, 328; Ronald Hutton, *Charles II, King of England, Scotland, and Ireland* (Oxford, 1989), *passim*.

CHAPTER THREE

Court, Country and the Origins of Party

Precisely when we can begin to talk about the emergence of party politics in England is a difficult question. Although the terms Whig and Tory did not come in to common usage until the Exclusion Crisis, the issues which divided the two groups did not suddenly burst onto the scene with Titus Oates' revelations of a Popish Plot in the late summer of 1678: there had been growing fears about 'popery' and 'arbitrary government' throughout the 1660s and 1670s; the idea of excluding the Duke of York from the succession because of his Catholicism had been raised as early as 1674; and during this period we see increasing polarisation along political and religious lines both in Parliament and in society at large. From the late 1660s contemporaries were beginning to talk in terms of a clash between the Court (the supporters of a strong, royal executive) and Country (the champions of Parliament), and by the early 1670s most people were prepared to acknowledge the existence of Court and Country 'parties'. Writing in 1682, Edmund Bohun asserted that the Commons during the last session of the Cavalier Parliament 'were divided into two great Parties . . . the Court-Party and the Country-Party';[1] indeed, in 1677–8 the future Whig leader, the Earl of Shaftesbury, had been able to divide both Houses of Parliament fairly evenly between those who were 'vile' (supporters of the Court) and those who were 'worthy' (supporters of the Country).[2]

To what extent, then, did the Court–Country groupings that had emerged by the mid-1670s anticipate the later partisan strife between Tories and Whigs? Most historians see a constitutional struggle between Court and Country, or between the royal executive and Parlia-

ment, as the dominant theme in politics in Charles II's reign, providing a basic continuity between the pre-Popish Plot era and the Exclusion Crisis. J. H. Plumb, for example, has written that during this time
'greater control of Parliament by the executive or greater independence from it became the crux of politics', whilst Weston and
Greenberg see the main conflict in politics as being between those
who believed the King was the only supreme governor within the
realm, and those who thought he shared his sovereignty with Parliament.[3] Nowadays scholars tend to be sceptical as to whether we can
talk about 'parties' before 1679: not only were the Court and Country
factions not as coherent and well-organised as we once thought, but
also politics at this time, so J. R. Jones maintains, 'were largely contained within the restricted arenas of Whitehall and Westminster',
allowing little potential for the mobilisation of nationwide support on
behalf of common and publicly stated objectives. Jones has also asserted that it would be wrong to see the Tory party as an outgrowth
of the Court interest which the Earl of Danby had sought to construct
in the mid-1670s: 'Toryism, when it developed as a reaction to the
introduction of Exclusion in May 1679, represented a fresh start.'[4]
Most would agree, however, that the first Whigs were the ideological
heirs of the Country opposition of the mid-1670s; indeed, many of
the leading Country spokesmen of the mid-1670s, who came to arti-
culate the case against royal absolutism, were to be prominent members of the first Whig movement.[5]

It will be the argument of this chapter that the political developments of the 1660s and 1670s were crucial for the subsequent development of party strife. Most of the components of the Exclusion Crisis,
it will be maintained, were already in existence before the crisis actually broke, so that what happened after the revelations of the Popish
Plot amounted not so much to a fresh start but rather to an intensification of old struggles. But our understanding of this period has been
hampered by an over-concentration on constitutional sources of conflict. In fact there were two main sources of political tension in this
period: a constitutional one, centring around the powers of the Crown
and the strength of the executive, which led to tensions between
Court and Country; and a religious one, centring around the nature of
the Church establishment and the issue of Dissent. Sometimes they
combined to reinforce each other, at other times they cut across each
other, to produce a complex system of political allegiances, as people
shifted from Court to Country depending on how they saw their religious interests could best be secured. I shall start this chapter by looking
at the development of Court–Country tensions, which were stimulated

by the fears that the Court was inclined towards popery and arbitrary government. I shall then look at the beginnings of party organisation, and suggest that the Court and Country groupings of the 1670s pioneered the techniques of party management which were to be used by the Whigs and Tories after the Popish Plot. Finally, I shall examine the importance of the issue of Dissent, and demonstrate the complex way in which religious issues cut across constitutional ones. It will be argued that the origins of the Tory–Whig divide are to be found less in the Court–Country tensions but rather in the religious tensions generated by the controversy over the nature of the Church establishment.

FEARS OF POPERY AND ARBITRARY GOVERNMENT AND THE EMERGENCE OF COURT–COUNTRY TENSIONS

In his *Account of the Growth of Popery*, written at the end of 1677, Andrew Marvell alleged that there had been a design carried on for 'diverse years . . . to change the lawful Government of England into an Absolute Tyranny, and to Convert the Established Protestant Religion into down-right Popery.' This design he traced back to 1665, outlining the various factors which had caused disaffection from the Court over the previous twelve years: the pro-Catholic leanings of the Court; the attempt to draw England into the orbit of Catholic France; concerns about the threat to the independence of Parliament; and the alleged effort to establish rule by a standing army. Marvell was, of course, writing political propaganda rather than offering an impartial analysis of the sources of political tension during the 1660s and 1670s. He glossed over the very real differences in the various royal administrations of this period, leaving the impression that there was more coherence to the designs of the Court during this time than in reality there was. Nevertheless, Marvell's *Account* does help explain why, by the late 1670s, many had grown to be so suspicious of the Court, and on the surface his chronology seems to fit well with the emerging polarisation in English politics which contemporaries recognised was taking place.

The re-emergence of a conflict between Court and Country can be traced back to the latter years of Clarendon's administration. The disappointments of the second Dutch War of 1665–67 brought about the first major political crisis for the Court, and enabled the opposition in Parliament to make successful challenges to the royal prerogative in two crucial respects. Clarendon was impeached for his mismanagement of the war effort (a direct attack on the King's prerogative of choosing his own ministers), whilst in addition the Commons, suspecting that the funds granted for the prosecution of the war had been misappropriated or embezzled, sought to extend its control over the purse strings by establishing a Parliamentary commission to inspect accounts of extraordinary revenue and expenditure. Underlying the crisis of 1667 was a fear that the Court was leaning towards popery and a more arbitrary style of government. The troops which were hurriedly raised in June 1667, ostensibly to protect England against coastal attack, brought allegations of a design to establish rule by a standing army; indeed, it was rumoured that the Duke of York had advised Charles to raise money without Parliament and to use the new army to keep order. The Commons unanimously voted for the immediate disbandment of the troops. There was also suspicion that the mismanagement of the war may have been due to the Catholic leanings of the Court. A number of members of the royal entourage were of the Roman faith, including the Queen and Queen Mother, a number of ladies of pleasure, and several of the King's friends and advisors. The religious leanings of the royal brothers themselves were not above suspicion. As early as February 1661 Pepys recorded his concern over the possibility that the Duke of York or his family might one day 'come to the Crowne' because he was 'a professed friend to the Catholiques'.[6] The King's Declaration of Indulgence of 1662, which had sought to grant religious toleration to both Protestant Dissenters and Catholics through the use of the prerogative power, provoked an outcry against popery, and not only did Parliament force the King to withdraw the Indulgence, but proceeded to introduce bills to prevent the growth of popery.[7] The number of Catholics at Court became a cause for concern when France joined the Dutch in the war against England in 1666, and when the Dutch sailed up the Medway in June 1667 and destroyed the naval base at Chatham, there were rumours that this was part of a Court conspiracy to advance the cause of popery. As a result, a further bill was brought to prevent the growth of popery.[8]

Fears of popery and arbitrary government reached a heightened intensity in the early 1670s as a result of developments during the administration of the 'Cabal' (1667–73) – so-called after the initial letters of five of the chief ministers of the period, Clifford, Ashley (the future Earl of Shaftesbury), Buckingham, Arlington and Lauderdale. Although immediately after the fall of Clarendon England became involved in an alliance with the Protestant powers of Sweden and the Netherlands against France, the Court soon broke out of this triple alliance and moved into a partnership with France. Under the terms of the Treaty of Dover of 1670, Charles agreed to join Louis XIV in a war against the Dutch in return for French subsidies; Charles had also secretly promised that, in return for further subsidies, he would declare himself a Roman Catholic as soon as his affairs permitted. Suspicions about the true nature of the treaty were aroused when, on 15 March 1672, two days before the declaration of war against the Dutch, Charles issued a Declaration of Indulgence suspending all the penal laws in force; the Indulgence not only allowed Protestant Dissenters to take out licences to hold public meetings, but also permitted Roman Catholics to worship in their own houses. The presence in England of troops raised to fight the Dutch (they were intended to be used to invade Holland once the Dutch fleet had been defeated in the Channel), troops which, moreover, were headed by a French General, Count Schomberg (albeit that Schomberg was a Protestant and of German extraction), gave further cause for alarm. Moreover, all these initiatives were taken without consulting Parliament. Burnet thought 'the whole conduct shewed a design to govern by the French model', whilst according to a contemporary pamphleteer, the French alliance and Dutch War were part of a conspiracy to establish absolutism and Catholicism by means of the army, with French subsidies enabling the King to become independent of Parliament.[9]

These developments led to an outcry in Parliament against popery and arbitrary government when it reconvened in February 1673. The royal use of the suspending power to grant toleration was attacked, the Commons voting that 'penal statutes, in matters ecclesiastical, cannot be suspended but by Act of Parliament', and Charles withdrew his Indulgence in March. The army was attacked, and in the session which met in October the Commons passed a resolution that 'the continuing of any standing forces other than the Militia, is a great Grievance and vexation to the people'.[10] Concern about the number of Catholics who held commissions in the armed forces and places at Court led to the passing of the Test Act on 20 March, which required all holders of civil and military office to take the Anglican sacrament and make a declaration against transubstantiation. The passage of the Act of 1673 was not only a further challenge to the King's freedom to choose his own ministers, but it also brought to a head the question of the Catholicism of the heir to the throne. Since Charles had not managed to father any legitimate children, the current heir was the King's brother, James, Duke of York. York had probably been converted to

Catholicism as early as 1669, but he made his first public affirmation of his new faith by his failure to take the Anglican sacrament at Easter 1673, and in June he resigned his office as Lord High Admiral under the terms of the Test Act. (A subsequent Test Act of 1678 disabled Catholics from sitting in either House of Parliament, although in this instance the Duke of York was explicitly excluded from its provisions.) Matters were made worse by York's marriage to a Catholic princess, Mary of Modena, in September 1673. By his first wife, Anne Hyde (who died in 1671), James had had two daughters (Mary and Anne) who were being brought up as Protestants. But their claim to the succession would be superseded by any son he had by his second marriage, and if that son were brought up a Catholic (as seemed likely) then there was the prospect of a never-ending succession of Catholic monarchs in England. It was at this time, therefore, that the Catholic succession first became a burning issue in English politics.

A manuscript libel of January 1674, addressed to 'the Lords and Commons in Parliament', vividly reflects many of the fears held by contemporaries. It starts by condemning the French alliance and the raising of the army as part of a plot, and accused 'those who have at present the chief direction of affairs' of 'a wicked and treasonable design to subvert the fundamental laws of this Kingdom by introducing Popery and setting up an arbitrary government'. Then reflecting on how 'dangerous' it would be 'to have the Crown placed on a Popish head hereafter', it asks whether 'it be not high time to consider the settling the succession of the Crown so as may secure us and our posterities from those bloody massacres and inhuman Smithfield butcheries, the certain consequences of a Popish Government?' The House of Lords busied itself considering bills to protect the Protestant religion and to restrict the powers of the Duke of York, if he ever became King, and on 10 February the Earl of Carlisle even proposed a measure that in future any prince of the blood who married a Catholic without the consent of Parliament should be excluded from the succession.[11]

The fall of the Cabal was followed by a period when the administration was trusted to Thomas Osborne, soon to be created Earl of Danby. Although Danby attempted to dissociate the Court from the previous pro-French and pro-Catholic policies, the system he developed of giving rewards and pensions to loyal supporters aroused more suspicions that the executive was seeking to establish arbitrary government by subverting the independence of the Commons. That Danby's aim was to tame Parliament seemed confirmed when in April 1675 he introduced a Test Bill, by which all members of both houses and all office-holders were to be required to make a declaration that taking up arms against the King was not lawful upon any pretence whatsoever, and to swear not at any time to endeavour the alteration of the government in Church or State. Shaftesbury, who had now moved into opposition, saw this as part of a wider design to make the government 'absolute and Arbitrary' and to establish rule by a standing army, that would so reduce Parliament's power as to leave it only 'as an instrument to raise Money'.[12] When in the winter of 1677–8 troops began to be raised for a war against France, many MPs, sceptical of the sincerity of the about-turn in foreign policy, began to fear that the army might be used against Parliament.

The pronouncements of those who defended the Court further reinforced the impression that there was a design to establish royal absolutism. As Mark Goldie has shown, the championship of patriarchal and divine-right monarchy became a staple of Restoration royalist apologetic, long before the Tories decided to resuscitate Filmer's *Patriarcha* in 1680. John Locke complained of 'a generation of men', that had sprung up after 1660, 'who would flatter princes with an Opinion, that they have a Divine Right to absolute Power'.[13] Such views became particularly prominent during the periods of the Cabal and Danby's ascendancy. Burnet commented how, at the time of the 1672 Indulgence, 'court-flatterers were always magnifying absolute government'.[14] Under Danby, High Church clerics busied themselves preaching up theories of divine right and non-resistance, whilst the government's hired political hacks made similar points. Marchamont Nedham, for example, maintained that the Kings of England enjoyed 'a Paternal, absolute Divine Right'.[15]

By the mid-1670s we see the emergence of a well-articulated Country platform in opposition to the Court's alleged absolutist intentions. This Country opposition championed mixed monarchy and a balanced constitution, with power shared between the three estates of King, Lords and Commons, and a citizen militia in preference to a standing army. Two of the leading Country spokesmen were the Earl of Shaftesbury and the Duke of Buckingham, both of whom had been ministers during the Cabal and both of whom were to be leading figures in the exclusionist movement. Because it was feared that the Commons had already been too corrupted by Danby to act independently, a crucial role in preserving the balanced constitution was seen to belong to the upper chamber.[16] Yet for the balance to be maintained, it was also essential to secure the independence of the Commons from Court management. An attempt was made in April 1675 to pass a bill forcing all office-holders to relinquish their seats in the Commons, though without success.[17] The opposition also demanded the dissolution of the Cavalier Parliament, on the argument that it was no longer truly representative: the Parliament had sat so long that the people had been 'cut off from their liberty of electing', since a significant proportion of the population had not been old enough to vote at the last general elections of 1661.[18] A motion made by Sir Harbottle Grimston in the House of Commons on 25 October 1675 for the King 'to set a period to this Parliament' died for lack of support, but a similar motion introduced in the upper chamber on 20 November produced a heated debate, when Shaftesbury maintained that the frequent sitting of Parliament was required by law. The motion was only narrowly defeated by fifty votes to forty-eight.[19]

Instead of dissolution, the Privy Council decided to prorogue Parliament for fifteen months. However, two statutes from Edward III's reign had laid down provisions that Parliament should meet every year, so the Country opposition now maintained that since this Parliament had been prorogued for a period in excess of twelve months it was *ipso facto* dissolved. Such an argument was first made by Francis Jenks, a London linendraper, in a speech given at the elections for sheriffs in June 1676, where (probably at the instigation of Buckingham) he urged the Corporation of London to petition the King for a new Parliament. At the same time, Jenks maintained that the Catholics were conspiring to burn London and assassinate Charles in order to set his brother on the throne, allegations which directly anticipated Titus Oates's subsequent account of the Popish Plot.[20] This line of attack was resumed by Buckingham, Shaftesbury, Salisbury and Wharton when Parliament reassembled in February 1677, and in a number of pamphlets produced at this time. The opposition maintained that the security of English liberties was tied up with this cause, for if the King could ignore the statutes requiring him to meet Parliament once a year, then he could override any laws he desired. As Buckingham put it in the Lords on 15 February, 'Either the Kings of England are bound by the Acts mentioned of Edw[ard] 3. or else the whole Government of England by Parliaments, and by Law is absolutely at an End'.[21] In a pamphlet contribution to this debate, Denzil Holles responded to the argument that prorogation was a matter solely for the royal prerogative by maintaining that Acts of Parliament might not only restrict that, but 'can bind, limit, restrain and govern the Descent and Inheritance of the Crown itself, and all rights and titles thereto', a claim which directly anticipated the justification for Exclusion later to be made by the Whigs.[22]

With the growth of opposition, there seems to have been a resurgence of republicanism. Despite the reimposition of censorship after 1662, a certain amount of republican literature can be found throughout the Restoration period. For the first dozen years of the Restoration, however, much of this literature was associated with the alleged plots of radical sectarians who had never been happy with the return of monarchy. What is interesting is that there seems to be a flourishing of republican literature (and especially poetry) in the mid-1670s, a period of Charles II's reign comparatively free from plots (rumoured or otherwise). This literature often circulated in manuscript form, especially in the taverns or in the newly fashionable coffee-houses of London, and much of it reveals not a doctrinaire commitment to non-monarchical forms of government, but instead carries the suggestion that people who had initially welcomed the Restoration were now turning against monarchy in disillusionment. One poem of 1674 spoke of 'the miracle' of Charles's restoration, 'the wish'd-for blessing which Heaven sent', which has now become England's 'curse and punishment'. The poem threatened to send Charles and his brother back to Breda, 'Where, spite of all that would restore you, Turn'd commonwealth, we will abhor you'.[23] Another poem from 1677, which appears to have been read aloud by its publisher in London for the edification of passers-by, spoke of how the gods 'have repented the King's Restoration'.[24]

The preceding discussion should already warn us that the political conflicts between Court and Country were not totally confined to Whitehall and Westminster, and even though there was nothing approaching the level of public excitement on a nationwide scale that we associate with the Exclusion Crisis, nevertheless the 1670s did witness the re-emergence of a pattern of extra-institutional politics, at least in the capital, which was to have important implications for the future. Jenks's speech at the hustings for the shrieval elections in 1676, and the cultivation of public opinion through the circulation of propaganda aimed at a mass audience, testify to the opposition's preparedness to take politics out into the streets. It was during this decade that the ritualised pope-burning processions began. The first occurred on 5 November 1673, when young men of the capital burnt effigies of the Pope and his cardinals, in reaction to the Duke of York's non-compliance with the Test Act and his marriage to a Catholic princess. In 1676 and 1677, similar pope-burnings were staged on 17 November, this being the anniversary of Queen Elizabeth's accession and hence of England's deliverance from the regime of the last Catholic monarch, Queen Mary.[25] According to Samuel Parker, when Shaftesbury and Buckingham pressed for the dissolution of the Cavalier Parliament in

February 1677, 'a prodigious rabble' of their supporters gathered out-side the House, so that 'if they had happen'd to have carried their point, they had a mob ready to proclaim through the city with trium-phant shouts and huzzas, that the Parliament was dissolv'd'.[26]

In the absence of any general election between 1661 and 1679, the opportunities for those in the localities to have any impact on national affairs were limited. Although there were a large number of by-elec-tions during the life of the Cavalier Parliament, most constituencies experienced these only infrequently, and some never at all. Some communities successfully managed to revive a mode of consensus poli-tics for a brief period after the Restoration, Herefordshire being a not-able case in point. By the mid-1670s, however, partisan tensions were beginning to emerge in a number of areas. In Herefordshire the con-sensual mode had been broken by 1675, as evidenced by the divisive by-election at Weobley in that year. Towards the end of 1675 one observer noted how the county had become divided between 'the close designing party' and those of 'the Crown side'.[27] In counties such as Norfolk and Hampshire, clearly identifiable Court and Country interests had emerged by the mid-1670s.[28] We should not exaggerate this trend; in many localities factional disputes continued to be primarily about local issues, although even such local issues could take on wider implications. Thus a number of corporations during the 1660s and 1670s were involved in a struggle against oligarchical con-trol by the local gentry which mirrored at the local level Country opposition to the growth of oligarchy at the centre. The Crown's attempt to subvert the corporate self-sufficiency of Liverpool, for example, explains why the assertion of municipal self-sufficiency took on strong anti-Court identifications, and helped pave the way for the emergence of staunch Whiggery in this corporate borough.[29] But it was particularly when religious disputes took on local ramifications that political consensus proved difficult to sustain, a point to which we shall return later in this chapter.

THE BEGINNINGS OF PARTY ORGANISATION

So far we have traced the emergence of tensions between the Court and the Country centring around the fears of popery and arbitrary government. Yet can we talk about the existence of Court and Country 'parties', in the sense of political groupings which were or-

ganised and disciplined – and if so, from when? The initiative in organisation was taken by the government. Clarendon, the ministers of
the Cabal, and Danby all found it necessary to engage in some degree
of Parliamentary management in order to facilitate the doing of the
Court's business. Many of the techniques employed by these three
different administrations were similar: the attempts by ministers to use
family and local connections to establish a loyal following in Parliament; the offer of financial incentives to support the Court, either in
the form of gifts of money, pensions, or the promise of office; and the
promise to introduce legislation which would favour certain powerful
sectional interests, if they were prepared to stand by the Court in
other matters. Management lists were drawn up prior to an anticipated
division to identify those members of the House who might be sympathetic to the Court, and ministers made direct approaches to certain
MPs to try to persuade them to vote in a particular way (a technique
which anticipated the later whip system).[30]

Having said this, it is probably fair to suggest that we cannot talk
about the existence of a Court party prior to the mid-1670s. Clarendon's administration was perpetually troubled by factional disputes
within the Court, and although his essays at management brought
some successes – notably the repeal of the Triennial Act in 1664 – the
fragility of whatever organisation the Chancellor had been able to construct was revealed by the circumstances of his own impeachment and
downfall in 1667.[31] Likewise under the Cabal there was just not
enough unity amongst the chief ministers to allow us to talk about a
Court party. The most significant advances in management during this
period were undertaken by Clifford, but he was handicapped by the
fact that he never controlled all sources of patronage, often competing
with other ministers – notably Buckingham – for access to the King's
favour.[32]

Danby's efforts at management were both more systematic and
more extensive than anything which had been tried before. He pushed
all the old techniques to the limit – approaching MPs, drawing up
management lists, and exploiting his connections amongst personal
friends and his innumerable relatives who found their way into the
House during his ascendancy. Danby also had a form of patronage at
his disposal unavailable to his predecessors: as a result of his reform of
the excise, conducted as part of his policy of financial retrenchment,
he secured control of the payment of pensions from the excise
revenue, and found himself in a position to be able to distribute these
pensions to MPs in order to consolidate his support in the House. He
also did much to build up a Court party in the House of Lords, and

was the first minister to resort to whipping in the upper chamber to any significant degree. Yet even under Danby there were limits to what the Court could achieve. Many of the King's servants or office-holders in the Commons had in fact been appointed before Danby's rise to power, and since such offices were typically a gift for life, there was little any administration could do if such office-holders decided to turn against the Court. Not all gifts or offices should be seen as bribes; the receiver often regarded them as a just compensation for services rendered in the past, rather than as a way of tying up their freedom of political action in the future. Since many members of Parliament had suffered financially during the Civil War, or as a result of the land settlement of the Restoration, or were owed money by the Crown, there were a large number of people who felt they were entitled to some form of compensation from the government. The offer of per-quisites rarely seems to have persuaded MPs to vote against their con-sciences; most who received them continued to behave as their past political behaviour would lead us to suspect. Probably the main pur-pose of Danby's alleged system of 'bribery' was not to persuade oppo-nents to change sides, but to ensure that known sympathisers would attend the House and support the administration.[33]

The question of whether we can describe the Country opposition as a party is even more problematic. In the 1660s there was little unity amongst those who opposed the Court; this group comprised both place-seekers, who merely wanted to bring down the administration in order to get power for themselves, and mere back-benchers, and even these were divided between old Cavaliers and old Parliamentarians. In October 1673 Sir William Temple recognised four distinct groups who were in opposition to the Court: the anti-ministers, those who wanted to break Buckingham, Lauderdale and Arlington; a more moderate group, who wanted to secure the business of religion and break the war with Holland; those who were prepared to vote the Crown money, although not give it unless peace were made; and a group led by Shaftesbury in the Lords, who wanted to persuade Charles to divorce Catherine of Braganza.[34] Even under Danby, the Country opposition lacked the degree of cohesion and leadership necessary for it to qualify as a party. K. H. D. Haley has warned that we should not see Shaftesbury as the leader of the Country opposition – he often failed to carry with him opponents of the administration in the House of Commons, and often disagreed with other leading Country spokes-men on the question of tactics.[35]

Nevertheless, we do see the beginnings of some degree of organisa-tion amongst the opposition, which was to be a significant portent for the future. Different groups of opposition members started meeting together to plan tactics, often in a favourite London tavern either just before or during a Parliamentary session.[36] The famous Green Ribbon Club, which met at the King's Head Tavern in Chancery Lane, was founded in 1674, and became a meeting place not just for opposition MPs, but also radical lawyers, London politicians, and publicists.[37] During the Exclusion Crisis the Green Ribbon Club played a crucial role in the Whig propaganda campaign, and in particular appears to have helped sponsor the pope-burning processions of 17 November. Whether it had already assumed this role prior to the Popish Plot is unclear; however, the pope-burnings that took place in the 1670s do seem to have had the backing of wealthy patrons, judging by their expense.[38] In the Lords, Shaftesbury and other leading Country peers used similar managerial techniques to Danby, writing to absentees asking them to attend or send in their proxies, and holding private meetings to discuss tactics to be employed in the upper chamber.[39]

There definitely was a growing conflict between the Court and Country during the first two decades of Charles II's reign, and by the mid-1670s the two groupings had developed a rudimentary organisational structure. It is debatable whether the degree of organisation was sufficient to allow us to talk about Court and Country parties; what is certain, is that this Court–Country conflict did not anticipate the later split between Tories and Whigs. At various times in the 1660s and 1670s future Whigs can be found allying themselves with the Court and future Tories with the opposition. The future leading Whigs, Buckingham and Shaftesbury, had gone into opposition only in 1673; until then, they had sided with the Court. Some of those who opposed the Court in the mid-1670s were later to side against the Whigs and Exclusion, including the Marquis of Halifax, Sir Thomas Clarges and Sir William Coventry. More generally, High Anglicans, who were to form the mainstay of Tory support after 1679, can often be found supporting the Country position in the 1660s and 1670s; in contrast, those sympathetic to Dissent, who were later to fall in overwhelmingly behind the Whigs, can often be found supporting the Court.

The reasons for this are that the issues which caused tensions between Court and Country were not the same as those which generated conflict between Tories and Whigs. For example, the Country suspicion of corruption and mismanagement could be shared by people of all political persuasions. For obvious reasons, old Puritans were critical of the profligacy and moral degeneracy of the Court, and many of the printed attacks on Court licentiousness in the 1660s and 1670s were produced by Nonconformists.[40] Yet this was a grievance shared by many Anglican gentry, especially during the troubled economic times of the second Dutch War: experiencing high taxation at a time when falling prices for grain and cattle and a decline in rents was squeezing their incomes, the landed squirearchy became very critical of the extravagance and luxury of the Court and the corruption of government officials.[41] Likewise hostility towards a standing army was not a position peculiar to Parliamentarians and future Whigs. Cavaliers had welcomed the Restoration because they thought it would mean a return to legal government, and one of their biggest grievances concerned the role played by the Army in the government of the realm during the 1650s. The demand for the immediate disbandment of troops following the conclusion of peace with the Dutch in 1667 was in fact led by old Cavaliers, such as Sir Thomas Tomkins, although they were joined in their attack by Parliamentarians. In the 1670s future opponents of Exclusion, such as Sir Thomas Clarges, Sir Thomas Littleton and Sir William Coventry, joined with future Exclusionists, such as Sir Thomas Lee, William Lord Russell and William Sacheverell, in the campaign against standing armies.[42] But the main reason why Court–Country tensions did not anticipate the later Tory–Whig divide was due to religious issues, which often served to cut across constitutional tensions between the Crown and Parliament.

CONFLICT OVER THE CHURCH

In addition to the threat of political tyranny posed by the popish and absolutist leanings of the Court, many were also concerned about the religious tyranny of the restored Anglican establishment. As we have seen, at the Restoration a severe code had been set up penalising Dissent, and although persecution was not continuous, when the penal laws were being enforced the plight of the Nonconformists could be desperate. Dissenters were liable to heavy fines, which if they could not meet would result in their goods being distrained. Many spent time in jail, either for failure to pay fines, or for refusing to take oaths of allegiance, where the conditions were often so bad that some died. With much justification, Nonconformists repeatedly complained that persecution was a threat to 'liberty and property', that it destroyed their 'lives, liberties and estates'.[43]

Particular resentment was focused on the bishops, most of whom were champions of religious intolerance. Many of them, indeed, held an exalted view of the clerical estate, defending the High Church vision of divine-right episcopacy, which maintained that only the bishops – and not the King – had the power to judge faith and religious truth.[44] The religious tyranny of the established Church was also regarded as popish. It is important to recognise that anti-popery was not the same thing as anti-Catholicism; popery was anything that was tainted by association with the Pope or the Church of Rome, and the charge of popery could be levied against sound Protestants who were believed to be acting upon popish principles. There were many popish practices within the Church of England, Nonconformists complained, such as kneeling at the name of Jesus, or using the sign of the cross in baptism. Persecuting people for their religious beliefs, they further argued, was a popish principle. The High Church views of the bishops seemed to be a rejection of the erastian tradition on which the Reformation had been based, which had set up the monarch as supreme head of the church, and appeared to be similar to papal claims of clerical infallibility.[45]

Religious persecution did not create tensions between Dissenters and Anglicans; rather the tensions that were generated were between those who were sympathetic towards Dissent and those who were not. These tensions cut deep into society. The nature of law-enforcement in early modern England, which was heavily dependent on unpaid local officials and members of the local community, meant that many sorts of people were caught up in the question of whether to enforce the laws against Nonconformists. Zealous Anglicans were often happy to seize the initiative in prosecuting Dissent, be they JPs, village constables, or local inhabitants who came forward as informers. Others declined to act, even if this meant that they would be reprimanded or fined for neglect of duty.[46] In areas where Dissenters were able to retain the support of local Anglicans, their plight could be significantly eased. In boroughs where sympathy for Dissent remained strong, Nonconformists were even able to evade the provisions of the Corporation Act and play an important part in local politics. In Coventry, although the Clarendon Code had the effect of removing the younger and poorer Dissenters from office, the older and wealthier ones were able to hold onto their positions. Between 1660 and 1687 some 28 per cent of those annually elected to office were Dissenters.[47] In many west country boroughs, despite effective purges in the early 1660s, Nonconformists were finding their way back into corporation politics in the late 1660s and early 1670s.[48] The political clout of Dissent was particularly noticeable in London, where by the 1670s there were significant numbers of Nonconformists serving not just on the Common

Council, but even as aldermen. Moreover, many of the London Dissenters active in the Corporation were wealthy financiers and investors
– for example, some 35 per cent of the directors of the Levant Company, the East India Company, and the Royal African Company from
1660–88 were Dissenters.[49] Given the noticeable presence of Dissent
amongst the commercial and manufacturing classes of the towns, many
people came to fear that religious persecution would be bad for England's economy. As Slingsby Bethel argued in 1671, liberty of conscience was essential for advancing the trade and wealth of the
country; peace would only force traders and manufacturers 'to flye
their Countries, or withdraw their stocks'.[50] What is clear is that the
sufferings of Nonconformists could provoke the sympathy of many
moderate Anglicans, and as a result the number of people who desired
to see some relaxation of the penal code was much larger than the
numerical strength of Dissent would suggest. In addition, Dissent was
not lacking a voice in Parliament. Only a small minority of MPs and
peers were actually Nonconformists, but to these must be added a
much larger number of old Parliamentarians and old Puritans who had
conformed at the Restoration, plus a younger generation of Low
Church Anglicans, all of whom were sympathetic to Dissent. Of the
859 members who at various times sat in the Cavalier House of Commons it has been estimated that at least 322 were either Nonconformists, conforming Nonconformists, or Low Church Anglicans.[51]

Nonconformists had good reason to feel betrayed by the Restoration religious settlement, and persecution did lead some of the more
radical types into plotting against the state, with the aim of bringing
down the monarchy and re-establishing a republic.[52] When the royal
government seemed to be allying itself with the intolerant Anglican
establishment, as it did, for example, under Danby, and as it was to do
again after 1681, hostility towards the Church readily translated into
hostility towards the monarchy. Yet for much of the 1660s and 1670s
Charles II seemed a better friend to Dissent than his Cavalier Parliament. Whether Charles sincerely believed in the principle of religious
toleration is questionable; he was probably concerned mainly with the
political advantages to be gained by playing off the High Anglican and
pro-Dissent factions against each other. But he had promised liberty of
conscience in his Declaration from Breda in April 1660, and in the
early years of his reign he made several efforts to fulfil this promise,
notably with his attempted Declaration of Indulgence in 1662. During
the 1660s Charles showed himself prepared to promote a number of
former Puritan opponents of the Crown to prime jobs in his administration (amongst them Ashley Cooper, the future Earl of Shaftesbury),[53]

whilst during the years of the Cabal enemies of Church – including Catholics, such as Clifford, and Protestants, such as Shaftesbury and Buckingham – virtually seized control of the royal administration. In 1668, Charles agreed to help introduce measures for toleration and comprehension in Parliament – the former was the project of the Buckingham circle (which included Cromwell's former chaplain, Dr John Owen), whilst a comprehension bill was drafted by Sir Matthew Hale, a former Cromwellian judge who was now Lord Chief Baron of the Exchequer. When in 1672 Charles sought to achieve toleration through the royal prerogative, he was backed all the way by Shaftesbury and Buckingham. It is hardly surprising, therefore, that we often find Nonconformists appealing to the Crown in their opposition to the penal laws, claiming that persecution was expressly against the King's wishes. It was not the Crown or the royal prerogative that was the enemy, but the Cavalier Parliament.[54] Thus for passing the second Conventicle Act in 1670 Parliament was accused of committing the 'highest treason', because the Act subverted the fundamental law, which was to preserve lives, liberties and properties. It was also claimed that the Act was an imposition upon the King, since it was 'expressly against . . . [his] printed Declarations and Promises for Indulgence.'[55]

Those who expected the Restoration to mark the triumph of Cavalier Anglicanism were deeply alarmed at developments in the 1660s and early 1670s. Believing themselves to be the allies of strong monarchy, they were nevertheless horrified by the prospect that the King's natural constituency might be overthrown by the King himself. As an anti-exclusionist tract of 1679 put it, 'the complaint against the Court was first the suffering of the Cavaleers onely, and not the Fanaticks, because their Dad's were then uppermost, and rul'd the roast'.[56] Cavalier Anglicans were particularly bitter because they felt that their former enemies had an edge in the struggle for preferment largely as a result of the fortunes which they had been able to amass (at the expense of the Royalists) during the civil wars and Interregnum. Such resentment was exacerbated during the Dutch War, when they saw Presbyterian members of the banking and merchant communities amassing huge profits through their involvement in war finance, whilst the landed interest suffered as a result of heavy taxation.[57] In addition to all this, the King seemed to be threatening the legal security of the Church establishment.

As a result, Cavalier Anglicans became involved in a desperate struggle to keep the King in line, and in doing this they came to champion Parliament's role as a check on the royal executive. It was the Anglican interest in Parliament, led by the bishops in the upper chamber, who led the opposition to Charles II's Declaration of Indulgence of 1662. In a letter to the King in December 1662, Gilbert Sheldon, at that time still Bishop of London, reminded Charles that only Parliament had the power to establish a toleration, and accused him of taking 'liberty to throw down the laws of the land at your pleasure'.[58] The High Church bishops and the Anglican gentry in Parliament managed to defeat the Court-backed schemes for toleration and comprehension in 1668, taking a stance in defence of the Church 'as by law established'. Sir John Vaughan argued that comprehension would 'subvert the present government' and 'raise new troubles by destroying the laws'. Colonel Sandys said that toleration would necessitate a standing army: I 'never knew a Toleration, without an army to keep all quiet'. Lord Fanshawe maintained that considering what 'villainies' the Nonconformists had committed during the 1640s and 1650s, it was essential that 'the laws be put in execution against them', so that they could 'be brought under'.[59] Such hostility from Parliament temporarily forced Charles to revert to the Cavalier policies of the Clarendon years. In 1670 he agreed to the passage of the second Conventicle Act, in order to placate the Parliamentary opposition and obtain a much needed grant of supply.

It should not be assumed that we see a simple reversal in political allegiances whenever the Crown supported toleration, with the Cavalier–Anglican interest going into opposition and the old Puritan–Parliamentarian interest aligning itself with the Crown. Some Cavalier Anglicans continued to put loyalty towards the Crown before the Church, whilst for some Nonconformists and sympathisers to Dissent suspicion of popery and arbitrary government prevented them from supporting prerogative attempts at achieving toleration. A number of those who opposed the Indulgence nevertheless hoped that some degree of relief could be achieved for Nonconformists in a Parliamentary way, and supported the attempt to pass the bill for the Ease of Protestant Dissenters introduced into the House of Commons following the King's withdrawal of his Indulgence in 1673. Allegiances were further complicated by the question of how dependent different individuals were on the Court. The complex pattern of political positions which resulted from the Crown's pursuit of toleration can be seen by looking at the response to the Declaration of Indulgence of 1672. For example, Sir Thomas Lee, a friend of Dissent who was later to be a supporter of Exclusion, opposed the Indulgence, arguing that the King had been misinformed about his prerogative and that he could not suspend the penal laws.[60] But there were other future Whigs who supported the Indulgence and the use of the royal suspending power on religious grounds. In addition to Shaftesbury and Buckingham, we have someone like Sir Robert Howard, a man who thought that the Church could be perfectly safe without compelling everyone to absolute conformity, and who maintained that since 'neither Life, Liberty nor Estates which is each Mans Property was infringed' by the Indulgence, it was not illegal.[61] The response of the Nonconformist community is particularly interesting. Presbyterians of the old school, amongst them Richard Baxter and Adam Martindale, were suspicious of the fact that indulgence was also granted to Catholics. Quakers, and some Baptists, refused to take out licences to preach under the terms of the Indulgence, because they felt they would acknowledge the legitimacy of the Conventicle Act by accepting dispensations from it. Yet most Nonconformists did avail themselves of the toleration afforded by the Indulgence, including Martindale himself. Some explicitly defended the King's prerogative, arguing that the King, as head of the Church, did have the power to suspend ecclesiastical laws. [62]

The Anglican response to the Indulgence was also mixed. Some Court Cavaliers, such as Heneage Finch and Henry Coventry, felt obliged to defend on principle the question of the King's discretionary power, even though they had little sympathy towards Dissenters and were opposed to weakening the Church establishment by granting religious toleration. That bitter enemy of Dissent, the Anglican cleric Samuel Parker, took the official Court line that an indulgence was necessary at this time, in order to soothe discontent at home whilst England was at war. Parker appears to have shared the erastian belief that the King exercised supreme power in ecclesiastical affairs; as Bishop of Oxford under James he was to support the Indulgence of 1687. Most of the Anglican gentry in Parliament, however, opposed the Indulgence. Edward Vaughan thought that the Indulgence was illegal: it was 'a repeal of forty Acts of Parliament', and 'if this Declaration signifies any thing, the Church of England signifies nothing'.[63] So did the majority of the bishops, who encouraged their clergy to preach against popery and to magnify the authority of the laws.[64]

What is important to stress is that the enemies of Dissent were also fierce enemies of popery. The Nonconformists, High Anglicans believed, were really seeking the same ends as the Catholics, because both sought to undermine the established Church of England. Tolerating Dissent, it was argued, would only lead to the growth of popery:[65] this was not only because toleration would so weaken the Church, as to make her less able to carry on her struggle against the Antichrist, but also because all the schemes for religious toleration ad-

vanced under Charles II were designed primarily to promote freedom
of worship for Catholics. What made the Anglican charge of popery
against the Dissenters so compelling was the fact that on a number of
occasions during the 1660s and 1670s Nonconformists did work in
alliance with the papists to promote their mutual interests. Catholic
and old Puritan politicians worked together in opposition to Clarendon in the 1660s, and also during the years of the Cabal. During the
mid-1670s Presbyterian politicians were working with Catholics to oppose Danby's religious policy and to try to bring about the dissolution
of the Cavalier Parliament. We even find the Earl of Shaftesbury prepared to work with the Duke of York; the Catholic heir joined with
the Lords in an address for the King to dissolve the Parliament in the
autumn of 1675. In May 1675 Cheshire MP, Richard Legh, reported
how 'the Papists and Presbyterians join heartily against the Church of
England', whilst in October of that year, the Speaker of the Commons, Edward Seymour, commented how there was a 'strict conjunc-
tion between the Fanatic and Papist, to dissolve this Parliament'.[66]

The foregoing context enables us to reassess the nature of the polarisation that happened under Danby. It is misleading to think of
Danby as trying to organise a Court party, if by that we mean a party
constructed with the aim of managing the King's business more effectively in Parliament. Rather, Danby set himself up as 'the patron of
the church party and of the old cavaliers', as Burnet put it,[67] with the
aim of trying to make the King and the Court pursue an Anglican
policy. Danby wanted to secure the Anglican establishment from the
double threat of popery and Dissent, and to this end threw himself
into an alliance with the High Anglican bishops. Although he made
himself indispensable to the Crown by putting the royal finances in
better shape, in many respects he pursued policies which were at odds
with Charles II's personal preferences. He sought to enforce the penal
laws against all those outside the established Church – Catholics as
well as Protestants. A Recusancy Commission was established to collect fines from Catholic gentlemen who had hitherto been left largely
unmolested, Catholic priests were banned, and papists were even
removed from Court. Danby sought to take England out of the
French orbit by conducting an alliance with the Dutch. In 1677 a
marriage was concluded between Princess Mary, York's daughter and
the second in line to the throne, and William of Orange, the Calvinist
Stadtholder of Holland. Danby also confronted the problem of how to
protect the Anglican Church in the eventuality of a popish successor.
In February 1677 a bill was introduced into Parliament for 'securing
the protestant religion': the bishops were to take charge of the educa-

tion of the royal children, and in the advent of a Catholic monarch, the bishops were also to be given control over ecclesiastical appointments.[68]

The pursuit of an Anglican policy did have the effect of winning back some Cavalier Anglicans who had drifted into opposition in the 1660s and early 1670s, but not all of them. A significant number continued to be suspicious of the Court, and remained in opposition until the Exclusion Crisis. During the mid-1670s, however, the Country opposition came to be increasingly dominated by those who were hostile to the intolerant Anglican establishment. Detractors made much of Shaftesbury's shift into opposition following his dismissal in 1673, calling him a Machiavellian and turn-coat politician. Yet in fact there was a consistency to his actions: throughout the 1660s and 1670s he showed himself to be violently opposed to the pretensions of the bishops and passionately committed to the defence of Nonconformists. Likewise the Duke of Buckingham, both as a minister of the Cabal and as a leading opponent of the government in the mid-1670s, consistently sought to achieve liberty of conscience for Protestant Dissenters. Shaftesbury and Buckingham were alarmed at developments under Danby not because they were, by instinct, enemies of the royal executive, but because Danby was working in alliance with the bishops to try to extirpate Dissent and cement the hegemony of the Anglican interest. This was why Danby's attempt in 1675 to force peers to swear an oath against endeavouring to alter the Church and State was so frightening. Shaftesbury represented it as part of a design to reserve all power in the kingdom to 'the High Episcopal Man, and the Old Cavalier'; this design had started with the repressive statutes of the 1660s, and since the 'great churchmen' had now managed to capture control of the King's administration, they were in a position, at last, to perfect their clerical tyranny.[69] The central significance of anti-episcopalianism to the Country platform of the mid-1670s cannot be stressed enough: Buckingham also launched an abusive assault on the bishops in the debate over the Test,[70] whilst Marvell's *Account* was in essence a bitter attack on Danby's alliance with the High Church establishment. Out-of-doors, the most visible supporters of the Country position were Nonconformists or friends of Dissent. In Herefordshire it was reported that the Country interest was composed of 'those that do not love the Church'.[71] Many of the most fiercely contested by-elections were fought over the issue of the Church and Dissent, the most well-documented example being that of Dorset in 1675.[72] And many of Shaftesbury's and Buckingham's allies in the City of London in the mid-1670s were religious Nonconformists.[73]

Yet if the partnership of Church and government led those who sympathised with Dissent into an extreme anti-Court position, the attitude of Country spokesmen towards the royal prerogative remained ambivalent, precisely because Danby's policies could be represented as being detrimental to the Crown. As one peer argued in the debate over the Test, to swear an oath that the Church was unalterable was a violation of the royal supremacy: if the Church could not be altered by laws agreed to by the King and Parliament, then the effect of the Test would be to 'Sett up the Mitre Above the Crowne'.[74] Danby's proposals of 1677 for dealing with the Catholic succession likewise seemed to challenge the royal supremacy and give too much power to the bishops. Thus the Country opposition vehemently opposed these attempts to limit the King's ecclesiastical prerogative, arguing that the bill would 'pull off the crown from the King's head', and they succeeded in defeating the measure.[75]

CONCLUSION

It is crucial to understand political developments during the 1660s and 1670s in order to set the context for the emergence of party strife during the Exclusion Crisis. The first two decades of the Restoration era saw growing fears about popery and arbitrary government, and concern that the Catholic Duke of York might one day succeed his brother was already an issue by the mid-1670s. The revelations of the Popish Plot created such a political storm not because they introduced a terrifying new dimension into politics, but because they confirmed already deeply felt anxieties. We also see during this period moves towards party organisation, and the beginnings of extra-Parliamentary activity co-ordinated by the opposition to try to bring pressure on the government. The playing-out of religious tensions between those who supported the intolerant Anglican establishment and those sympathetic to Dissent also forms a vital backdrop to the subsequent battle between Whigs and Tories, for, as will be seen in the next chapter, this battle was fought as much over the issue of Dissent as it was over Exclusion. However, Charles II's own ambivalent attitude towards the Church, and the shifting policies of the different Court administrations between repression and attempts to promote toleration, meant that the constitutional and religious issues interacted with one another to produce a complex pattern of political allegiances. In a tract of 1675, Shaftesbury aptly described the way in which the conflict between Court and Country had been complicated by the struggle, as he termed it, between the old Roundheads and the old Cavaliers. Writing shortly after the attempt by Danby and the bishops to impose a non-resistance Test on the Lords, Shaftesbury was convinced that the greatest danger to English law and liberty came from the prerogative and from the bishops, and that the best way to restrain prerogative was to give liberty to the Protestant Dissenters. But he also recognised that the Cavalier was such

> a Byggot to the Bishops, that he forces his Loyalty to strike Sail to his Religion, and could be content to pare the Nails a little of the Civil Government, so you would but let him sharpen the Ecclesiastical Tallons; which behaviour of his so exasperates the Round-head, that he on the other hand cares not what Increases the Interest of the Crown receives, so he can but diminish that of the Miter: so that the Round-head had rather enslave the Man, than the Conscience; the Cavalier rather the Conscience than the Man.[76]

What the analysis in this chapter suggests, therefore, is that the origins of the Tory–Whig divide are to be found not so much in the Court–Country tensions that had been developing in the 1660s and 1670s, but rather in the religious conflict between Church and Dissent. If we wish to trace the roots of Toryism, we shall find them in the Cavalier-Anglican attachment to the Church and State as re-established by law at the Restoration. It is sometimes thought that the Tories did not really emerge as a party until the 1690s, because it was only after the Glorious Revolution that they were able to take a stance independent of the Crown. Yet, as we have seen, the Cavalier-Anglican interest often acted independently of the Court in the Restoration period, especially when it saw the need to defend the Church from attack by the executive. Although by instinct champions of strong royal government, Cavalier Anglicans did not believe that the royal prerogative could be used to undermine the legal security of the Church of England; in this respect, there was always a strong Country dimension to Cavalier Anglicanism. It was this interest which Danby sought to turn into a 'party' in the mid-1670s, and the policies he pursued in many respects directly anticipated the Tory platform of the Exclusion Crisis: an alliance with the Anglican establishment, and especially the bishops; the pursuit of both Catholic and Protestant enemies to Church and State; and an attempt to deal with the problem of the Catholic heir by providing additional legal securities to protect the established Church should the Duke of York become

King. On the other hand, the widely held assumption that the first Whig party emerged out of the earlier Country opposition needs some reconsideration. It is true that by the mid-1670s this opposition had come to be dominated by future Whigs, that the organisational structure it was developing was to be built upon by the Whigs during the Exclusion Crisis, and that its ideological stance in opposition to popery and arbitrary government directly anticipated many of the arguments of the exclusionists. But even in the mid-1670s, the opposition was still a loose coalition of forces hostile to Danby: sympathisers to Dissent, who were in particular critical of the pretensions of the bishops; Anglicans, who as yet remained more fearful of popery and arbitrary government than they were of Dissent; and Catholics, who had little to gain from the aggressively anti-Catholic stance now being pursued by the Court. The revelations of the Popish Plot, followed by the downfall of Danby and the introduction of Exclusion, broke any common ground these disparate forces once had, with the result that Whiggery was to emerge largely out of the pro-Dissent and anti-episcopalian interest associated with Buckingham and Shaftesbury.

REFERENCES

1. Bohun, *An Address to the Free-Men and the Free-Holders of the Nation* (1682), p. 64.
2. K. H. D. Haley, 'Shaftesbury's Lists of the Lay Peers and Members of the Commons, 1677–8', *BIHR*, **43** (1970), pp. 86–105.
3. Plumb, *The Growth of Political Stability in England 1675–1725*, p. 32; Weston and Greenberg, *Subjects and Sovereigns: The Grand Controversy over Legal Sovereignty in Stuart England*, ch. 6.
4. Jones, 'Parties and Parliament', in J. R. Jones (ed.), *The Restored Monarchy 1660–1688*, pp. 58–9, 65–6, 70.
5. J. G. A. Pocock, *The Machiavellian Moment: Florentine Political Thought and the Atlantic Republic Tradition* (Princeton, 1975), ch. 12; Lois G. Schwoerer, *'No Standing Armies!': The Anti-Army Ideology in Seventeenth-Century England* (Baltimore, 1974), ch. 6.
6. Pepys, *Diary*, **II**, p. 38.
7. *CJ*, **VIII**, pp. 440, 449, 452, 463; Miller, *Popery and Politics in England, 1660–1688*, p. 101.
8. Pepys, *Diary*, **VIII**, pp. 264, 269–70; CJ, **IX**, pp. 4, 10; *CSPD, 1667*, p. 196; Miller, *Popery and Politics*, p. 105.
9. Burnet, *History*, p. 228; Pierre Du Moulin, *England's Appeal from the Private Cabal at White-Hall* (1673).

10. Grey, *Debates*, **II**, pp. 26, 399.
11. *CSPD, 1673–5*, pp. 128–32; Miller, *Popery and Politics*, pp. 133–4; Haley, *The First Earl of Shaftesbury*, pp. 358–60; Jones, *Charles II: Royal Politician*, p. 113.
12. Shaftesbury, *Letter from a Person of Quality*, pp. 1–2; Haley, *Shaftesbury* ch. 18.
13. Mark Goldie, 'John Locke and Anglican Royalism', *Political Studies*, **31** (1983), pp. 61–85; John Locke, *Two Treatises of Government*, Peter Laslett (ed.)(Cambridge, 1960, student edition, 1988), **I**, para. 3, p. 142.
14. Burnet, *History*, p. 228.
15. [Marchamont Nedham], *A Pacquet of Advices and Animadversions Sent for London to the Men of Shaftesbury* (1676), p. 43.
16. Pocock, *Machiavellian Moment*, pp. 406–16.
17. Grey, *Debates*, **III**, pp. 53–8; Betty Kemp, *King and Commons, 1660–1832* (1957), p. 23.
18. Burnet, *History*, p. 258; [Denzil Holles], *The Long Parliament Dissolved* (1676), p. 4.
19. Grey, *Debates*, **III**, pp. 341–6; [Shaftesbury], *Two Seasonable Discourses*; Haley, *Shaftesbury*, pp. 400–1.
20. Gary S. De Krey, 'London Radicals and Revolutionary Politics, 1675–1683', in Harris et al. (eds), *The Politics of Religion in Restoration England*, pp. 138–40; Haley, *Shaftesbury*, pp. 409–10; Jones, *Charles II*, pp. 120–1.
21. *The Duke of Buckingham's Speech; Spoken in the House of Lords, Feb. 15th 1676. Proving that the Parliament is Dissolved* (Amsterdam, 1677), p. 8. Cf. [Holles], *Long Parliament Dissolved*; Haley, *Shaftesbury*, pp. 417–19.
22. [Denzil Holles], *Some Considerations Upon the Question, Whether The Parliament is Dissolved By its Prorogation for 15 Months?* (1676), p. 26.
23. [Andrew Marvell?], *The History of Insipids* (1674), in *POAS*, **I**, pp. 243–51.
24. PRO, KB 10/1/5, ind. of Joseph Browne for publishing 'A Dialogue Between the Two Horses'; *POAS*, **I**, p. 282. The poem was probably by John Ayloffe.
25. *The Pope Burnt to Ashes* (1676); *Correspondence of the Family of Hatton, 1601–1704*, E. M. Thompson (ed.) (2 vols, 1878), **I**, p. 157; *CSPD, 1677–8*, p. 446.
26. Samuel Parker, *History of His Own Time*, trans. Thomas Newlin (1727), pp. 403–4.
27. *CSPD, 1675–6*, pp. 460–1; Key, 'Politics beyond Parliament', chs 5, 6.
28. J. M. Rosenheim, 'Party Organization at the Local Level: The Norfolk Sheriff's Subscription of 1676', *HJ*, **29** (1986), pp. 713–22; Rosenheim, *Townshends of Raynham*, pp. 35–46; Coleby, *Central Government and the Localities: Hampshire 1649–1689*, ch. 6.
29. Michael Mullett, 'The Politics of Liverpool, 1660–88', *Transactions of the Historical Society of Lancashire and Cheshire*, **124** (1973), pp. 31–56.
30. Jones, 'Parties and Parliament', pp. 51–3; J. R. Jones, 'Court Dependents in 1664', *BIHR*, **34** (1961), pp. 81–91; E. S. De Beer, 'Members

of the Court Party in the House of Commons 1670–1678', *BIHR*, **11** (1934), pp. 1–23; Andrew Browning, 'Parties and Party Organization in the Reign of Charles II', *TRHS*, 4th series, **30** (1948), pp. 21–36; *Idem, Thomas Osborne, Earl of Danby and Duke of Leeds, 1632–1712* (3 vols, Glasgow, 1951), **III**, appendix III.

31. Seaward, *The Cavalier Parliament and the Reconstruction of the Old Regime, 1661–1667*, esp. chs 4, 9.
32. Maurice Lee, *The Cabal* (Urbana, 1965), p. 122.
33. Browning, *Danby*, **I**, pp. 167–73; *Idem*, 'Parties and Party Organization'; Andrew Swatland, 'The Role of the Privy Councillors in the House of Lords, 1660–1681', in Jones (ed.), *Pillar of the Constitution*, (1989), pp. 62–6; Barry Coward, *The Stuart Age* (1980), p. 277; Plumb, *Growth of Political Stability*, pp. 47–8; *A List of One Unanimous Club of Voters in His Majesties Long Parliament* (1679); Haley, *Shaftesbury*, p. 388.
34. *Essex Papers*, Osmund Airy (ed.) (1890), **I**, pp. 131–2; K. H. D. Haley, *William of Orange and the English Opposition 1672–4* (Oxford, 1953), pp. 134–5; Clayton Roberts, 'Sir Richard Temple's Discourse on the Parliament of 1667–1668', *HLQ*, **20** (1956–7), pp. 137–44.
35. Haley, *Shaftesbury*, pp. 353, 398, 410, 412–13.
36. Plumb, *Growth of Political Stability*, p. 33; Haley, *Shaftesbury*, pp. 351–2.
37. J. R. Jones, 'The Green Ribbon Club', *Durham University Journal*, **49** NS 18 (1956), pp. 17–20.
38. Miller, *Popery and Politics*, p. 184; Harris, *London Crowds*, p. 93.
39. Swatland, 'Role of Privy Councillors', p. 66.
40. Harris, *London Crowds*, pp. 80–1; John S. T. Hetet, 'A Literary Underground in Restoration England: Printers and Dissenters in the Context of Constraints', unpub. Cambridge PhD thesis (1987), pp. 168–71.
41. Seaward, *Cavalier Parliament*, pp. 242–5, 297.
42. Schwoerer, '*No Standing Armies!*', pp. 71, 96, 98. I disagree with Schwoerer's conclusion that 'opposition to standing armies reflected a Whig philosophy of government'. *Ibid.*, p. 95.
43. Tim Harris, '"Lives, Liberties and Estates": Rhetorics of Liberty in the Reign of Charles II' in Harris et al. (eds), *Politics of Religion* pp. 217–41.
44. Goldie, 'Locke and Anglican Royalism', pp. 77–8.
45. Bodl. Lib., MS Tanner 36, fol. 144; [Charles Wolsley], *Liberty of Conscience upon its True and Proper Grounds* (1668), pp. 11, 40–1; George Whitehead, *The Christian Progress* (1725), p. 497.
46. Harris, *London Crowds*, pp. 19–21, 70–3; Tim Harris, 'Was the Tory Reaction Popular?: Attitudes of Londoners towards the Persecution of Dissent, 1681–6', *London Journal*, **13** (1988), pp. 106–20; Seaward, *The Restoration 1660–1688*, pp. 57–9.
47. Hurwich, 'Fanatick Town', p. 31.
48. Norrey, 'Restoration Regime', pp. 809–12.
49. Gary S. De Krey, 'The London Whigs and the Exclusion Crisis Reconsidered', in Lee Beier, David Cannadine and James Rosenheim (eds), *The First Modern Society: Essays in English History in Honour of Lawrence Stone* (Cambridge, 1989), pp. 463–6.

50. Slingsby Bethel, *The Present Interest of England Stated* (1671), pp. 13, 16–17; Nicholas Tyacke, 'The "Rise of Puritanism" and the Legalizing of Dissent, 1571–1719', in Ole Peter Grell, Jonathan I. Israel and Nicholas Tyacke (eds), *From Persecution to Toleration: The Glorious Revolution and Religion in England* (Oxford, 1991), pp. 34–6.

51. Henning (ed.), *The House of Commons 1660–1690*, **I**, p. 52.

52. Greaves, *Deliver us from Evil: The Radical Underground in Britain, 1660-1663* Richard L. Greaves, *Enemies under his Feet: Radicals and Nonconformists in Britain, 1664–1677* (Stanford, 1990).

53. Seaward, *Cavalier Parliament*, pp. 54–5.

54. Harris, *London Crowds*, pp. 76–7; Goldie, 'Locke and Anglican Royalism', pp. 82–3.

55. [Nicholas Lockyer], *Some Seasonable and Serious Queries upon the Late Act against Conventicles* (1670), p. 13; *The Englishman* (1670), pp. 8–11.

56. G. P., *The Moderate Parliament Considered* (1679), p. 3.

57. Seaward, *Cavalier Parliament*, pp. 244–5, 297.

58. Burnet, *History*, p. 134; Osmund Airy, 'Notes on the Reign of Charles II', *British Quarterly Review*, **67** (1883), p. 333.

59. Grey, *Debates*, **I**, p. 110; John Milward, *Diary*, Caroline Robbins (ed.) (Cambridge, 1938), pp. 215, 216, 219, 221; Seaward, *Cavalier Parliament*, p. 69; Harris, *London Crowds*, pp. 86–7; Jones, *Charles II*, p. 84; Lacey, *Dissent*, p. 58; W. G. Simon, 'Comprehension in the Age of Charles II', *Church History*, **31** (1962), p. 445.

60. Grey, *Debates*, **II**, p. 19.

61. *Lyme Letters 1660–1760*, Lady Newton (ed.) (1925), p. 52; Grey, *Debates*, **II**, pp. 21–2.

62. *Reliquiae Baxterianae*, Part III, pp. 99–101; Martindale, *Life*, pp. 198–9; *Vindiciae Libertatis Evangelii* (1672); Miller, *Popery and Politics*, p. 118; F. Bate, *The Declaration of Indulgence, 1672: A Study in the Rise of Organised Dissent* (1908), pp. 85–91; Lacey, *Dissent*, pp. 64–7.

63. Grey, *Debates*, **II**, p. 21.

64. Burnet, *History*, p. 207; Andrew Marvell, *The Rehearsal Transpros'd* (1672), p. 268.

65. Milward, *Diary*, p. 214.

66. Burnet, *History*, p. 258; *Lyme Letters*, p. 63; Grey, *Debates*, **III**, p. 345; Bohun, *Address to the Free-Men*, pp. 36–44; Richard Davis, 'The "Presbyterian" Opposition and the Emergence of Party in the House of Lords in the Reign of Charles II', in Clyve Jones (ed.), *Party and Management in Parliament, 1660–1784* (Leicester, 1984), pp. 1–35; Haley, *Shaftesbury*, pp. 370–402; Miller, *Popery and Politics*, pp. 136–7, 142–3; John Miller, *James II: A Study in Kingship* (1978, 2nd edn, 1989), pp. 78–9.

67. Burnet, *History*, p. 248.

68. Goldie, 'Danby, the Bishops and the Whigs', in Harris et al. (eds), *Politics of Religion*.

69. [Shaftesbury], *Letter from a Person of Quality* (quote on p. 1).

70. Andrew Marvell, *Letters and Poems*, H. M. Margouliouth (ed.) (2 vols, Oxford, 1971), **II**, p. 343.

71. *CSPD, 1675–6*, p. 461.
72. Henning, *House of Commons*, **I**, p. 211.
73. De Krey, 'London Radicals', p. 137.
74. Bodl. Lib., MS Rawlinson D 924, fols 298–9.
75. Goldie, 'Danby, the Bishops and the Whigs', pp. 85–6.
76. [Earl of Shaftesbury], *A Letter from a Parliament-Man to his Friend, Concerning the Proceedings of the House of Commons This last Session, begun the 13th of October, 1675* (1675), in *State Tracts: Being a Farther Collection of Several Choice Treatises Relating to the Government* (1692), pp. 53–4.

CHAPTER FOUR
The Exclusion Crisis

In the autumn of 1678 Titus Oates made his revelations of a Popish Plot to kill the King and massacre thousands of English Protestants. The story was a pack of lies, but such was the paranoia about Catholicism that few English Protestants doubted its veracity, and the Plot had alarming implications. What if Charles were to die suddenly, and be succeeded by his brother? How secure could English Protestants expect to be under a Catholic monarch? The successful exploitation of the Plot brought about the collapse of the system of government established by the Court in the 1670s; the Cavalier Parliament was dissolved and Danby fell from power, under the threat of impeachment. A pressure group emerged, soon to be known as the Whigs, which sought to get the Catholic heir excluded from the succession; those who opposed this policy came to be known as Tories. Between 1679 and 1681 three Parliaments were called (the last at Oxford), into each of which the opposition introduced Bills of Exclusion against the Duke of York. Yet the struggle for Exclusion was not limited to Westminster; it was also fought out in elections, in the press (the lapsing of the Licensing Act in 1679 led to a flood of pamphlets, broadsides and newspapers, as both sides sought to justify their positions), in petition campaigns, and in the streets, as the Whigs sought to mobilise mass support for their cause in order to pressurise Charles into yielding to their demands. Charles managed to forestall Exclusion through the timely use of his prerogative powers for determining the calling, proroguing and dissolution of Parliament, and in the end defeated the movement by his refusal to call Parliament again after 1681. Some Whigs were prepared to countenance popular resistance to achieve their aims: there were revelations of a Whig Plot in 1683 (the Rye House Plot), and indeed there was a rebellion in the west country led by the Duke of Monmouth in 1685. But few Whigs were willing to go to such extremes, and lacking a Parliamentary focus, and being perpetually harassed by a government who saw them as political subversives, the first Whigs were effectively crushed before the end of Charles II's reign.

It was during this time, then, that the language of party, and the terms Whig and Tory, became entrenched in English political vocabulary. So what divided the Whigs and Tories during the Exclusion Crisis? An older historiographical tradition tended to paint a picture of two fairly cohesive parties being born out of the crisis following the revelations of the Popish Plot, divided by their divergent attitudes towards the problem of the Catholic succession and rival interpretations of the constitution. The Whigs, because they maintained that Parliament had the right to alter the succession, were the champions of Parliamentary sovereignty, and advocates of constitutional or limited monarchy. They were also the party of the people, exploiting popular fears of Catholicism, and purporting to stand in defence of the lives, liberties and estates of the Protestant subjects of the realm. The Tories, in contrast, were the champions of hereditary, divine-right monarchy, who denied that the powers of the Crown could be limited in any way by Parliament. They were also an anti-populist party. Today, such views seem more questionable. J. R. Jones has argued that the first Whigs had no 'coherent political philosophy', but were a loose coalition of disparate forces, consisting of Country politicians, a few constitutional and religious radicals, and a group of political adventurers, with little in common beyond the desire for Exclusion.[1] Others have stressed the conservative nature of the first Whigs, arguing that most were not interested in remodelling the constitution, but merely wanted to preserve strong monarchy under a Protestant King,[2] although there has been a reaction against this view of late, as some have sought to reinvest the first Whigs with their true revolutionary credentials.[3] Most recently, some scholars have argued that the Whigs and Tories cannot be described as 'parties', since they possessed little internal unity, and that there was considerable overlap not only in the ideology, but also in the personnel, of the two groupings. Jonathan Scott, for example, has asserted that 'there were no whig and tory "parties" in 1678–83 partly because the "whig" (anti-court) majority of 1678–80, and the "tory" (loyalist) majority of 1681–3 were mostly the same people. . . . From 1678 to 1683 people remained convinced of an imminent threat to the church and government: in 1681 they changed their minds about where the greatest threat was coming from.'[4] In addition, it has been suggested that the crisis of 1678–83 was not really about Exclusion, but about contemporary fears and grievances, such as over Charles II's pro-French foreign policy, over attempts by the Court to interfere with the independence of Parliament, and over the Church of England.[5]

Whether we can talk about the emergence of party politics during the Exclusion Crisis depends on how rigid a definition of party we adopt. Certainly there continued to be some fluidity in political allegiances, and the structures of party politics were not as well developed as they were to become during the eighteenth century. Nevertheless, the crisis over the succession did produce a polarisation between two fairly well-identified sides, both of which had distinct political ideologies and possessed a rudimentary degree of organisation – a situation which by contemporary standards can appropriately be described as a party conflict. However, the party battle was about much more than Exclusion; it involved a whole range of issues which had been sources of political tension since the Restoration. Part of our confusion over the nature of party politics at this time has arisen from an over-concentration on constitutional issues. Constitutionally, both sides embraced a broad spectrum of positions. Within the Whig movement there were some radicals, and even republicans, a larger group of Parliamentary constitutionalists, but also many who wanted to preserve strong monarchy in England, as long as that monarch was a Protestant. Likewise, whilst some Tories championed divine-right, royal absolutism, the majority believed in legal monarchy and the rule of law, and in this respect had much in common with the more moderate Whigs. The key divide came over the issue of the Church, with the Whigs being the party sympathetic to Dissent, and the Tories the party of intolerant Anglicanism. It is also necessary to stress that the Tories were as violently anti-Catholic as the Whigs, even if they believed that the Church of England could be safe under a popish successor. Although it remains fair to describe the Whig position as populist, as the crisis progressed the Tories did pick up considerable support amongst the mass of the population, as people grew less concerned about the prospect of a popish successor, and more alarmed at the threat posed to the Church of England by the Whigs and their Nonconformist allies. As a result, England became sharply polarised, but the divide was not so much a reflection of divergent attitudes towards the relative powers of the Crown and Parliament, but rather of divergent attitudes towards the issue of Dissent.

THE WHIGS AND EXCLUSION

We should start by considering how central the issue of Exclusion was to the political strife that developed after the revelations of the Popish Plot. Between November 1678, when the Cavalier Parliament first reconvened after the Popish Plot scare, and the dissolution of the Oxford Parliament in 1681, a number of proposals for dealing with the problem of the Catholic succession were discussed. The government's solution was to place limitations on the powers of a popish successor, so that 'he may be disabled to do any harm'. Thus on 30 April 1679 Charles II suggested that all ecclesiastical benefices and promotions in the gift of the Crown should be removed from the control of a Catholic King, and that under a popish successor the power of appointment to civil and military offices should be transferred to Parliament. Other expedients suggested during the Exclusion Crisis were that there should be a regency, with the Princess of Orange ruling in James's name, that the Duke of Monmouth, the King's eldest illegitimate son, should be declared legitimate, or that Charles should obtain a divorce, so that he could re-marry and father a legitimate Protestant heir.[6]

It was not until 11 May 1679, several months after Oates's initial revelations, that an Exclusion Bill was introduced into the Commons. However, this delay cannot be blamed upon the failure to recognise Exclusion as a potential solution to the problem of a Catholic successor. Exclusion had been on the political agenda since the mid-1670s, and shortly after the Plot broke the idea was revived again in Council. It was Charles II who was determined to prevent Exclusion being put forward as the way to deal with the Catholic succession, and on 9 November 1678 the Commons was informed by its Speaker, Edward Seymour, that Charles would not consider any bills as tended 'to impeach the Right of Succession'.[7] In the face of such explicit royal hostility, there were obvious reasons why the opposition did not dare bring in an Exclusion Bill immediately, not least because of the risk of alienating moderate opponents of the Court by pursuing such an extreme measure too quickly. Parliament's investigations into the Plot, however, revealed that the Duke of York's Catholicism had 'given the greatest countenance and encouragement to the present conspiracies and designs of the Papists against the king, and the Protestant Religion', as a vote of the Commons put it on 27 April 1679,[8] and that he might have been mixed up in the Plot himself. As soon as the opponents of the Court felt their case was strong enough to launch an attack on the Catholic heir, despite Charles II's hostility, they introduced an Exclusion Bill. The offer of limitations did have some success in buying off the more moderate members of the opposition in the spring of 1679, but most of the opposition believed that such schemes would be unworkable, and suspected they were an attempt 'to delude the people', as MP William Sacheverell put it.[9] Once Exclusion had been introduced, opinion tended to polarise over the issue of whether the Duke of York should be barred from the succession. Exclusion was pursued with vigour in the Parliaments of 1680 and 1681, and only a few members of the opposition continued to favour the alternative of expedients. It is difficult to deny, therefore, the importance of Exclusion to the political crisis which developed in the aftermath of the Popish Plot; nevertheless, it must be emphasised that the crisis was not just about Exclusion (a point to which we shall return later).

Caution is also required when considering whether the first Whigs were a party. Certainly the old view that the Earl of Shaftesbury led an efficient and well-organised party-machine has to be corrected. Shaftesbury may have been a leading Whig, and an active proponent of the exclusionist cause (both inside and outside Parliament), but he was not *the* leader of the Whigs, and at times can be found at odds with other key figures in the Whig movement. He was not even a member of the Green Ribbon Club, which was once thought to be the organisational cell of the first Whigs, although it should be noted that various relatives, servants and close political associates of his were.[10] We also have to recognise the existence of different factions within the Whigs – the Shaftesbury–Russell interest can perhaps be contrasted with the Sidney–Capel one – and of tensions between moderates and extremists.

Nevertheless, the first Whigs evinced a degree of organisation which was impressive and sophisticated by the standards of the day, and which suggests that the world of 1679–81 was much more recognisably one of party politics than had been the world even of the 1670s. Members of the opposition movement frequently met in taverns or coffee-houses to co-ordinate tactics, and a total of twenty-nine different Whig clubs have been found in London alone during the Exclusion Crisis. Along with the Green Ribbon Club, they included clubs held by Shaftesbury at the Swan in Fish Street, the Angel Tavern, near the Old Exchange, the Queen's Arms and the Nag's Head, and a club held at the Salutation Tavern in Lombard Street by the Duke of Buckingham. Some of the London clubs tapped into a rudimentary provincial network; the Green Ribbon Club, for example, had sister societies in Oxford, Taunton and Bristol (the Horseshoe Tavern), whilst Buckingham's Club at the Salutation had close contacts with the west country.[11] The clubs played an important role in the mobilisation of public opinion. The Green Ribbon Club was believed to be responsible for distributing Whig propaganda throughout the country, and although its precise control over the output of the Whig press is unclear, it did number several prominent publicists amongst its ranks, whilst it also appears to have sponsored the activities of Henry Care, the author of the exclusionist periodical, *A Weekly Pacquet of Advice from Rome*. The club also helped sponsor the pope-burning processions of 17 November, which were elaborately stage-managed affairs, costing £100 or more to put on.[12] A fair amount of co-ordination went into electoral campaigns. Wealthy Whig magnates, such as Shaftesbury, Buckingham, Wharton, and Grey, brought all their influence to bear to ensure the return of sympathetic candidates, whilst electoral agents were also employed to campaign on behalf of Whig candidates at the polls.[13] In Bristol, the Mermaid and Horseshoe Taverns served as electioneering clubs, gathering support for exclusionist candidates.[14] The Whig petitions of 1679–80, calling for the sitting of the second Exclusion Parliament (which Charles II kept prorogued for over a year), were organised from the centre, with printed sheets being sent down from London into the provinces where local agents would busy themselves obtaining signatories.[15]

The Whigs viewed Exclusion as essential because they felt the 'lives, liberties and estates' of Protestants could not be safe under a popish successor.[16] Whig propaganda recalled what life had been like under Mary Tudor, England's last Catholic monarch, when Protestants had been burnt at the stake for heresy, but more lurid and fanciful images of the types of atrocities Catholics might commit were also invoked: papists ravishing wives and daughters; children being eaten or having their brains dashed out against the walls; mothers being put to the sword; and people being hung by their feet or even boiled alive.[17] Although such arguments helped to fuel anti-Catholic paranoia, the Whig case for why a Catholic had to be barred from the succession was based on much more sophisticated political arguments. The thrust of their position was that a Catholic ruler would be compelled to govern in an arbitrary and despotic manner, after the fashion of Louis XIV of France, and ride roughshod over the interests of his subjects. It was argued that subjects obeyed their King partly as a matter of religious conscience, so that if the King's religion were different the bonds of obedience would be broken.[18] Unable to rely on the support and co-operation of his Protestant subjects, a Catholic monarch would have to abandon Parliament, and instead rule through a standing army. In the past, the Duke of York had shown himself to be in favour of a more autocratic style of monarchy and impatient with Parliament. As one pamphleteer put it: 'is it not too notoriously known, that the D. hates our Parliaments with an implacable hatred . . . if he Succeed, adieu to all Parliaments; must you not expect to be Ruled by Force'.[19] Moreover, a Catholic King would be forced as a matter of principle to attempt to undo the Reformation, and make us 'Vassals again to the Romish Yoke'.[20] Again, this was something that could only be done by force. Government by a standing army would mean an end to the rule of law. It would also be expensive, and require such a heavy burden of taxation as to reduce English people to desperate poverty.[21] In short, York's 'vehemence in exalting the Prerogative (in his Brother's time) beyond its due bounds and the principles of his Religion which carry him to all imaginable excesses of Cruelty' meant that 'he must be excluded'.[22]

THE CONSTITUTIONAL POSITION OF THE WHIGS

The case for Exclusion was justified, first and foremost, in terms of the possible disasters that might befall England should there be a Catholic successor. Yet was there more to the exclusionist platform than this? Were the Whigs concerned only with a potential threat, sometime in the future, or did the logic of their position involve a fundamental criticism of constitutional arrangements as they existed under Charles? Or, to put the question another way, how radical were the first Whigs?

The Parliamentary Whigs liked to portray their position as constitutionally conservative, claiming that they wanted to preserve strong monarchy, not weaken it. As the Earl of Huntingdon said in a debate on Exclusion in the Lords on 15 November, 1680, 'there is not a man in this House, I am confident, who is for the passing of this bill who is not most zealous for the support of this monarchy and the King in his royal prerogatives'. The Exclusion Bills of 1679–81 did not impinge upon the Crown's powers in any way; they merely proposed that James should be removed from the succession, so that on Charles's death the throne should pass to the next in line (which would mean Princess Mary), as 'if the Duke of York were naturally dead'.[23] Some would have liked to see the succession settled on the Duke of Monmouth, but none of the Exclusion Bills explicitly endorsed such a proposition, and it is now generally agreed that very few Whigs espoused Monmouth's cause before the dissolution of the Oxford Parliament. Whigs repeatedly, and quite rightly, argued that the various alternatives to Exclusion suggested by the Court were far more injurious to the royal prerogative. As Sir Robert Clayton said in a speech in the Oxford Parliament of March 1681, 'all the Expedients I have heard of . . . seem all to be a breach of the Constitution of the Government'.[24] A tract of 1681 opposed limitations by arguing that any laws passed to prevent a popish successor from introducing popery would have to so 'tye up his hands' as 'must ruine his Prerogative, and put the executive Power of the Laws into the hands of the People', whilst another charged 'the Court expedient managers' with 'setling a Republick'.[25]

We should be wary of taking Whig self-professions of conservatism at face value, since it would have been a tactical mistake for the exclusionists to admit that their real aim was a fundamental restructuring of the powers of the monarchy. There were some republicans or commonwealthmen within the Whig movement, who may have hoped that Exclusion would be a prelude to more radical constitutional reform. A number of leading Whigs had been supporters of the regimes of the 1650s, including Shaftesbury himself, or else had come from families who had opposed the Crown during the Civil War. So too had many members of the Green Ribbon Club, which also included amongst its membership known republicans such as Slingsby Bethel, Richard Nelthorp, Nathaniel Wade, and the poet John Ayloffe, author of much of the republican doggerel of the 1670s. Buckingham's club at the Salutation was filled with republicans, many of the Whig activists in London could boast radical histories stretching back to the Interregnum, whilst those involved in the Rye House Plot and Monmouth Rebellion included stern critics of the monarchy such as Algernon Sidney and the one-time Leveller, John Wildman.[26]

On the other hand, it is significant that some of the most outspoken critics of the monarchy tended to distance themselves from the policy of Exclusion. Henry Neville, a classical republican, who had been a member of John Harrington's republican Rota Club in the late 1650s, produced a work shortly before the Oxford Parliament of 1681 in which he opposed Exclusion and argued instead for a drastic limitation on the powers of the monarchy: if the monarch had no real power to act independently, it would make no difference whether he was a Protestant or a Catholic.[27] John Wildman also preferred limitations to Exclusion.[28] And if we look at the group normally considered to be the most radical amongst the Whigs, those who were prepared to countenance plotting after the Oxford Parliament of 1681, we find that even here a number of them seem to have had fairly traditional views of the constitution. Thus in addition to radicals such as Wildman, Sidney, and Ayloffe, there were other plotters such as Robert Ferguson, William Lord Russell, and Sir Thomas Armstrong, who appear to have wanted not a republic, but merely the establishment of Protestant monarchy in England, with the Duke of Monmouth as King.[29]

If it is fair to suggest that most Whigs probably did not wish to move in the direction of a commonwealth, it would be wrong to conclude that they were happy with Charles II. Indeed, the exclusionist position was as much bound up with an indictment of the style of government under Charles II, as it was with concern about what might happen when his brother became King. The first Whigs were desperately alarmed by Charles's preference for a pro-French foreign policy, and there was a sense in which their belief in an international popish plot to subvert Protestantism in England was justified. The seventeenth century had seen Protestantism on the retreat in many parts of Europe, and the Whigs felt it was the duty of the English King to uphold the dwindling Protestant interest in Europe, rather than ally himself with the powers of the counter-Reformation against Calvinist nations such as the Dutch.[30] At the time of the opening of the first Exclusion Parliament, Shaftesbury wrote a paper pointing to the threat posed by the French, and warning that Protestant Europe could not look for help from the English Court whilst 'a Popish successor' was 'so near at hand'.[31] One author stated that 'the Protestant States flatter themselves extreamly, if they be perswaded, That . . . the Progress which the work of the Reformation hath made in Europe' had so weakened the papal enemy, that 'he is not to be feared any more', and argued for a union of the northern Protestant nations of England, Holland and Sweden to withstand the Catholic challenge.[32] Others complained that England's economic interests were being jeopardised by French expansionism, and urged the necessity of taking swift action against the French King.[33]

The Whig position also embraced many of the grievances voiced by the Country opposition in the 1670s. Thus the exclusionists attacked placemen, denounced electoral corruption and bribery, and argued for annual Parliaments – although in response to Charles II's latest tactics they insisted that Parliaments 'should not be Prorogued or Dissolved till all the Petitions, and Bills before them were answered and Redressed'.[34] They maintained that England was a mixed monarchy, where sovereignty was shared by the King, Lords and Commons, and that Parliament enjoyed a very large share of the law-making power.[35]

The Earl of Shaftesbury, writing in 1679, claimed that 'The Parliament of England is that Supreme and absolute Power, which gives Life and Motion to the English Government'.[36] Such views were rooted in the belief that Parliament was the representative of the people, and that its acts were based upon popular consent as given by the electorate. Many Whig writers championed the theory of the ancient constitution – most notably James Tyrrell, William Petyt and Algernon Sidney – arguing that Parliaments predated the Norman Conquest, and that English constitutional liberties could be traced back to Anglo-Saxon times.[37]

There were obvious reasons why the Whigs chose to exalt Parliament at this time, since they dominated the House of Commons, and between 1679–81 it seemed that they stood a good chance of achieving what they wanted through Parliament. Yet it would be a mistake to see the Whigs (as a whole) as a Country party. Not only had some future exclusionists backed the Court during the last years of the Cabal, but a number of leading Whigs accepted positions to Charles's remodelled Privy Council of 1679, when Charles sought to broaden the basis of his support by bringing into the government some of his political opponents. Moreover, we have already seen how some future supporters of Exclusion had in the past acted in ways which seemed to undermine the notion of Parliamentary sovereignty, notably with regard to the Declaration of Indulgence of 1672. Without wishing to denigrate the sincere attachment to Parliamentarianism or the Country platform which many Whigs undoubtedly possessed, it must be recognised that a fair number of exclusionists had shown themselves throughout their careers prepared to work with either Court or Country, King or Parliament, in order to achieve their political ends.

Some scholars have maintained that the radicalism of the first Whigs can be seen in their championship of a wider electoral franchise; Richard Ashcraft has gone so far as to suggest that their position on the suffrage came close to that of the Levellers.[38] Such a view seems questionable. It is true that we can find instances of Whigs arguing for an extension of the franchise. For example, the exclusionist candidates won the election at New Windsor in February 1679 when the House of Commons set aside the return made by the Corporation and declared in favour of an unlimited inhabitant franchise. In the borough of Aldborough in Yorkshire, the Tory member, Sir John Reresby, was defeated when the vote was extended from the burgage-holders to all the inhabitants paying scot and lot (which extended the number of voters from nine to sixty-six).[39] But there are counter-examples of

Whigs favouring a narrower franchise than the Tories. At the South-wark election of 1681 the Whig candidates – one of them being Slingsby Bethel, whom contemporaries styled a republican – argued that the poll should be restricted to those who paid poor rates, whilst the Tories wanted all householders to vote. The Tories won the argument and, as a result, the election.[40] Another republican, Algernon Sidney, who stood for Amersham between 1679 and 1681, argued for a narrowing of the franchise from all inhabitant householders to only those paying scot and lot.[41] Concern about the Court's potential to manipulate elections led Shaftesbury in 1679 to draft proposals which would have drastically reduced the size of the electorate, on the grounds that the majority of electors were 'of a mean and abject Fortune' who, lacking 'that discerning faculty, which Electors in such weighty concerns ought to have', were easily 'Corrupted and Seduced by the inveiglements of a little Mony, or a Pot of Ale'. A similar scheme for limiting the franchise was put forward by John Wildman (an ex-Leveller himself) in 1689.[42] In the existing state of research it is probably best to conclude that the attitude towards the franchise – for both parties – was determined less by questions of principle (Leveller or otherwise), but by more pragmatic considerations (which franchise would enable us to win the election?).

In the light of the evidence presented above, we can see why some historians have denied that the Whigs had a coherent political ideo-logy, and been dismissive of their credentials as being either a radical or a populist party. Such a reaction is going too far. A different per-spective is gained if we move away from central politics and look at Whig agitation at the local level. In London, for example, the Whigs argued for a radical reform of the City's constitution, which would have greatly extended democratic rights within the Corporation.[43] More generally, however, I would suggest that the radicalism of the first Whigs is to be found less in their advocacy of specific constitu-tional reforms, and more in their use of the natural law tradition to criticise duly constituted authority. Although Whigs looked for histori-cal precedents to show that Parliament had the power to alter the succession, their position ultimately rested upon an appeal to natural law and reason, and could be justified in these terms alone. One MP insisted that even if there were no precedents to support the case for the Exclusion Bill, 'the Law of Nature . . . would afford us sufficient arguments' for its passage.[44] One pamphleteer asserted that 'it is con-trary to the Law of Nature and Reason, to suppose that the King and Parliament together cannot alter the Succession'. If the heir was a fool, a madman, a Turk, or a heretic, he continued, ruin would inevitably follow if the government was put into his hands, and government was ordained for the benefit of the public, not for its destruction.[45] Underlying the Whig position was the belief that government existed for the good of the people, and that the King derived his authority 'from the Consent of the people': 'Every form of Government is of our Creation and not Gods, and must comply with the safety of the people in all that it can'.[46] Since the people could not be safe under a Catholic monarch, the Duke of York had to be barred from the succession. As the Lord Cavendish put it, since government 'is intended for the safety and protection of those that are Govern'd', then 'it follows, naturally, that the Succession of Princes in Hereditary Monarchies, can not be binding, nor ought to be admitted, where it proves manifestly inconsistent with those ends'.[47]

It is sometimes claimed that the Whigs had a restricted definition of the term 'people', and that by it they meant only men of property: hence the reason why they always linked their defence of liberty with a defence of property. Yet property, as many Whigs used the term, meant more than just real estate – people had a property in their laws, in their liberties, in their lives, and all these would be threatened by a popish successor. The laws and liberties of England, as one exclusionist pamphleteer put it, preserve 'inviolable the rights of the meanest peasant'.[48] The prime strategy of the Whigs was to show Charles II that the people of England were determinedly opposed to a Catholic succession. This is why they did their utmost to encourage anti-Catholic demonstrations (such as the famous pope-burnings of 17 November), popular petitions and addresses to the Crown, and instructions to newly-elected MPs informing them how their constituents wanted them to act in the ensuing Parliament. Whatever his views on the franchise, Shaftesbury was extremely active in encouraging these manifestations of public opinion. The Whigs in Parliament also defended the people's right to petition the Crown.[49] In short, the whole logic of the exclusionist position reveals that they believed that subjects had the right to tell their rulers how they should act – whether that be through their representatives in Parliament, by petition, or by demonstrations. As one Whig put it, it was the people's 'Birth-right and Priviledge [to petition], and the King's Honour, to receive the Supplications of his People'.[50]

The logical extension of this position was that the subjects had the right to resist a King who did not rule in the interests of his subjects. The Whig position, therefore, was not only populist, but also radical, in the sense that contemporaries understood the term. As Tories repeatedly complained, the Whigs maintained that 'Royal Authority is

Originally and Radically in the People'. The people committed 'onely
the Administration of such Power as is radically in them to others', so
that 'upon the Male-administration of the Power so delegated, they
may revoke the Delegation, and take all the Power into their own
hands again'.[51] The most famous articulation of the Whig radical
populist position is John Locke's *Two Treatises of Government*, most of
which was probably composed between the dissolution of the Oxford
Parliament in March 1681 and the revelations of the Rye House Plot
in June 1683. In essence Locke had a contract theory of government:
legitimate government was founded in individual consent, and those in
authority merely exercised a position of trust, to protect people in
their lives, liberties and estates. If they broke that trust, the people had
the right to resist them. Locke located sovereignty in the legislature,
but like many Whigs, he was also critical of Parliament, being well
aware that it too could betray its trust, as the experience of the Cavalier Parliament had shown. And although the *Two Treatises* were a
contribution to the exclusion debate – indeed, much of the *First
Treatise* is given to a refutation of the divine-right, hereditary principle
and the argument that the succession to the throne was unalterable –
Locke's main concern was not so much with the possible tyranny that
might come under a popish successor, but with the present misgovernment of Charles II. It was the reigning monarch, and not his heir, that
needed to be resisted.[52]

The number of Whigs who were prepared to carry the implications
of their populist position to its radical conclusion, and urge the
necessity of resistance after the failure of the Parliamentary Exclusion
movement, was probably greater than we once thought. However, it
has to be conceded that such radicals were still a minority, and that
most Whigs shied away from such extremes.[53] Does that mean we
have to abandon the search for any coherence in the exclusionist
movement, and conclude that the first Whigs were united on little else
besides their shared attachment to Exclusion? From a purely constitutional perspective, the answer would probably have to be yes. But
then again the Exclusion Crisis was not purely about constitutional
issues. The Tories were concerned not merely with the subversive
threat the Whigs posed to the structure of authority within the State;
they were particularly concerned with the threat the Whigs posed to
the established Church of England. If we look at the Whig attitude
towards the re-established Church, we find that there was a great deal
of coherence behind their platform, and it further emphasises the fact
that the Exclusion Crisis was not just about a potential threat in the
future, but was a crisis over a very deep-seated problem which had

been a fundamental cause of conflict in Restoration politics – the issue of Dissent.

THE WHIGS AND THE ISSUE OF DISSENT

Many leading figures in the first Whig movement were united by a shared history of opposition to the intolerant High Anglican establishment – such as Shaftesbury, Buckingham, and Russell, to name three of the most obvious examples. The Whig Green Ribbon Club was composed mainly of people who were critical of the Church establishment, many being Nonconformists themselves, amongst them men such as Henry Booth, the Trenchards, Slingsby Bethel, Richard Goodenough, Richard Nelthorp and Sir William Waller. Most of the Whig publicists or propagandists were Dissenters: Henry Care, the author of the famous exclusionist periodical, the *Weekly Pacquet of Advice from Rome,* was a Presbyterian; of the publishers of Whig newspapers, Langley Curtis and Richard Janeway were moderate Nonconformists, whilst Benjamin Harris and Francis Smith were Baptists; and there were also a number of Baptist printers, such as John Darby and George Larkin. Nonconformists were active in campaigning for Whig candidates at the polls, whilst many of the London Whigs were Dissenters.[54]

Most Whigs were critical of the intolerance of the Church establishment. They repeatedly argued that it was necessary for Protestants of all persuasions to unite to meet the challenge of popery.[55] As one author implored, 'the Breach betwixt the Church of England and other Protestants of different Perswasions' must be healed: 'neither of you can ever be safe if you do not both unite and joyn hand in hand against the Common Enemy, viz. the Papists and Popery'.[56] Some form of religious toleration had to be achieved; Protestant unity, as one pamphleteer claimed, was the 'main (and indeed chief) business' at this time.[57] In particular, the Whigs wanted the repeal of the savage Elizabethan statute of 1593 against seditious sectaries (the Act of 35 Elizabeth), they promoted a bill to distinguish Protestant from Catholic recusants (to prevent Nonconformists suffering under the old Elizabethan recusancy laws), and also supported measures for comprehension and religious toleration.[58]

The Whigs had to be rather careful in the way they dealt with the issue of the established Church. Since they portrayed themselves as the defenders of the Protestant interest, and since it was essential for them to win over moderate Anglican opinion, they had to claim that they had the best interests of the Church at heart. Having said this, it is surprising how outspoken they were in their criticism of the Anglican establishment. This was in part because it was the High Church clergy who were the fiercest opponents of Exclusion. The Whigs held the bishops responsible for the defeat of the second Exclusion Bill in the House of Lords in November 1680, and it was even mooted that a bill should be introduced 'to exclude the Bishops' votes, as they show themselves enemies to the Commons'.[59] A poem which circulated in manuscript at this time suggested that

> . . . the best of Expedients the Lords can propose
> the Church to preserve and Ruine her foes
> Is not to lett Lawne Sleeves our Parliaments fill
> but to throw out the Bishops that threw out the bill.[60]

Whigs accused all the enemies of Exclusion as being at heart sympathisers to popery, even though they might profess to be Church of England men, and the extreme opposition that many High Churchmen had to any compromise with the Protestant Nonconformists led the Whigs to accuse the Tory clergy of preferring to risk 'setting up the Mass, rather than shake hands with a Presbyterian'.[61]

Hostility towards the bishops and the Tory clergy went deeper than the fact that they opposed Exclusion. More extreme Whigs saw the Church establishment as part of the long-term Popish Plot to extirpate true religion in England. The re-established Church, they argued, contained too many relics of popery. Although the Church hierarchy might hate the Pope, they had nevertheless 'received Popery', by encouraging superstitious ceremonies, by attacking sound Protestant doctrines, and by persecuting people for their religious beliefs. As one writer claimed, 'Arminianism, Free-Will, General Redemption, Falling from Grace, denying a free, personal, eternal election, are all hatched in Hell, and are the Pope's foundation'.[62]

THE TORIES AND THE DEFENCE OF THE SUCCESSION

Those who opposed Exclusion, or the Tories as they soon came to be known, were less well organised than the Whigs. No individual or group of individuals readily stand out as leaders of the movement:

there was no obvious or recognised successor to the role Danby had filled since the mid-1670s. Some of the leading opponents of Exclusion were holders of Court office, such as Halifax, the second Earl of Clarendon (Henry Hyde), Laurence Hyde (the Earl of Rochester from 1682), Sir Leoline Jenkins, and Edward Seymour. But it is important to recognise that the Tories were not a Court party: only a few held positions in the central administration, even fewer were dependent upon the Crown for their election to Parliament, whilst some opponents of Exclusion, such as Sir William Coventry, Sir Thomas Thynne (the future Lord Weymouth), Sir Thomas Clarges, and Halifax himself had been active in the Country opposition against Danby in the 1670s.[63] The Tories would not have seen themselves as a party; they believed everyone should be loyal supporters of the Crown, and saw it as their task to win back the support of moderates who, as a result of the Popish Plot scare, had temporarily been deceived into supporting the factious opposition (a task which, as we shall see later, they fulfilled with some success).

Nevertheless, it is possible to detect some co-ordination behind the anti-exclusionist campaign. Licenser of the press, Sir Roger L'Estrange, played a vital role in the propaganda war against the Whigs, writing many pamphlets and producing his own Tory newspaper, *The Observator*. It was rumoured that L'Estrange was financed in part by a pension from the King and partly by voluntary contributions from loyalist bodies such as the Bristol Artillery Company and the clergy of Worcester. Francis North, Lord Chief Justice of Common Pleas and a close advisor of the King, also helped co-ordinate Tory propaganda; in his papers there are a set of guidelines for a treatise to be written 'for undeceiving the people about the late popish plott', in which he lays down many of the main arguments which opponents of Exclusion repeatedly employed.[64] There were Tory printers and newspaper publishers, such as Nathaniel Thompson, Henry and Joanna Brome, and Benjamin Tooke. Although there was no equivalent to the Whig Green Ribbon Club, there were a number of Tory clubs, especially in London; L'Estrange frequented one at Sam's Coffee-House in Ludgate, whilst the Duke of Ormonde held another in the same area.[65] Some of these clubs served electoral ends. At the time of the elections to the second Exclusion Parliament in September 1679, one Whig pamphleteer recalled how the London Tories 'press on by many Clubs and Meetings, where they make their Party as industriously as a newly Commissioned Captain labours to compleat such a number of Souldiers, as may enable them to pass Muster, and have right to Pay'.[66] And although Tory ideology was as rich and varied as that of the

Whigs, we can recognise a distinctive Tory identity, one centred around an attachment to Church and State as by law established.

The basic premise of the case against Exclusion was that English monarchs ruled by divine right and therefore the hereditary succession could not be broken. To support this argument the works of Sir Robert Filmer were revived: his most famous tract, *Patriarcha*, which had been written during the reign of Charles I, was published for the first time in 1680. Filmer had maintained that the King's power came directly from God, and that God had given the world to Adam, and his heirs in succession, exclusive of the rest of posterity. It was therefore the case, as one Tory pamphleteer put it, that 'no Human Power can hinder the Descent upon the Right Heir of the Crown. The Descent makes the King'.[67] A similar point was made by Sir Leoline Jenkins, in a speech in the House of Commons on 4 November 1680: 'I am of opinion that Kings of England have their Right from God alone, and that no Power on Earth can deprive them of it'.[68] Tories refuted the natural law argument for Exclusion, by denying that there was any original contract between the King and his people, which made the former accountable to his subjects if he failed to rule for the public good. Kings were accountable only to God, and could not be resisted by their subjects.

At first glance it appears that the Tories were royal absolutists. Filmer maintained 'To Majestie or Sovereignty belongeth an Absolute Power not to be subject to any law'.[69] As another author put it, there was an 'Obligation upon Subjects not to start from their Allegiance to their Soveraigns'.[70] Some Tories clearly got carried away with their enthusiasm for the monarchy. One writer urged Charles II not to let 'the French King be a greater monarch than yourself . . . shew yourself as absolute over your people as he is'.[71] One Bristol gentleman allegedly expressed his opinion in January 1680 that 'The King is unwise to govern by a Parliament', and wondered why 'He doth not raise an Army, and govern by the Sword', claiming that several Somerset gentlemen were ready to assist the King, and that the Bishop of Bath and Wells had gone to acquaint him of this.[72] Yet to style the Tories as advocates of royal absolutism obscures more than it reveals, since most writers made important qualifications to any of their absolutist statements. Thus one author, whilst maintaining that 'God is the immediate Author of Soveraignty in the King, and that he is no Creature of the People's making', nevertheless stressed that he was not arguing 'for a Dispotical Soveraignty, an absolute Power, such as the great Turk this day exercises over his Subjects: I maintain only such Royal, Paternal Soveraignty, as we and our Ancestors have lived long, and happily under'.[73] Another writer, having first asserted that God was the author of government, and denied that people were by nature free born, went on to put the question 'May Princes then Reign without controul?', to which he replied that 'the most Absolute Prince is subject to the Laws of his God, his own Conscience, and the Rules of Common Justice . . . for Princes are tied and circumscribed in the exercise of their Power by Laws'. The problem was, subjects had no recourse if the King broke the laws: he did not forfeit his authority as a result, and he was restrained not 'by the Efficient and Compulsive Part of them [the Laws], but by the Exemplary only'.[74]

It is important to recognise, however, that Tories tended to urge obedience to the legally constituted government of England. That England was ruled by a divine-right monarch, many felt, could be proved not only by the laws of God, but also by the laws of the land. The King enjoyed certain prerogatives by law, which meant that he had immense powers, but his prerogatives were also bounded by the law. 'Active obedience' was therefore 'to be yielded to the King as Supream, in *omnibus licitis*, in all things lawful'.[75] The qualification that obedience was due to lawful government was typically made, even by those who seemed to be urging a high degree of subservience by the people to their rulers. As one critic of Exclusion wrote, 'if Almighty God in his Providence should please to send us a Popish Prince, The best way to preserve the Protestant Religion in the Purity of her Doctrine, is not only to admit him, but submit to his just Authority in all his Lawful Commands'.[76]

The implications of what this position meant for Tories were not to be faced until James II's reign, when the King did start acting illegally. During the Exclusion Crisis, Tories argued that the King was doing everything legally, and so the legalist argument was used to reinforce the claim that subjects were obliged to remain loyal to the Crown. It was also used to defend the Catholic succession; the Duke of York had a legal title to the throne, he had done no wrong, and so he could not have his legal rights taken away from him. As Sir Leoline Jenkins put it in a speech on Exclusion in the Oxford Parliament, 'No Bill was ever offered in Parliament so much against the Justice of the Nation. Here is a great Prince condemned before he is heard.'[77] Or as one writer asked, 'is the Cry of Law and Justice . . . intended so particularly for the People, that the King must have no share?'[78] Yet the law would also protect English subjects under a popish successor, since the Protestant religion was 'sufficiently guarded by several Acts of Parliament, which he can never repeal'.[79] What could the Duke of York do when he became King? 'Can he make Laws, or alter the constitution of the Government, without the consent of a Parliament?'[80] Protestantism was bound to be safe under a Catholic successor, since 'All our Laws are in favour of that Religion that is Established, which could never be repealed but in Parliament'.[81] The government had even been prepared to offer additional legal safeguards in the advent of a popish King, but these had been rejected by the exclusionists.

This Tory stress on the security given to the Protestant religion by Acts of Parliament is worth emphasising, since it is the Whigs who are usually regarded as the champions of Parliament during the Exclusion Crisis. Did not the Tories show themselves in many respects to be enemies of Parliament? The Tories certainly denied the Whig principle of co-ordination, that the King shared his powers with the Lords and Commons: it was 'a breach upon the best Constitution of Government in the World', to assert that 'the soveraign Power lieth in the Commons'.[82] They rejected the theory of the ancient constitution, and defended the King's prerogative power of determining the sitting of Parliament. As the Cambridge scholar, Dr Robert Brady, was to show, Parliaments were created by the Crown in the late-medieval period, and had historically always been dependent upon the Crown for their sitting; they were therefore subordinate to the King, who alone was sovereign.[83] Yet most Tories were not against Parliaments *per se*; they were just against Whig-dominated Parliaments. What the Tories wanted, as John Verney wrote in July 1679, at the time of the dissolution of the first Exclusion Parliament, was 'an honest Church of England Parliament'.[84] In his Declaration issued in April 1681, explaining why he had dissolved the previous two Parliaments, Charles II expressed his resolve 'to have frequent Parliaments', and although he did not in fact fulfil this promise, he clearly recognised that it was something which, not only his opponents, but also his supporters wanted to hear.[85] As one Tory newspaper put it at the same time, 'I hope we shall have a Parliament yet that will heal all'.[86] One pamphleteer claimed he desired 'as heartily as any one in England, the frequent Meetings of Parliament', though he cautioned that 'experience tells us, That Parliaments may Erre as well as Kings'.[87] Tories continued to hope for a Parliament well into the period of the Tory Reaction which followed the defeat of Exclusion. In January 1683 one correspondent, commenting how the situation in London was much better now than it had been for a long time, concluded by saying 'we want only A Parliament that we may trust'.[88]

Although Tories opposed the Whig demand to exclude a popish successor, they repeatedly maintained that in doing this they were seeking to protect the realm from popery and arbitrary government. The starting point for their line of reasoning was the depiction of the Whigs as Nonconformists and republicans whose real aim was to destroy the Church and State as by law established. 'All honest men', one pamphleteer wrote, 'believe the Popish Plot, and have a Detestation both against the Principles and Practises of Popery'. But the 'Commonwealth Protestants' and the Dissenters had used the Plot 'to play their Old Game again', namely, 'the Alteration and Ruine of the Government established both in Church and State'.[89] In doing this, the Whigs were seeking the same aims as Catholics, and acting on popish principles themselves. As one author put it, 'the Papists would destroy our Church and State; so would the Common-Wealthsmen: the Papists would set up Popery and absolute Monarchy; the other an Amsterdam Religion, and Arbitrary Government in the hands of many'. Then drawing parallels between what had happened in the 1640s, this author pointed out that whereas the Catholics had continually plotted against our monarchy, only the commonwealthmen had ever succeeded in killing a King.[90] Dethroning a King was a jesuitical principle.[91] The Calvinists had learnt their theories of resistance from Catholic or Jesuit writers, a point which was historically quite accurate. As one clergyman put it in a sermon delivered on 30 January 1679, 'let presbyterians remember this', that their doctrine 'that kings were to give an account to the people . . . is from the Pope, and let us know that all popery is not only among them that call themselves papists, but that such among us as doe inveigh most bitterly against the name, doe as hotly own the thing as anyone bred all his lifetime at a Pope's Feet'.[92] The Whig pursuit of toleration, it was felt, would seriously undermine the integrity of the Church of England, and inevitably work to the advantage of Catholics. After all, the Nonconformists and Catholics had worked together for toleration in the past (most notably in 1672), and it could be plausibly argued that 'Popery could never come into England, unless the Phanatiques let it in at the back door of Toleration'.[93] It was also claimed that the political turmoil caused by the Whigs and Nonconformists at this time could only serve the interest of France and the international cause of popery, since it would be impossible to protect ourselves or our Protestant neighbours from the international threat whilst we were fighting amongst ourselves at home. As Edmund Bohun later recalled, the only service performed by the Whig Parliaments 'was to the French King; for our Allies beyond Seas seeing that No Assistance was to be Expected from England, Surrendered their strongest Towns to him for the Asking, and so suffered the worst effects of War in Peace'.[94]

By alleging that the exclusionists intended to revive the common-wealth, the Tories were able to suggest that the Whigs were the true promoters of arbitrary government. As John Nalson put it, during the 1640s and 1650s the Dissenters had 'governed with the most arbitrary injustice imaginable', they had overturned normal constitutional proce-dures, and set up 'their uncontrolled will and pleasure' as 'theirs and our only law'. In the 1650s laws had been passed without the consent of a Parliament, so that England had been governed essentially by the will of the Protector.[95] One broadside, set out as a dialogue between Cromwell and the Pope, had Cromwell confessing 'Have not I Trans-grest all the Laws of God and Man? Did not I subvert a State? Change its Religion and Government, Murder its Prince . . .?' Yes, the Pope agreed, but you were only the executioner of 'the Roman contrivan-ces'.[96] In 1678 L'Estrange produced a lengthy tract entitled *Tyranny and Popery Lording it over the Lives, Liberties and Estates both of King and People*, which was in essence a detailed chronicle of various irregu-larities and abuses suffered in England and Scotland during the middle decades of the seventeenth century. The Tories also argued that rule by a standing army would be more likely under the Whigs than under a popish successor. During the Commonwealth England had been ruled by a standing army.[97] Charles's Declaration of April 1681 stated that Exclusion would make it 'necessary to maintain a Standing Force, for the Preserving the Government and the Peace of the Kingdom'.[98] If toleration to Protestant Dissenters had been granted, Bohun main-tained, such feuds would have started amongst the different sorts of Protestants, and between them and the Catholics who were excluded, 'that nothing but a standing Army would have been able to have kept us in any tolerable quiet'.[99]

The way to avert the Whig threat, the opponents of Exclusion argued, was through a strict enforcement of the law, and especially the penal laws. Charles's Declaration of April 1681 confirmed that the 'impartial Execution of Our Laws' was 'the best Support, both of the Protestant Interest, and the Peace of the Kingdom'.[100] One writer, blaming the political troubles of the entire reign on papists, sectarians, Fifth Monarchists, atheists, and cunning old statesmen, none of whom had been able to live happily under the restored regime, concluded that if only the laws had been properly enforced against popish recu-sants and sectarians, these troubles would never have happened.[101] Bohun recommended 'an Universal Execution of the Laws against the Dissenters, Especially those against Conventicles', which he saw as 'the Seed-places where factions are nursed up till they may be strong enough to graple with and overturn the Government of Church and State'.[102]

In certain respects, then, the political outlook of the Tories was similar to that of the Whigs. They, like the exclusionists, claimed to be against popery and arbitrary government, for the rule of law, and defenders of (what they saw as) Parliament's true role in the constitution. There were obvious tactical reasons for this use of similar rhetoric. At the beginning of the crisis, the Whigs had won over moderate Anglican opinion, and to defeat Exclusion, this had to be won back, something which could only be done by appealing to the political sensibilities of this group. But we should be wary of concluding that political consensus therefore existed in this society, or that in ideological terms there was very little difference between Whigs and Tories. For in seeking to win back moderate Anglican opinion, the Tories helped polarise the conflict of the Exclusion Crisis around the issue of Dissent. If we look at the respective attitudes towards the Church establishment of the two parties, then we can see that indeed they were separated by a wide ideological gulf.

Tories and Whigs also diverged in their attitudes towards the people, for the Tory position was essentially an anti-populist one. 'It is high Impudence in any Subject', Tories felt, to take it upon himself to advise the King 'how and when to execute his Power'.[103] They inveighed against the rabble-rousing tactics of the Whigs, playing on the fears of mob rule and popular government in the 1640s and 1650s, and accused the Whigs of seeking to level all social hierarchies.[104] This is not to suggest that the Tories were unconcerned with public opinion; indeed, they were well aware of the need to win public support for their position, and much of their propaganda was targeted at the masses. But the basic position of the Tories was paternalistic: ordinary people had gained little in the 1650s, when they had suffered from high taxes, economic dislocation, and an attack on their traditional pastimes from Puritan magistrates and politicians, and they would be much better off if they stuck to their allotted role in society and allowed their betters to get on with the job of ruling.[105] Nevertheless, in the Tory attack on the populist stance of the Whigs we occasionally find glimpses of an awareness of the inequities in the political system, especially with regard to the question of the representative nature of Parliament. We have already seen how, mainly for pragmatic reasons, Tory candidates at the polls were occasionally prepared to defend a wider franchise than the Whigs. One of the most bitter attacks on the nature of the franchise system came from a certain Captain Thorogood, who was a defender of the hereditary succession. Attacking the Whig claim that the people, through Parliament, were able to change the government, Thorogood asserted:

that the Parliament as now usually Elected, is not at all the Representative of the People. . . . For none have Votes in Elections, but Free-holders of at least forty Shillings a Year, and Citizens and Burgesses, and consequently all Lessees for Years, Grantees of Annuities for Years: Men that live upon the Interest, and Product of their Money: The greatest part of the Clergy, all Soldiers, and Seamen in general, most of the young Nobility and Gentry. . . And in fine, the whole number of Labourers, Servants, Artificers, and Tradesmen, not residing in, or at least free of Cities and Boroughs, are totally excluded.

Thorogood asked 'what can be more unequal, not to say unjust', than that 'the far greatest part of the Nation, that are Passengers in the great Ship of the Commonwealth . . . should be debarred their right of choosing a Master or Pilot, to whose Skill and Care they commit their common safety'? He further complained about the inequities in the distribution of Parliamentary seats, with sparsely populated areas often having the right to return more MPs than more densely populated ones, and also bemoaned the fact that MPs were often not local men, had no idea how their constituents felt, and that they often gained votes 'by Bribes, Treats, and many unlawful Artifices'. But the whole thrust of Thorogood's argument was not to argue for franchise reform, but to show that the Whig-dominated Parliament could not claim to be speaking the voice of the people, and was just another part of his reasoning why a popish successor should not be excluded.[106]

DIVISIONS IN PARLIAMENT AND 'OUT-OF-DOORS'

So far we have looked at the ideological divide between the parties. It is now necessary to consider how the party divide worked itself out in practice, not just at the high political level, but also in society at large. The Tories had the better of things in the House of Lords. The Exclusion Bill came before the peers on only one occasion, on 15 November 1680, and it was rejected at its first reading. Out of one hundred peers present that day, it has been estimated that only thirty favoured Exclusion, whilst seventy were against it (including all four-teen bishops then present).[107] The Whigs, by contrast, dominated the House of Commons. When the House voted on the second reading of the first Exclusion Bill on 21 May 1679, out of a total of 509 members (the House at the time was four short of its proper complement), 207 (41 per cent) were for the bill, 128 (25 per cent), were against it, whilst 174 (34 per cent) were absent.[108] We have no recorded divisions on the second Exclusion Bill, but it has been estimated that of those elected to the second Exclusion Parliament in the autumn of 1679, the opponents of the Court comprised 58 per cent and its supporters 42 per cent, whilst the estimates for those elected to serve in the Oxford Parliament are 62 per cent and 38 per cent respectively.[109]

The Whig domination of the Commons suggests that they were stronger amongst the electorate. The number of General Elections in such a short space of time gave the electorate a chance to express their political sympathies on a scale which they had not enjoyed for many years. The last General Election prior to the Popish Plot, that of 1661, had produced contests in eleven counties and thirty-two boroughs. In the General Election of March 1679 there were contests in seventeen counties and eighty-four boroughs, in that of October 1679 in sixteen counties and sixty-one boroughs, and in 1681 in nine counties and forty-five boroughs.[110] By the time of the elections to the Oxford Parliament, a new practice had developed of the electorate issuing instructions to their new members, informing them how they should act in the upcoming Parliament. We should, of course, be wary of assuming too direct a correlation between the outcome at the polls and the political preferences of those with the right to vote. Although there is little evidence of direct interference in elections by the Court, both parties used whatever means were at their disposal to secure favourable returns, and charges of undue influence, bribery and electoral irregularities were numerous. As a general rule, however, the Whigs tended to do better in the larger, more open constituencies, which were more difficult to control, although there were some exceptions (as the Tory success in Southwark in all three elections between 1679 and 1681 testifies). There was no clear geographical pattern to the distribution of allegiance; support for and opposition to Exclusion appears to have been distributed fairly evenly across the country.[111]

Many constituencies were divided, and often success at the polls was achieved only after a bitterly fought contest. The sources of tension within a given constituency could be numerous, and might not involve questions of national policy. Thus some contests were fought primarily over local issues. At others, where national concerns played a part, Court-Country issues were often more important than Exclusion, although it probably does not make sense to push this distinction too far, since there was a considerable overlap in the Country and Whig positions, and opposition towards a Court candidate was typically also a sign of support for Exclusion, as the Court had come out so strongly in defence of the hereditary succession.[112]

What historians have failed to stress sufficiently is that many of the most fiercely contested elections were fought over the issues of the Church and Dissent. Although there were a few Whig clergymen, most of the clergy opposed Exclusion, and they used their influence at election time to campaign on behalf of Tory candidates. As a result, Whig electoral propaganda was often fiercely anti-clerical, urging constituents that they should not listen to the opinions of their clergy when it came to politics. As one author pointed out, the clergy had a vested interest in supporting a popish successor. Arbitrary power would raise them, whilst depressing the laity; 'Popery will add to their Benefices Absolution-Money, Indulgence-Money, Purgatory-Money, and a hundred other Perquisites, besides all the Abbey-Lands, and take nothing from them but their Wives'.[113] This anti-clericalism can be detected at the polls. At the Essex election in August 1679 the supporters of the Whig candidates came to the polls crying not only 'no Courtier, no Pensioner', but also 'no popish Clergy' and 'no bishops, no bishops'. The clergy who turned up to vote for the Court candidates were called 'Dumb Dogs, Jesuitical Dogs, Dark Lanthorns, Baal's Priests, Damned Rogues, Jacks and Villains, the Black Guard, the black Regiment of Hell'.[114] Cries of 'No Clergy, No Bishops' greeted the return of the Whig candidates at the Oxford election of 1681. At the Exeter election of February 1679 religious issues were mixed with local ones. One of the Whig candidates, William Glyde (himself a former mayor and leader of the Nonconformist interest in the City), insinuated to the commonalty that the City chamber had encroached upon their rights, which he promised he would restore if elected. At the poll, a huge crowd gathered (including many non-voters) crying 'Down with the Church! Down with the Chamber!', and threatened those who had come to vote for the Court candidates. At the Bedfordshire election of 1681 religious concerns were joined with Country grievances and a demand for Exclusion. Here the freeholders presented the successful Whig candidates with a paper asking them to defend the subject's right to petition for redress of grievances, to strive for regular meetings of Parliament, the repeal of the Act of 35 Elizabeth, the maintenance of the Protestant religion, the abolition of popery, and the exclusion of a popish successor.[115]

By contrast, the Tories at the polls showed themselves concerned to protect the Church and State from the challenge of Dissenters. This was particularly true by the time of the elections to the Oxford Parliament. In March 1681 a number of constituencies delivered instructions to their newly-returned Tory MPs asking them, as the Cambridgeshire address put it, to use their 'utmost endeavour to preserve the Government of Church and State, as now by Law established'.[116] The Cheshire Tories, when their candidates were defeated at the polls in 1681, presented an address to the House of Commons asking for the execution of the 'wholesome laws' against Dissenters, who, they said, had perpetrated 'the barbarous murder of the best of kings'.[117] After the dissolution of the Oxford Parliament, the loyal party in Bristol sent an address to their Tory MPs, stating they were happy with the King's actions, and pledging their support

> for the due Execution of the Statutes in being, particularly that of the 35th Elizabeth made . . . against all Recusants and Dissenters whatever, their Prosecution being in our Opinion the only means (under God) to preserve the King's Person, Our Religion, Liberty and Property, from the secret machinations and hellish conspiracies of the wicked and ambitious, whether Papists or Fanaticks.[118]

The same partisan divisions can be seen if we look at extra-Parliamentary politics. The attempts by the Whigs to gain mass support for their cause have been fairly well-documented. They were able to collect large numbers of subscriptions to their petitions of 1679–80, urging that the King allow the prorogued Parliament to sit, asking that the Oxford Parliament be allowed to meet at Westminster, and calling for another Parliament after the dissolution of the Oxford one in March 1681. A monster petition from the inhabitants of London, Westminster and Southwark, which was presented to the King on 13 January 1680, formed a roll three hundred feet long and contained well over 16,000 signatures.[119] Twenty-thousand London apprentices allegedly put their hands to a petition for the sitting of Parliament presented to the Lord Mayor on 2 September 1681.[120] There were large-scale demonstrations on behalf of the Whig cause, particularly the famous pope-burnings of 5 and 17 November, not only in London but also in many parts of the provinces. According to one report, 200,000 people witnessed the burning of the Pope at Temple Bar in 1679. London witnessed a number of anti-York and pro-Monmouth demonstrations, and when the Duke of Monmouth went on a number of quasi-royal progresses in 1681–2, to bolster support for his pretensions to the throne, everywhere he went he received a rapturous reception.[121] Nonconformists or Nonconformist sympathisers seem to have played a prominent part in the Whig agitation 'out-of-doors'. Many of the signatories to the monster petition of 1679–80 are known to have been Dissenters or sympathetic to Dissent.[122] The petitions from the London Whig apprentices of 1681–2 were organised by an apprentice bookseller, John Dunton, who was probably a Presbyterian himself and who was soon to marry the daughter of the Presbyterian divine, Samuel Annesley, whilst many of the Whig demonstrations were co-ordinated by a Nonconformist apprentice called Mr Stilling-fleet. Sometimes anti-episcopalian sentiment can be detected in Whig demonstrations. During the disturbances in London on Gunpowder Treason Day 1682, a group took it upon themselves to destroy the sign of the Mitre hanging outside a tavern in Stocks Market, the crowd being encouraged by the Quaker, Edward Billing.[123]

Yet as the Exclusion Crisis developed, there was a definite growth in sentiment 'out-of-doors' in favour of the Tories. This was particularly so following the dissolution of the Oxford Parliament, when politics for all groups was of necessity driven out-of-doors. Although the Tories had organised abhorrences of Whig petitions in 1680, many of these were the result of the initiative of a few energetic Courtiers, although a few owed something to local initiative. Tory instructions to MPs issued at the 1681 elections were more spontaneous, but they were far fewer in number than their Whig counterparts. But the publication of Charles II's Declaration in April 1681, explaining why he had dissolved Parliament, prompted a nationwide response from Tories. A total of 210 loyal addresses were presented, from JPs, grand juries, militia officers, borough corporations, and local inhabitants – even from apprentices, in cities such as Norwich, Bristol and London – thanking the King for the promises contained in that Declaration that he would protect the Church of England, rule through an impartial execution of the laws, and continue to hold frequent meetings of Parliament. The mayor, aldermen, sheriffs and common councilmen of Gloucester, for example, told Charles II that they were ready to lose their lives in defence of 'your most Sacred Person, your lawful Successors, and the just Laws by which you govern both in Church and State'. The City of Winchester expressed their gratitude 'that Your Majesty will relieve the agrievances of Your People by frequent Parliaments, and make the Law of the Land Your Rule . . . [and] That Your Majesty will preserve the Church in its Rights, and the true Protestant Religion, as it is by Law established'. Eighty-five addresses came in from boroughs or counties where two MPs hostile to the Court had been elected to serve in the Oxford Parliament, and a further forty-one where one opposition MP had been elected, perhaps indicating a genuine shift in opinion in many localities.[124] There were further addresses in 1682 in abhorrence of Shaftesbury's alleged plans to form a Protestant Association to resist the Duke of York, should he become King, and more abhorrences of the Rye House Plot the following year. There were also a number of demonstrations in support of the Duke of York. When he landed in Yarmouth on 10 March 1682, on his return from Scotland, he received a rapturous reception, as he did when he entered Norwich and then London over the next few days.[125] As an alternative to the Whig pope-burnings, Tory groups in various parts of the country held their own presbyter-burning processions, normally on Restoration Day or Gunpowder Treason Day. An effigy of Jack Presbyter was burnt in Derby on 5 November 1681, whilst in Norwich on the following 29 May, a group burned the effigy of the Presbyterian publicist, Henry Care, with a paper fixed to its breast inscribed 'scisme, faction and restless rebellion'.[126] What is interesting is that these manifestations of pro-York and anti-Dissenter sentiment often occurred in areas where the Whigs and Dissenters had been strong. This was true of Bristol, Norwich, and Yarmouth.

Perhaps the most remarkable turn-around in public opinion occurred in London. A study of the elections to the Common Council, where all citizens could vote, show a steady drift of opinion away from the Whigs amongst the freemen as the crisis progressed. Thus the Whig majority on the Common Council that had existed at the beginning of the Exclusion Crisis had been lost by 1680, and the Tories steadily increased their majority over the next two years. Several thousand apprentices from the Strand area were engaged in a plan to burn 'the Rump' on 29 May 1680, although the Whig authorities managed to prevent this from coming to fruition. The years 1681–2, however, show a number of large-scale Tory addresses and demonstrations. One Tory address of June 1681 claimed to be signed by 18,000 apprentices; another of July 1682 boasted 12,000 signatories amongst the young freemen and apprentices. All the Tory addresses expressed a desire to protect the Church and State as by law established, and were fiercely anti-Nonconformist in nature. Similar sentiments can be detected in Tory demonstrations, where it was typical to toast the King and the Duke of York, and burn effigies of Jack Presbyter or leading Whigs.[127]

Although there was a definite rise in public support for the Tories as the Exclusion Crisis progressed, it would be wrong to suggest that the Whig consensus of 1678–80 had become a Tory one by 1681–3, or that the Whigs of the earlier period and the Tories of the later were largely the same people. Local studies show that by the early 1680s many communities had become polarised along Whig-Tory lines, and that these party rivalries affected all classes of people. In Cheshire a bitter conflict emerged within the governing elite, which culminated at the Assizes of September 1682 with a Tory grand jury accusing thirty-two leading Whig gentlemen of sedition because of their support for the Duke of Monmouth during his tour of the north-west.[128] Similar party divisions amongst the elite can be detected in Northumberland in the early 1680s.[129] In Herefordshire most of the political community – gentry, town-dwellers and freeholders – were split into Whig and Tory camps.[130] Many corporations – Bristol, London and Norwich being well-documented examples – were riven with partisan rivalries, from the mercantile elite, through to the middling traders and craftsmen, right down to the 'mob'. In London, for example, fierce rivalry developed between Whig and Tory crowds, and on a number of occasions they came into violent conflict, as they sought to gain dominance of the street. Thus on 5 November 1681, in addition to holding their own presbyter-burning processions, Tory groups sought to sabotage the Whig pope-burnings, and they managed to seize the Whigs' effigies in a number of places throughout the city. On Restoration Day and Gunpowder Treason Day the following year there were violent clashes between rival groups shouting 'A York, a York' and 'a Monmouth, a Monmouth'.[131]

CONCLUSION

The crisis of 1678–83 was about much more than Exclusion or fears of a popish successor; it brought to a head many of the problems which had bedevilled the monarchy of Charles II since the Restoration. Although the labels Whig and Tory did not become common usage until the early 1680s, the party struggle can only be understood in the context of the political, constitutional and religious conflicts that had been developing during the 1660s and 1670s – between the Crown and Parliament, Court and Country, Church and Dissent. It has been argued that the party divide should not be seen purely in constitutional terms. Whilst there were some Whigs who were radical Parliamentarians, and likewise some Tories who believed in unlimited monarchy, there was in fact a great deal of common ground between the constitutional outlooks of the more conservative Whigs and the moderate Tories. Moreover, it is essential to realise that both sides were deeply alarmed about the threat of popery and arbitrary government; they differed over where they saw the greater threat as coming from. A key source of divide appears to have been religion. The Whigs championed the cause of Dissent against the intolerance of the High Anglican establishment, and were concerned for the liberties of Protestants not just under a future Catholic monarch but also under Charles II.

The Tories, by contrast, were defenders of the Church of England as re-established at the Restoration, fierce enemies of Dissent, and were more worried about the threat posed to Church and State by the Whigs and their Nonconformist allies than they were by a popish successor.

A number of themes have emerged which need stressing. The first is that the account of the origins of party politics should not begin with the emergence of Court–Country groupings in the 1670s; indeed, it has been shown that it is not particularly helpful to see the Tory–Whig split in terms of the Court–Country dichotomy, since there were Whig politicians who at times had shown themselves willing to work with the Court, whilst there was always a strong Country dimension to Cavalier-Anglican or Tory ideology. Rather, the genesis of the party conflict can be traced back to 1660, and the various constitutional and religious problems that the Restoration left unsolved. Secondly, we have seen that it is wrong to dismiss the Tories as mere cronies of the Crown, whose doctrines of passive obedience and non-resistance would lead them to support anything the King did; rather, their position was defined in terms of loyalty to a particular vision of government in Church and State 'as by law established', an ideology whose roots went back to the Restoration, and we have already seen hints that Cavalier Anglicans were prepared to defend this vision against attack even from the Crown itself. Thirdly, this Cavalier-Anglican position was capable of generating much support amongst the population, as had been shown in 1660, and as was to be shown again in 1681–2. Although the Whigs were initially very successful in rallying the people in support for their position, as the Exclusion Crisis progressed there was a definite shift in public opinion in favour of the Tories. This revised picture of the nature of party strife in the reign of Charles II is vitally important for understanding political developments in the 1680s, the causes and nature of the Glorious Revolution of 1688–9, and what happened to party politics in the reigns of William and Anne, subjects explored in the remaining chapters of this book.

REFERENCES

1. Jones, *The First Whigs: The Politics of the Exclusion Crisis, 1678–83,* pp. 9–19, 214.
2. J. R. Western, *Monarchy and Revolution: The English State in the 1680s* (1972), p. 36.

3. Richard Ashcraft, *Revolutionary Politics and Locke's 'Two Treatises of Government* (Princeton, 1986); De Krey, 'The London Whigs and the Exclusion Crisis Reconsidered', pp. 457–82; *Idem*, 'London Radicals and Revolutionary Politics, 1675–1683', in Harris et al. (eds), *The Politics of Religion in Restoration England*, pp. 133–62.

4. Jonathan Scott, 'England's Troubles: Exhuming the Popish Plot', in Harris et al. (eds), *Politics of Religion*, p. 126; *Idem, Algernon Sidney and the Restoration Crisis, 1677–1683* (Cambridge, 1991). This last title appeared after the draft of this book had already been completed. Scott never defines what he means by party, and ignores the evidence of what party organisation did exist. Curiously, given the fact that Scott believes that the Whigs and Tories were the same people (a point for which no documentary support is offered), he is also prepared to recognise the existence of 'polarities of belief', and states that 'what polarity existed between the sides themselves, was ideological' (*Sidney and the Restoration Crisis*, pp. 14, 24).

5. In addition to the works by Scott cited above, see also Mark Knights, 'Politics and Opinion during the Exclusion Crisis, 1678–81', unpub. Oxford DPhil thesis (1989). Knights is more willing to recognise the existence of parties than Scott, although he stresses that they fluctuated in their strength and cohesiveness over this period.

6 Grey, *Debates*, **VII**, pp. 158–9; *Heads of the Expedient Proposed in the Parliament at Oxford* (1681); Goldie, 'Danby, the Bishops and the Whigs', in Harris et al (eds)., *The Politics of Religion*, pp. 87–8; Knights, 'Politics and Opinion', pp. 49–56; David Ogg, *England in the Reign of Charles II* (Oxford, 1934, 2nd edn, 1956), pp. 605, 615.

7. *CJ*, **IX**, p. 536; Hutton, *Charles II, King of England, Scotland and Ireland*, p. 364.

8. Grey, *Debates*, **VII**, pp. 150–1.

9. Grey, *Debates*, **VII**, p. 160. Cf. William Cavendish, Duke of Devonshire, *Reasons for His Majesties Passing the Bill of Exclusion* (1681), p. 5; [Algernon Sidney and William Jones?], *A Just and Modest Vindication of the Proceedings of the Two Last Parliaments* (1681), pp. 30–1, 33–4.

10. Pepysian Library, Magdalene College, Cambridge, Pepys Miscellanies, **VII**, pp. 465–91, 'Transcript of the Minutes of the Green Ribbon Club'.

11. Wood, *Life and Times*, **III**, p. 42; D. F. Allen, 'The Crown and the Corporation of London in the Exclusion Crisis, 1678–1681', unpub. Cambridge PhD thesis (1977), p. 179; *Idem*, 'Political Clubs in Restoration London', *HJ*, **19** (1976), pp. 561–80.

12. Harris, *London Crowds in the Reign of Charles II: Propaganda and Politics from the Restoration until the Exclusion Crisis*, pp. 100–1, 103–4.

13. M. D. George, 'Elections and Electioneering, 1678–81', EHR, **45** (1930), pp. 552–78; Lacey, *Dissent and Parliamentary Politics in England, 1661–1689,* ch. 6.

14. Jonathan Barry, 'Politics of Religion in Restoration Bristol', in Harris et al. (eds), *Politics of Religion*, p. 176.

15. Jones, *First Whigs*, pp. 115–22.
16. For Whig exclusionist ideology, see: B. Behrens, 'The Whig Theory of the Constitution in the Reign of Charles II', *CHJ*, **7** (1941), pp. 42–71; O. W. Furley, 'The Whig Exclusionists: Pamphlet Literature in the Exclusion Campaign', *CHJ*, **13** (1957), pp. 19–36; Finlayson, *Historians, Puritanism, and the English Revolution: The Religious Factor in English Politics Before and After the Interregnum*, ch. 5; Ashcraft, *Revolutionary Politics*, esp. chs 5, 6; Harris, *London Crowds*, ch. 5; *Idem*, 'Lives, Liberties and Estates'.
17. *An Appeal from the Country to the City* (1679), p. 1; *The Coronation of Queen Elizabeth* (1680), p. 5; *The Protestant Tutor* (1679); *A Scheme of Popish Cruelties* (1681).
18. Devonshire, *Reasons for His Majesties Passing the Bill of Exclusion*, p. 3.
19. *A Most Serious Expostulation with Several of my Fellow-Citizens* [1679], p. 4. Wing dates the tract as '1680?', but a manuscript addition to the copy in the University Library, Cambridge, dates it October 1679.
20. *A Letter from a Gentleman in the City, To One in the Country* (1680), p. 8.
21. *Appeal from the Country*, p. 2; *A Character of Popery and Arbitrary Government* [1681], p. 2.
22. [Sidney and Jones?], *Just and Modest Vindication*, p. 30.
23. *HMC, 78 Hastings*, **IV**, p. 303.
24. Grey, *Debates*, **VIII**, p. 309.
25. [Elkannah Settle], *The Character of a Popish Successour* (1681), p. 13; *A Letter from a Person of Quality to his Friend, Concerning his Majesty's Late Declaration* [1681], p. 8.
26. De Krey, 'London Radicals'; Scott, *Sidney and the Restoration Crisis*, stresses the importance of the republican challenge during the crisis of 1678–83.
27. Henry Neville, *Plato Redivivus* (1681), in Caroline Robbins (ed.), *Two English Republican Tracts* (Cambridge, 1969).
28. Maurice Ashley, *John Wildman, Plotter and Postmaster: A Study of the English Republican Movement in the Seventeenth Century* (1947), p. 223.
29. Robert Ferguson, 'Manuscript Concerning the Rye House Plot', in James Fergson, *Robert Ferguson – the Plotter; Or, The Secret of the Rye House Conspiracy and the Story of a Strange Career* (Edinburgh, 1887), p. 418; Ford Lord Grey of Wark, *The Secret History of the Rye House Plot and of Monmouth's Rebellion* (1685), p. 31.
30. Scott, 'England's Troubles'.
31. 'The Present State of the Kingdom at the Opening of the Parliament, March 6, 1679', in W. D. Christie, *A Life of Anthony Ashley Cooper, First Earl of Shaftesbury* (2 vols, 1871), **II**, pp. 281–3, 309–14; Haley, *The First Earl of Shaftesbury*, pp. 502–3.
32. Edmund Everard, *Discourses on the Present State of the Protestant Princes of Europe* (1679), pp. 3, 15–16.
33. *Mr Francis Jenks Speech Spoken Common Hall 24 June 1679* (1679), p. 1; Johannes Philanglus, *England's Alarm* (1679), p. 5.

34. [Sidney and Jones?], *Just and Modest Vindication*. p. 1; *A Letter from a Person of Quality to his Friend, Concerning his Majesty's Late Declaration*, p. 8; *A List of One Unanimous Club of Voters* (1679); Jones, *First Whigs*, pp. 53–4; George, 'Elections and Electioneering', pp. 569–72.

35. Weston and Greenberg, *Subjects and Sovereigns: The Grand Controversy over Legal Sovereignty in Stuart England*, ch. 7; Ashcraft, *Revolutionary Politics*, p. 213.

36. Earl of Shaftesbury, *Some Observations Concerning the Regulating of Elections for Parliament, Found Among the Earl of Shaftesbury's Papers after his Death* (1689), p. 5.

37. James Tyrrell, *Patriarcha Non Monarcha* (1681); William Petyt, *Jus Parliamentarium: Or, The Ancient Power, Jurisdiction, Rights and Liberties of the Most High Court of Parliament, Revived and Asserted* (written in the 1680s, first pub. 1739); Algernon Sidney, *Discourses Concerning Government* (written in the early 1680s, first pub. 1698); J. G. A. Pocock, *The Ancient Constitution and the Feudal Law: A Study of English Historical Thought in the Seventeenth Century* (Cambridge, 1957, reissue with a restrospect, 1987), ch. 8.

38. Ashcraft, *Revolutionary Politics*, pp. 164–9. Cf. Plumb, *The Growth of Political Stability in England 1675–1725*, pp. 41–2.

39. Henning, *The House of Commons, 1660–1690*, **I**, pp. 131, 469, 471.

40. *The Tryal of Slingsby Bethel Esq* (1681); Henning, *House of Commons*, **I**, p. 416.

41. *Smith's Protestant Intelligence*, no. 3, 4–8 Feb. 1680[/1]; Henning, *House of Commons*, **I**, p. 138; Scott, *Sidney and the Restoration Crisis*, pp. 159, 174–5, 183–4.

42. Shaftesbury, *Some Observations*, p. 11; Ogg, *England in the Reign of Charles II*, pp. 481–3; Ashcraft, *Revolutionary Politics*, pp. 165–6; Mark Goldie, 'The Roots of True Whiggism 1688–94', *History of Political Thought*, **1** (1980), p. 214.

43. De Krey, 'London Radicals'.

44. *An Exact Collection of the Most Memorable Debates in the Honorable House of Commons . . . October, 1680* (1681), p. 47; Ashcraft, *Revolutionary Politics*, p. 193. Cf. *A Letter from a Person of Quality to His Friend Concerning His Majesty's Late Declaration* [1681], p. 4.

45. J. P., *A Letter to a Friend in the Country: Being a Vindication of the Parliaments Whole Proceedings this last Session* [1679], p. 3.

46. [Thomas Hunt] *The Great and Weighty Considerations . . . Considered* (1680), pp. 9, 16.

47. Devonshire, *Reasons for His Majesties Passing*, pp. 2–3.

48. *Character of Popery and Arbitrary Government*, p. 2; Harris, 'Lives, Liberties and Estates'.

49. Grey, *Debates*, **VII**, pp. 369–70, 390–1.

50. *A Speech made by a True Protestant English Gentleman* [1679], p. 2.

51. *A Letter to a Friend. Shewing from Scripture, Fathers and Reason, How False that State-Maxim is, Royal Authority is Originally and Radically in the People* (1679); T. L., *The True Notion of Government* (1681), pp. 8, 12.

52. Locke, *Two Treatises*.

53. De Krey, 'London Radicals', pp. 146–55; Ashcraft, *Revolutionary Politics, passim*.

54. Harris, *London Crowds*, pp. 119–20; *Idem*, 'Revising the Restoration', in Harris et al. (eds), *Politics of Religion*, pp. 10–11; Lacey, *Dissent*, ch. 7; De Krey, 'London Radicals'; Scott, *Sidney and the Restoration Crisis*, pp. 128–9.

55. *An Answer to the Pretended Letter, To A Friend in the Country* [1680], p. 3.

56. *A Most Serious Expostulation*, p. 1.

57. J. B., *A Proposal Humbly Offered to the Parliament, For Suppressing of Popery* (1680), p. 2.

58. Henry Horwitz, 'Protestant Reconciliation in the Exclusion Crisis', *JEccH*, **15** (1964), pp. 201–17; Lacey, *Dissent*, pp. 144–5; Haley, *Shaftesbury*, pp. 618–19.

59. BL, Add. MSS 28,930, fol. 203; A. S. Turberville, 'The House of Lords under Charles II', Part II, *EHR*, **45** (1930), p. 62.

60. Christ Church, Oxford, Evelyn MSS, Box IV, no. 4, 'The Grave House of Commons'.

61. *Plain Dealing; Or, A Second Dialogue between Humphrey and Roger* (1681). See also Harris, *London Crowds*, pp. 124–9.

62. Philanglus, *England's Alarm*, p. 11.

63. Jones, 'Parties and Parliament', in J.R. Jones (ed.), *The Restored Monarchy 1660–1688*, pp. 65, 67; Henning, *House of Commons*, **II**, pp. 74–81, 157–63, **III**, pp. 565–6.

64. BL, Add. MSS 32,518, fols 144–52; Knights, 'Politics and Opinion', pp. 120–1.

65. Harris, *London Crowds*, pp. 132–3.

66. E. E., *London's Choice of Citizens to Represent them in the Ensuing Parliament* (1679), p. 2.

67. E. F., *A Letter from a Gentleman of Quality in the Country To His Friend* (1679), p. 4.

68. Cited in Edmund Bohun, *The Third and Last Part of the Address to the Free-Men and Free-Holders of the Nation* (1683), p. 98.

69. Robert Filmer, *The Power of Kings* (1680), p. 1. First published in 1648 as *The Necessity of The Absolute Power of all Kings: And in particular, of the King of England*, and reprinted in Johann P. Sommerville (ed.), *Sir Robert Filmer: Patriarcha and Other Writings* (Cambridge, 1991), pp. 172–83 (quote on p. 173).

70. *A Word to the Approaching Parliament of England, For the Settlement of the Nation* (1679[/80]), p. 7.

71. *An Apostrophe from the Loyal Party* (1681), p. 3.

72. *The Proceedings of the Grand-Jury of the City of Bristol, Upon an Indictment against Edward Flower* (1680), p. 2.

73. *A Letter to a Friend. Shewing from Scripture*, pp. 4, 8.

74. T. L., *True Notion*, pp. 26–7 (misnumbered pp. 18–19).

75. W. P., *The Divine Right of Kings* [1679], p. 2.

76. *Some Observations upon the Tickling Querie* (1681), p. 7.
77. Grey, *Debates*, **VIII**, p. 338.
78. *A Letter on the Subject of the Succession* (1679), p. 4.
79. B. T[horogood], *Captain Thorogood His Opinion of the Point of Succession* [1680], p. 9.
80. *Fiat Justitia* [1679], p. 2.
81. Bohun, *The Third and Last Part of the Address to the Free-Men*, p. 66.
82. *Advice to the Men of Shaftesbury* (1681), p. 2.
83. Robert Brady, *Introduction to the Old English History* (1684); *Idem, Compleat History of England* (1685); Pocock, *Ancient Constitution*, ch. 8.
84. *HMC, 7th Report*, p. 473.
85. Charles II, *His Majesties Declaration To All His Loving Subjects, Touching the Causes and Reasons that Moved Him to Dissolve the Two Last Parliaments* (1681), p. 9.
86. *Heraclitus Ridens*, no. 13, 26 Apr. 1681.
87. L. S., *A Letter to a Noble Peer of the Realm* [1681], p. 2.
88. Bodl. Lib., MS Ballard 39, fol. 5.
89. [John Nalson], *The True Protestants Appeal to the City and Countrey* (1681), p. 2.
90. *Advice to the Men of Shaftesbury*, pp. 1–2.
91. *Fiat Justitia*, p. 2.
92. Bodl. Lib., MS Rawlinson E 134, p. 325.
93. *Heraclitus Ridens*, no. 7, 15 Mar. 1680[/1].
94. Bohun, *The Third and Last Part of the Address*, pp. 115–16.
95. [John Nalson], *The Character of a Rebellion* (1681), pp. 4–5; [*Idem*], *The Complaint of Liberty and Property against Arbitrary Government* (1681), pp. 2, 3.
96. *Cromwell's Complaint of Injustice* (1681).
97. Nalson, *Complaint of Liberty*, p. 2; 'The Commonwealth Ruling with a Standing Army', frontispiece to [Sir Thomas May], *Arbitrary Government Display'd in the Tyrannick Usurpation of the Rump Parliament* (1683).
98. Charles II, *His Majesties Declaration*, p. 7.
99. Bohun, *The Third and Last Part of the Address*, p. 117. Cf. *Ibid.*, p. 119. The Tory view of the Whigs and Nonconformists as promoters of popery and arbitrary government is examined in more detail in Harris, *London Crowds*, ch. 6; Harris, 'Lives, Liberties and Estates'.
100. Charles II, *His Majesties Declaration*, p. 6.
101. F. K., *The Present Great Interest Both of King and People* [1679], pp. 1–3.
102. Bohun, *The Third and Last Part of the Address*, pp. vi–vii.
103. *Reasons Offered by a Well-Wisher to the King and Kingdom* (1680), p. 1.
104. *The Whig's Exaltation* [1682], in N. Thompson (ed.), *A Collection of One Hundred and Eighty Loyal Songs* (1685), p. 6; *Advice to the City; Or, The Whigs' Loyalty Explained* (1682).
105. Harris, *London Crowds*, pp. 131–3, 136–9, 208–11; *Idem*, 'Lives, Liberties and Estates', p. 233.
106. T[horogood], *Captain Thoroughgood His Opinion*, pp. 3–7.

107. E. S. De Beer, 'The House of Lords in the Parliament of 1680', *BIHR*, **20** (1943–5), pp. 27–8.

108. Andrew Browning and D. J. Milne, 'An Exclusion Bill Division List', *BIHR*, **23** (1950), pp. 205–25.

109. Henning, *House of Commons*, **I**, p. 65.

110. The reason for the decline in contests in the elections to the Oxford Parliament was in part a reflection of the fact that fewer Tory candidates were prepared to stand against the Whigs, feeling their task hopeless, and in part due to the fact that those who had stood in previous years felt they could not bear the cost of a third election in two years.

111. Henning, *House of Commons*, **I**, pp. 39, 64, 74, 106. Henning does find a slightly higher proportion of Whig MPs from the south-west in the first Exclusion Parliament (possibly due to the electoral influence of Shaftesbury), although not for the second and third Exclusion Parliaments. For elections, see also, Kishlansky, *Parliamentary Selection: Social and Political Change in Early Modern England*, chs 6, 7, *passim*. For instructions, see: Jones, *First Whigs*, pp. 167–73; *Vox Patriae* (1681).

112. Knights, 'Politics and Opinion', ch. 4.

113. *Plain Dealing; Or, A Dialogue between Humphrey and Roger* (1681).

114. *Essex's Excellency* (1679), p. 4; *A Faithful and Impartial Account of the Behaviour of a Party of the Essex Freeholders* (1679), p. 6; *CSPD, 1680–1*, p. 232; Bodl. Lib., MS Ballard 12, fol. 39; George, 'Elections', p. 557; Henning, *House of Commons*, **I**, p. 229.

115. Henning, *House of Commons*, **I**, pp. 126, 199, 360; Goldie, 'Danby, the Bishops and the Whigs', pp. 98–9.

116. *A True Account of the Election at Cambridge* (1681), p. 2. Cf. *Certain Proposals Humbly Offered by the Bayliff And Other Inhabitants of Cricklade* (1681); *The Southwark Address* (1681).

117. *VCH, Chester*, **II**, p. 117.

118. *Bristol's Second Address* (1681).

119. Knights, 'Politics and Opinion', ch. 5. All but 23 pages of the petition survive, and the extant sheets contain 15,734 signatories.

120. *The Address of Above 20,000 of the Loyal Protestant Apprentices of London* (1681).

121. Harris, *London Crowds*, ch. 7; David Cressy, *Bonfires and Bells: National Memory and the Protestant Calendar in Elizabethan and Early Stuart England* (Berkeley, 1989), p. 179; Philip Jenkins, 'Anti-Popery on the Welsh Marches'; Geraint Jenkins, *The Foundations of Modern Wales: Wales 1642–1780,* pp. 143–4; Robin Clifton, *The Last Popular Rebellion: The Western Rising of 1685* (1984), ch. 4.

122. Knights, 'Politics and Opinion', pp. 267–8.

123. Harris, *London Crowds*, pp. 177–9, 186–7.

124. *Vox Angliae; Or, The Voice of the Kingdom* (1681), quotes on pp. 3, 8; Knights, 'Politics and Opinion', chs 6, 7.

125. Bodl. Lib., MS Tanner 36, fol. 254; Michael Mullett, 'Popular Culture and Popular Politics: Some Regional Case Studies', in Clyve Jones,

(ed.), *Britain in the First Age of Party, 1680–1750: Essays Presented to Geoffrey Holmes* (1987), p. 131; Harris, *London Crowds*, pp. 170–1.

126. R. Clark, 'Anglicanism, Recusancy and Dissent in Derbyshire, 1603–1730', unpub. Oxford DPhil thesis (1979), p. 216; *The Domestick Intelligence: Or, News from both City and Country Impartially Related*, no. 108, 1–5 Jun. 1682.

127. Harris, *London Crowds*, pp. 164–80.

128. *VCH, Chester*, **II**, p. 115.

129. Margaret Smillie Child, 'Prelude to Revolution: The Structure of Politics in County Durham, 1678–88', unpub. University of Maryland PhD dissertation (1972), pp. 72–80.

130. Key, 'Politics Beyond Parliament', ch. 8.

131. Barry, 'Politics of Religion in Restoration Bristol'; De Krey, 'London Radicals'; De Krey, 'London Whigs and the Exclusion Crisis'; Evans, *Seventeenth-Century Norwich: Politics, Religion and Government, 1620–1690*, ch. 7; Harris, *London Crowds*, ch. 7.

CHAPTER FIVE

The Glorious Revolution

The reign of James II appeared to confirm the prediction made by the exclusionists that a Catholic King would mean popery and arbitrary government. James did prove determined to promote the interests of Catholics, and he did so largely through recourse to the prerogative powers of dispensing with or suspending the penal statutes. He upset the Tories, who had so vigorously defended his right to the succession, by attacking the Anglican monopoly in worship and education, and then by punishing recalcitrant Anglicans in a specially erected Commission for Ecclesiastical Causes; he enlarged his standing army, appointing a number of Catholics to prominent positions of command; and he interfered with local franchises and borough corporations in order to try to secure the election of a Parliament which would be subservient to his wishes. When the birth of the Prince of Wales in June 1688 raised the prospect of a never-ending succession of Catholic Stuart Kings, Whigs and Tories united to invite William of Orange, the husband of James's eldest daughter Mary, to come to England to secure her liberties and religion. In the face of foreign invasion, James panicked and fled the country in December 1688 (though it took him two attempts before he finally escaped to France), and in February 1689 a specially convened Convention Parliament established William and Mary as joint King and Queen and debarred all Catholics from the succession in the future. This was the Glorious Revolution. It seems that the policy of Exclusion, which had first been raised in 1673, and which had been a major political goal of the first Whigs, had at last come to fruition.

A crucial question to consider about the Glorious Revolution, therefore, is the extent to which it can be seen as a victory for Whig principles. The old Whig historians tended to see the Revolution as being the climax of the great struggle of the seventeenth century between the absolutist pretensions of the House of Stuarts and the cause of Parliamentary constitutionalism. Thus Macaulay thought that the Revolution 'finally decided the great question whether the popular element . . . should be destroyed by the monarchical element, or should be suffered to develop itself freely, and to become dominant'.[1] Modern scholars have tended to see the Revolution in a more conservative light, stressing the key role of the Tories in bringing about the Revolution and maintaining that the powers of the Crown were not significantly redefined in 1688–9.[2] Most recently, however, there has been a reaction against this conservative interpretation. Lois Schwoerer, for example, believes that the constitutional settlement of 1689 was an emphatic, though qualified, victory for Whig principles, since it established limited monarchy with ultimate sovereignty residing in the House of Commons.[3] And although disagreeing in significant respects with Schwoerer, W. A. Speck concludes that significant inroads on the royal prerogative were made by the Revolution settlement, and that 'the debate on the nature of the monarchy did end decisively in 1689 with the victory of those who argued that it was limited and mixed'.[4]

The Glorious Revolution is best seen not as a victory for one party, but as a compromise. The settlement which was worked out had to be palatable to all the leading protagonists: Whig and Tory politicians in the Lords and Commons; the Church Establishment and the Protestant Nonconformists; and the new monarchs themselves, William and Mary. There was a sense in which both Whigs and Tories made the Revolution, and could claim it as their own; but because of the compromises which had to be worked out, both were left feeling dissatisfied with the eventual outcome, something which helps to explain why partisan strife continued to grow in intensity after 1689. Yet part of our confusion over how to understand the Revolution stems from the inappropriate conceptual approach most scholars have adopted when assessing its significance. When considering whether the Revolution should be seen as a victory for Whig principles or not, historians have tended to take a constitutional frame of reference – the more a particular historian believes the Revolution settlement limited the constitutional powers of the Crown, then the more Whiggish the Revolution is said to be. The problems with such an approach should by now be apparent. We have already seen that there were times when the High Anglican interest, supposedly the natural allies of strong monarchy, sought to challenge the powers of the Crown in order to protect the interests of the established Church; we have also seen that Nonconformist and Whig politicians, who during the Exclusion Crisis became the champions of Parliamentarianism, had at times shown themselves prepared to defend the royal prerogative against Parliamentary limitation when it was being used to protect the interests of the Dissenters. Any assessment of the significance of the Glorious Revolution, therefore, must give due weight to the ways in which the tensions between the Church and Dissent interacted with the constitutional conflicts that shaped Restoration politics, and once we do this, the Revolution appears in a fundamentally different light.

If we ask who was responsible for defeating the drift towards popery and arbitrary government under James II, the answer has to be the Tory-Anglican establishment. The Whigs, as a political force, had been largely destroyed by the time of James's accession, and were in no position to mount an effective challenge to his rule. What needs to be explained is why Tory Anglicans, who had so strongly defended James's right to the succession during his brother's final years, and who have normally been seen as the Crown's allies in an attempt to establish royal absolutism in the early 1680s, should have turned so quickly against the King. The solution requires a reassessment of the nature of Toryism at this time; rather than seeing the Tories as royal absolutists, it is better to see them as conservative legal-constitutionalists, deeply committed to the rule of law and the Anglican Church. When James challenged both of these, Tory Anglicans inevitably sought to oppose him. In a sense, the Glorious Revolution began as an attempt to vindicate Tory principles. Unfortunately for Tory Anglicans, things got out of hand, and they had to concede much more than they would have wanted (most obviously on the central issue of the transfer of the Crown). But they also salvaged much, so that the new regime was established upon principles which were much more conducive to Toryism than is normally thought.

THE TORY REACTION AND THE ACCESSION OF JAMES II

Few English monarchs have come to the throne in as strong a position as did James II. Charles's failure to call Parliament after 1681 removed the Whig challenge in the Commons, and a series of purges of local corporations, livery companies, and lieutenancies effectively destroyed the local bases of Whig power, both in London and in the provincial towns. There was also a purge of the bench and of juries, which enabled the government to take legal recriminations against a number of leading Whigs, whilst their Nonconformist allies were harassed through a rigorous enforcement of the penal laws. These measures, collectively known as the Tory Reaction, meant that by 1685 the opposition alliance which had given rise to the first Whig party had largely crumbled. Many leading Whigs were dead: Shaftesbury had fled to Holland at the end of 1682, only to die in exile in January 1683; Sidney and Russell were both executed for their part in the Rye House Plot, whilst another conspirator, the Earl of Essex, killed himself in the Tower (although some suspected he had been murdered). Other Whigs had gone into exile, as too had some Nonconformists; those who remained in England were either in jail or under such close government surveillance that they were in no position to offer a serious challenge to the new King. Although the Duke of Monmouth and a number of other exiles did lead a rebellion in the west country in 1685, the rebels were unable to gain the support of any men of substance, and the ease with which the rebellion was crushed provides further testimony to the strength of the government's position at this time.

When Parliament met in May 1685 it proved to be overwhelmingly Tory in sympathy, there being only fifty-seven Whigs in a House of Commons totalling 513 members. It is true that the government used all the influence it could to secure the return of loyal members, and the purges of borough corporations at the end of Charles II's reign certainly had an electoral impact, but the election of such a loyal Parliament appears to have been more the result of a genuine reaction against the Whigs amongst the electorate than it was of Court manipulation. Thus we find that the Tories did best in the larger boroughs and in the counties, where they won over 90 per cent of the seats.[5] At his accession, James was not just powerful, but also popular. When he was proclaimed King in February, there was popular rejoicing throughout the realm. 'It is harde to be expected', wrote one newsletter writer, 'with what great joy and satisfaction his majesties have been proclaimed in most of the Citties', whilst the Earl of Peterborough thought that never had a King been 'proclaimed with more applause than he that raignes under the name of James the Second'.[6] At some of the elections in the spring there were anti-Whig demonstrations, such as at Newcastle, where crowds burnt the Bill of Exclusion and Shaftesbury's Association.[7] There were 'unspeakable expressions of joy' on St George's Day that year (23 April), the day of the coronation, in many parts of England and Wales, including an elaborate celebration at Lyme Regis, soon to be the place where the Monmouth rebellion would begin.[8] The King's birthday in October was also greeted with extravagant displays of loyalty, such as at Norwich, where church bells rang all day and bonfires blazed all night.[9]

The Crown was in such a strong position in 1685 because Charles II, in his last years, had taken a stance in defence of the Church of England as by law established, and was able to exploit the anti-Nonconformist prejudices of the Anglicans. The Tory Reaction is sometimes seen as the beginnings of the attempt to revive royal absolutism in England, and certainly in the years following the defeat of Exclusion supporters of the Crown encouraged an exalted view of monarchy. Anglican clergymen busied themselves with preaching up theories of divine right and non-resistance. In July 1683 the University of Oxford issued a judgment condemning certain doctrines thought to be 'destructive to the kingly government', amongst them the views that 'civil authority is derived originally from the people', that resistance to tyrants was legitimate, and that England was a mixed monarchy, with sovereignty vested in the King, Lords and Commons.[10] But it is better to see the ideology of the Tory Reaction as authoritarian rather than absolutist, since those who stressed obedience to the Crown typically also urged the need for obedience to the laws – the laws, that is, which had been established to protect both Church and State from the challenge of subversives. As John Allen, chaplain to the Bishop of Chester, put it in an Assize Sermon preached at Chester in April 1682: 'Let us be as zealous and couragious and industrious too, to support, and preserve the Government both in Church and State, as they [the Whigs and Nonconformists] are stubbornly bent, and furiously acted to demolish and destroy it: While we have good Laws, for God's sake, let us live and act according to them; and let them have their course upon All those, that do violate, affront, and defie them'.[11]

The aim during the Tory Reaction was to use the full weight of the law against those who were perceived to be enemies of the Church and State. Undoubtedly there was some bending of the law. In 1684, for example, the Whig conspirator Sir Thomas Armstrong, who already stood condemned as an outlaw, was peremptorily executed without a trial.[12] There were also some dubious legal procedures used in dealing with the Rye House plotters of 1683, the Monmouth rebels of 1685, and other Whig dissidents who faced legal recriminations in the 1680s, and all of these legal 'abuses' were complained about in the Declaration of Rights of 1689. But the rhetoric of those who defended government policy in the early 1680s was explicitly legalist in nature. In their sermons – and particularly the ones they delivered at the Assizes – Anglican clergymen continually stressed the need for judges, magistrates and juries to enforce the laws against the Nonconformists. John Standish, a royal chaplain, concluded his Assize sermon at Hertford in March 1683 by imploring his auditors to 'Govern according to Law; and make it your care, that our wholesome Laws be vigorously and impartially executed'.[13] The drive against corporations was carried out in the same spirit; the only reason why the Whigs and Nonconformists had grown so influential in corporation politics was because the Corporation Act of 1661 had not been properly enforced. Charles was acting quite legally in initiating the *quo warranto* proceedings against borough charters, and his primary aim appears not so much to achieve royal control over the borough electorate – boroughs which did not return MPs were also subject to attack – but rather to drive Nonconformists and their sympathisers out of the local magistracy and to secure the empanelment of juries who would be prepared to act against the Dissenters.[14]

Another important feature to note about the ideology of the Tory Reaction is that it was as fiercely anti-Catholic as it was anti-Nonconformist. As had been the case during the Exclusion Crisis, Tories and Anglicans repeatedly argued that the Nonconformists were acting on popish principles in seeking to destroy both Church and State. In a sermon on 9 September 1683 (the day of thanksgiving for deliverance from the Rye House Plot) Richard Pearson, rector of St Michael, Crooked Lane, London, told his congregation that there was no great difference between the principles of the fanatics and the Jesuits, since both were against the King (although Pearson, in fact, thought the fanatics were worse).[15] Edward Pelling, rector of St Martin, Ludgate, in a sermon given earlier that year on the anniversary of the execution of Charles I, spelt out how the Nonconformists had derived their resistance theories and king-killing principles from Catholic writers such as Mariana, Bellarmine and Azorius,[16] a point also made by the Oxford Decree of 1683.

It has been suggested that during the last four years of his reign Charles 'at last emerged as an unfettered sovereign', and that 'instead of having to solicit the support of his subjects, he now commanded their obedience'.[17] Such a view seems highly questionable. The strength of the Crown during the Tory Reaction was to a large degree dependent on the fact that Charles II was at last prepared to wear the mantle of King of the Anglicans, and he was very careful in soliciting their support. The Court was eager to use the legalist justification of

the reaction. After the Oxford Parliament, according to Lord Worcester, Charles promised to 'stick to that that is law, and maintain the
Church as it is now established . . . I will not be for the lessening of
it, and if I do I know I less my crown, for we must march together'.[18]
The combined effect of the purges and the anti-Nonconformist propaganda was to put power in the localities into the hands of people who
were determined to protect the Church and State from both popery
and fanaticism through a strict adherence to the rule of law. There was
a genuine enthusiasm for the campaign against Dissent from many sections of the English population, an enthusiasm which grew greater
after the revelations of the Rye House Plot in 1683. Magistrates, jurors
and local constables showed themselves increasingly willing to prosecute the laws against the Nonconformists.[19] Yet the very success of
the Tory Reaction placed fetters of a different kind on the Crown.
Tory Anglicans believed they had nothing to fear from a popish successor whilst those in control of the mechanisms of local government
were determined to enforce the laws designed to protect the Church.
There was no way that James's supporters in 1685 were going to help
him promote Catholicism by undermining the laws. Even during the
height of enthusiasm for the monarchy in the first half of the 1680s,
Anglican polemicists offered hints that their loyalty to the Church
came before their loyalty to the Crown. In an Assize Sermon delivered
at Leicester in 1682, Thomas Ashenden, rector of Dingley (Northants),
even went so far as to accuse the King of being too soft on Dissent:
'our present divisions, and our manifold menacing mischiefs', he argued, 'we may chiefly date from the late Toleration', which 'allowan-
ces proceed from Royal mercy', and he claimed that the strength for
rebellion had come 'from the Breasts of Royal Indulgence'.[20] The
loyalty which Anglicans professed to the Stuart monarchy was quite
specifically 'a church of England-Loyalty', as William Sherlock put it
in his sermon to James II's first Parliament on 29 May 1685. To be
'true to our Prince', he insisted, 'we must be true to our Church and
to our Religion', for 'it would be no Act of Loyalty to accommodate
or complement away our Religion and its legal Securities'.[21]

TORY-ANGLICAN OPPOSITION TO JAMES II

At the beginning of his reign, James issued a number of assurances that
he would 'preserve this Government, both in Church and State, as it

is now by Law established'.[22] Yet he soon showed that his word could not be relied upon. Shortly after his accession, he ordered the release of Catholics who had been imprisoned for refusing to go to church or for not taking oaths, and ordered the Exchequer to repay their fines. He used the Monmouth Rebellion as an excuse to increase the size of his standing army, from the 8,565 troops inherited from his brother, to a total of 19,778 by the end of the year. He also commissioned a number of Catholic officers, in violation of the 1673 Test Act, which required commissioned officers to take the Anglican communion and abjure transubstantiation. James maintained that he could issue dispensations from the provisions of this Act by the royal prerogative, an opinion which was upheld by the judges in the test case of Godden *v.* Hales in June 1686, although it required a purge of the judicial bench to achieve a verdict favourable to the Crown. Armed with this decision, James proceeded to promote more Catholics to offices under the Crown, not just in the army but also in civilian posts. In July, for example, five Catholics were appointed to the Privy Council. He also encouraged his Catholic subjects to worship openly.

At all stages James met with opposition from Tories and Anglicans. On 27 May 1685, only a week after Parliament had convened, a grand committee of the House of the Commons (comprising some 330 members) agreed to address the King calling for the enforcement of the laws against 'all Dissenters whatsoever from the Church of England', including Catholics. This time, in the face of opposition from the Crown, the Commons eventually drew back, and rejected the committee's recommendation. The second session of Parliament, which began on 9 November, saw an attack on the standing army, the Commons refusing to vote supply for the additional forces that had been raised over the summer, and instead resolving to bring in a bill to reform the militia. Since some historians see the anti-standing army platform as essentially a Whig position before the Glorious Revolution, it is worth stressing the Tory dimension to the opposition in 1685. In the Commons, Sir Thomas Clarges moved that 'a standing Army is destructive to the Country', whilst his fellow Tory, Edward Seymour, declared that 'the safety of the Kingdom doth not consist with a standing force', adding (in a way which anticipated Tory arguments used after 1689) that 'all the profit and security of this Nation is in our Ships, and had there been the least ship in the Channel', Monmouth could never have landed. Seymour also condemned the commissioning of officers 'not taking the Tests', alleging 'it is dispensing with all the laws at once', whilst in the Lords speeches against the employment of Catholics in the Army came from staunch Anglicans such as Nottingham and the Bishop of London.[23] On 20 November, after a stormy session lasting less than two weeks, James prorogued this Parliament, never to call another one.

Following the prorogation of Parliament in November 1685 it was the Anglican establishment which took the initiative in opposing James's policies. The London clergy, led by their bishop, Henry Compton, met frequently to co-ordinate an anti-Catholic propaganda campaign, and virtually once a week some new book or sermon appeared against popery.[24] When James issued his *Directions to Preachers* in March 1686, ordering the clergy to steer clear from such controversial topics in their sermons, they refused to comply. As a result, the Commission for Ecclesiastical Causes was established to deal with recalcitrant clergy, its first act being to suspend Henry Compton from his bishopric for refusing to discipline John Sharp, Dean of Norwich and rector of St Giles in the Fields, for preaching against popery. Compton, it is worth noting, had voted against Exclusion in the Lords in November 1680. Whilst the Anglicans campaigned against popery, the Dissenters remained largely quiet, much to the disgust of the exiled Nonconformist divine, Robert Ferguson.[25] James met with similar intransigence when he attempted to use his dispensing power to break the Anglican monopoly over education. When he tried to force the trustees of Charterhouse school to give a scholarship to a Roman Catholic, the trustees, headed by the staunch Anglican Tories such as Danby, Ormonde, Sancroft and Compton, refused.[26] The Fellows of Magdalen College, Oxford, refused James's attempt to foist a Catholic President on them in March 1687 (electing one of their own fellows instead, whom James immediately deposed), and when they subsequently refused to accept James's nomination of Samuel Parker, Bishop of Oxford, the Commission for Ecclesiastical Causes was used to deprive twenty-five of them of their fellowships.[27]

James also met with opposition from Tory magistrates. At the end of April 1686 the Tory lord mayor of Bristol took it upon his own initiative to disturb the celebration of the mass by a group of English Catholics, committing the priest and all those present to prison. When those arrested threatened the lord mayor that they would inform the King how they were dealt with, he defiantly replied that he would save them the trouble and do it himself.[28] In London, the Tory lord mayor tried to stop work on the construction of a Catholic chapel in Lime Street, and when the eventual opening of the chapel provoked rioting, he was reluctant to take action to suppress the disorders. The trained bands, which were under the control of the Tory-Anglican lieutenancy, and which during the Exclusion Crisis had been efficient

in suppressing the activities of Whig and Nonconformist crowds, refused to act against the crowds who gathered to prevent people from
attending the mass, believing that since the professed purpose was
'only pulling down Popery', they could not 'in conscience hinder'.[29]

Such opposition from his former Anglican and Tory allies persuaded
James to try to forge an alliance with the Dissenters, in the hope that
the disabilities under which they suffered would give them common
cause with the Catholics to support the removal of the penal laws.
Moves towards toleration began during 1686, when James used his
prerogative powers to grant a large number of pardons and remissions
of fines (especially to Quakers), and even allowed individuals to obtain
dispensations from the penal laws. In April 1687 he issued a Declaration of Indulgence, whereby in one fell swoop he suspended all the
penal laws, the Test Acts and the Corporation Act.[30] He then started
to purge corporations and commissions of the peace, replacing Tory
Anglicans with Catholics, Dissenters and former Whigs, and began a
drive to secure the return of a Parliament which would formally repeal
the Test Acts and penal laws. James's initial attempts to woo Dissenters
and erstwhile Whigs, it is now being recognised, were more successful
than we used to think. It is true that some Nonconformists were suspicious of the King's motives, and were concerned about the legality
of the suspending power. The Presbyterian, Daniel Williams, persuaded a meeting of London Dissenting ministers not to present an
address of thanks to the King for the Indulgence, and argued that 'it
was better for them to be reduced to their former hardships, than
declare for measures destructive of the liberties of their country'. Yet
most Dissenters did avail themselves of the relief afforded by the Declaration, and some eighty addresses of thanks were presented by various Nonconforming ministers and churches; addresses even came in
from the Quakers, who had refused to have anything to do with
Charles's Indulgence of 1672.[31] From the diocese of Norwich Archbishop Sancroft learned that the Dissenters had 'greedily swallowed the
bayt', and had celebrated the news of the Indulgence 'with bells and
bonefiers'.[32] A number of Whigs showed themselves prepared to colla-
borate with James. Amongst them were Henry Care (a Presbyterian,
and author of the Exclusionist periodical, the *Weekly Pacquet of Advice
from Rome*), who became James's chief propagandist in promoting the
cause of religious toleration, and Sir William Williams, who became
James's solicitor-general (and who was to lead the prosecution of the
seven bishops in 1688). Other Whig collaborators included prominent
exclusionists such as Silius Titus, Lord Brandon, James Vernon, Ralph
Montagu, Sir Francis Winnington, and William Sacheverell, several

erstwhile members of the Green Ribbon Club, such as Henry Trenchard, Edward Nosworthy, Nathaniel Wade, and Henry and William
Trinder, several Nonconformist divines, such as Stephen Lobb and
Vincent Alsop, and some Quakers, notably William Penn. In London,
the Nonconformist Sir John Shorter became lord mayor, whilst outside the capital, many Whigs and Dissenters who were intruded into
the remodelled corporations co-operated with James's policies. In
Wales, old republican soldiers and even some of the former disciples of
the Fifth Monarchist, Vavasor Powell, accepted places on the remodelled bench in 1687–8, much to the horror of local Tories, who portrayed the new magistrates as 'the old gang' of 1641.[33]

James hoped that Anglican principles of passive obedience would
induce members of the Church establishment to stand by him. Few in
fact did. Some bishops, notably those who owed their promotions to
James (such as Thomas Cartwright of Chester and Samuel Parker of
Oxford), supported the Indulgence, and encouraged their clergy to
deliver addresses of thanks for that part of Declaration in which James
promised he would continue to protect the Church of England. They
did not always meet with success, however; Parker's clergy, for
example, refused to sign the address.[34] Most of the bishops did their
best to dissuade their clergy from subscribing any such addresses. The
Archbishop of Canterbury, William Sancroft, composed a lengthy
statement of 'Reasons against Subscription', in which he condemned
the Indulgence for 'endeavouring to abrogate Lawes for their [the Dissenters'] sake', laws which, he added, 'perhaps cannot be repealed'.[35]
One government pamphlet complained how scarcely any of the Anglican clergy could find it in their hearts to thank the King, 'and those
Few that pretend to do it, have proceeded so Awkwardly in their
Acknowledgments, as renders them of very little Value, since in the
same addresses they also pressed for 'the continuance of those Penal
Laws, which diametrically oppose . . . the Royal Indulgence'.[36]

James had no better luck in securing the acquiescence of the Anglican gentry. In late 1687 he began polling the deputy lieutenants and
JPs to see if they would assist him in obtaining the election of a Parliament committed to the repeal of the penal laws and the Tests. Only
about one quarter of those asked said that they would, and many of
these were Catholics or Nonconformists. About a third said unequivo-
cally that they would not support the repeal, and even the doubtfuls
expressed their opinions in such a way as to leave no doubt about the
strength of their reservations. The result was particularly disappointing,
given the fact that the magistracy had already been purged by both
Charles and James.[37] There were even attempts by Anglican groups to

prevent the Dissenters from enjoying the toleration they were offered after 1687. At Mildenhall in Suffolk in the spring of 1688, a parson threatened to bring a Nonconformist minister before a JP for preaching a sermon, saying that it should cost him £20 (the fine for preaching at a conventicle under the terms of the 1670 Act, whose operation had just been suspended). On another occasion he brought with him a constable and several others, saying 'I shall make you leave your Singing'. We also have reports of Anglican crowds at York and at Sandwich in Kent riotously disturbing Nonconformist meetings.[38]

The issuance of James's second Declaration of Indulgence on 27 April 1688 brought the impending crisis to a head. This time James instructed the bishops to order all their clergy to read the Declaration from the pulpit on two successive Sundays. Seven bishops – Sancroft (of Canterbury), Trelawny (Bristol), Lloyd (St Asaph), Turner (Ely), White (Peterborough), Ken (Bath and Wells) and Lake (Chichester) – petitioned the Crown asking to be excused from reading and distributing the Declaration. The bishops were sent to the Tower on the grounds that their petition was seditious libel. As a result of their stance, very few clergy read the Declaration. At their trial, the bishops were found not guilty, and the decision was greeted with popular demonstrations throughout the country.[39]

In short, James faced a concerted campaign of civil disobedience from his Anglican subjects in response to his undermining of the laws protecting the Church of England. What is remarkable is that the initiative here was taken by the High Anglican clergy, who should have been the natural allies of the Stuart monarchy, and who had staunchly defended James's title to the throne during the Exclusion Crisis. In contrast, most Whigs and Nonconformists (who had remained in England) either kept quiet or actively collaborated with James. Indeed, Anglicans were forced to engage in a propaganda campaign to try to prevent the Whigs and Nonconformists from falling too much in line with government policy.

The case of the seven bishops was an important turning point in the development of events leading up to the Revolution, marking the defeat of James's attempts to win Nonconformist support for his policies of toleration. Anglican polemicists had promised that they would allow the Dissenters some degree of toleration, if they helped them protect the Church of England from the Catholic onslaught, whilst the bishops in their petition affirmed that they did not act 'from any want of due tenderness to Dissenters, in relation to whom they are willing to come to such a temper as shall be thought fit, when the matter shall be considered and settled in Parliament and Convention'.

Most Dissenters decided to rally behind the bishops in their opposition to the second Declaration of Indulgence, proclaiming that they wanted 'liberty by law'. A delegation of ten Nonconformist ministers even visited the bishops in the Tower on 10 June, saying 'they could not but adhear to them as men constant in the Protestant faith'.[40] Whig lawyers, such as Treby and Somers, served as counsel for the defence in the bishops' trial, a curious development considering the mutual antipathy between bishops and Whigs during the Exclusion Crisis.

The situation was further transformed by the birth of James's son on 10 June, which raised the spectre of a never-ending succession of Catholic monarchs. It was on the day that the bishops were acquitted, 30 June, that the famous seven – Bishop Compton, the Earl of Danby, Lord Lumley, Edward Russell, Henry Sidney, and the Earls of Devonshire and Shrewsbury – sent an invitation to William of Orange pledging their support if he brought a force to England against James. Whilst the invitation came from men who represented both Tory and Whig opinion, most of those who conspired with William in Holland were in fact outlawed Whigs. Yet William was made well-aware that the crisis in England which had led to his invitation had been brought about mainly by the opposition of the Anglican interest, something he implicitly recognised in his invasion propaganda. Radical Whigs in William's circle wanted to limit William's appeal to Whigs and Dissenting groups, and John Wildman urged that the invasion manifesto be couched in these terms. But most realised the tactical disadvantages of doing this, and insisted that the manifesto would have to appeal to the nobility, the gentry, most of the clergy, and 'all the high church party'. In the end, William's invasion manifesto, which was based to a large extent on a draft sent to him from England by Danby, emphasised grievances that had a special appeal for Anglicans and Tories. Thus his *Declaration of Reasons for Invading* focused on the violations of the Test Act, the creation of the Commission for Ecclesiastical Causes, the suspension of the Bishop of London, the affair of Magdalen College, the dispensing and suspending powers, and the attack on the corporations in 1687–8.[41]

If the key role in opposing James's pro-Catholic policies came from the Anglican establishment, and in particular from the clergy, how did they justify doing this, given their professed attachment to the principles of non-resistance and passive obedience? Supporters of James repeatedly charged the Church with hypocrisy. As one satirical poem put it: 'Though of Passive Obedience we talk like the best, 'Tis prudence, when interest sways, to resist'.[42] Yet Anglicans had always allowed for passive resistance, in the sense of non-compliance with the

ungodly commands of the sovereign, so long as one peacefully accepted the punishments for one's disobedience. In a sermon preached
at the Reading Assizes in July 1681, John Okes, whilst stressing the
need for obedience to magistrates, also stated that if the magistrate
commanded something 'that is manifestly impious, and contrary to the
know will of God', we should not obey.[43] Similarly, as we noted
earlier, Tory-Anglican writers during the Exclusion Crisis had typically
stressed that obedience to the monarch was due in 'all lawful things'.
A broadside written towards the end of the 1680s defended the
Church of England against the charge that their stress on obedience
and subjection had been pressed so far as 'to set up arbitrary Power,
and the Will of the Prince, above Law'. This was 'a misrepresentation
of the true Doctrine of Obedience taught in our Church; which was
oppos'd to Faction and Sedition, not to a Legal Government: For
Obedience is a Duty owing to setled Governments, administered by
Legal Methods . . . but does not extend, nor was ever so intended,
to the subversion of Laws, and our civil and religious Rights, at the
Will of the Prince'.[44] The way the Anglicans responded in James's
reign was in perfect conformity to their principles. The Magdalen
College affair, for example, provides a classic example of passive resistance. As the fellows told the King in September 1687, 'the Electing
the Bishop of Oxford' was 'directly contrary to their statutes, and to
their positive oaths', and although 'they were as ready to obey the K.
in all things that lay in their power', they 'could not apprehend it in
their power to obey him in this matter'.[45] But they nevertheless
peacefully suffered the consequences of their action – the ejection
from their fellowships. Likewise the bishops stood prepared in 1688 to
accept the penalties for their non-compliance. In such cases, non-compliance was not so much an option but, many felt, an obligation, since
Anglican clergymen were duty-bound to protect the Church from the
attacks of an heretical King. As George Hickes wrote in May 1687, in
reference to the Magdalen College affair, 'non r[esistance] is always a
duty, and noncomp[liance] very often is'.[46]

But if many Anglicans thought passive resistance to James II both
proper and necessary, they certainly had no intention of seeking to
dethrone a legitimate, hereditary monarch. They hoped that under
pressure James would make concessions. In a meeting with the King
on 3 October 1688, the bishops asked James to dissolve the Commission for Ecclesiastical Causes, and promise never to erect 'any such
court again', to 'desist from the Exercise of such a Dispensing power
as hath of late been used' (the determination of which was to be left
to Parliament), to restore the corporations and the universities, and to

give office only to those who were legally qualified. In short, they wanted to 'set all things back upon the foot they were at his coming to the crown'. They did ask the King to call a free Parliament, in which provision could be made for a 'due liberty of conscience' for all Protestants, although they linked this with the demand that the Church of England should 'be secured according to the Act of Uniformity', suggesting that 'due liberty of conscience' was to be very limited indeed.[47] This attempted Anglican Revolution very nearly succeeded. The Commission for Ecclesiastical Causes was abolished on 5 October, some of the corporations (including London) recovered their charters, and the old fellows of Magdalen College were restored. James also promised free elections. These developments, however, were pre-empted by William's invasion preparations and his eventual landing on 5 November, which forced James to delay his plans to call Parliament.

Most Whigs welcomed William's invasion, but the reaction of Tory Anglicans was more mixed. Two prominent Tories, Danby and Compton, had been involved in the invitation to William, the bishops refused to bow to pressure from James to issue a repudiation of the invitation, whilst in the provinces a number of leading Tories rallied to William's cause.[48] There were some, however, who thought that the invasion came too close to the active resistance which Tories and Anglicans had for so long condemned. The Earl of Nottingham, a Tory who was to make his peace with the Revolution, nevertheless opposed the invitation, condemning it as 'high treason, in violation of the Laws . . . and that allegiance which I ow'd to the Soveraigne and which I had confirm'd by my solemn oath'.[49] When William arrived in England he met with pockets of resistance in various parts of the country from Tory groups.[50] Even those Tory Anglicans who welcomed William's assistance had no desire to see him gain the Crown. In his invasion manifesto, William had made no mention of intending the throne for himself, and had avoided any attacks on James, but instead had blamed the King's evil counsellors, and promised to call a free Parliament to settle the affairs of the Kingdom. Danby later insisted that he had never intended things to go 'so far as to settle the Crown on the Prince of Orange'.[51]

During the last weeks of 1688 James's regime began to disintegrate. Faced with desertion amongst his nobility and gentry and within his army, and with the outbreak of violent anti-Catholic rioting in London, James panicked, and decided to try to flee the country on 11 December.[52] Even his last act of desperation proved a failure; James was ignominiously stopped by fishermen at Faversham, Kent, who recognised his travelling companion, Sir Edward Hales (Governor of the

Tower), but failed at first to recognise the King. James was brought back to London on 16 December, where the enthusiastic reception he received from the crowds who lined the streets, made the King think that the people's anger 'was not at his person, but at his religion'.[53] James's attempted flight, however, effectively destroyed any hope that a settlement might be reached which would enable James to preserve his throne. William of Orange, whatever his initial intentions might have been when coming to England, was now determined to obtain the English Crown for himself, and he secured James's second, and this time enforced, removal from his Kingdom on 23 December. The interregnum produced by the King's removal facilitated a sudden and dramatic resurgence of the Whigs. On 26 December William summoned an irregular assembly of commoners, comprised of the surviving MPs from Charles II's last Parliament, the lord mayor and Court of Aldermen, and fifty representatives of the Common Council of London. The Tory members of James's Parliament of 1685, however, were deliberately ignored; as a result, William obtained a predominantly Whig assembly.[54] At least temporarily, William had established himself as regent of the realm, whilst the Tories had lost the initiative which they had possessed until very recently in the campaign against James.

THE REVOLUTION SETTLEMENT

The Revolution settlement was worked out in the Convention Parliament which assembled on 22 January 1689. The Convention not only transferred the Crown to William and Mary, but also laid down certain terms for the new rulers in the document known as the Declaration of Rights, and if the offer of the Crown was not strictly speaking conditional upon William and Mary's acceptance of these terms, it was clear that everyone expected that they were to abide by them. The Declaration of Rights was eventually given statutory force with the passage of the Bill of Rights in December, which included a further proviso that no Catholic could inherit the Crown.

The elections to the Convention were the least contentious of any of the general elections held under the later Stuarts: few of the contests which did occur were fought along party lines, and a number of constituencies returned one Whig and one Tory unopposed.[55] As a result, the two parties ended up being fairly evenly matched. In the House of Commons there were 174 known Whigs to 156 known Tories, along with 183 new members. The Whigs perhaps enjoyed an overall majority, since the House chose as its Speaker Henry Powle, who had generally sided with the opposition during the Exclusion Parliaments, over the Tory candidate, Sir Edward Seymour. If so, it was a majority of moderate Whigs. Powle himself had not been an exclusionist; he voted against the first Exclusion Bill in 1679, and consistently favoured the policy of limitations on a popish successor. The Whigs dominated the two Commons' committees established to consider the terms upon which the Crown should be offered to William and Mary: of forty-three men involved in drafting the Declaration of Rights, twenty-nine were Whig and fourteen Tory. The Tories, however, enjoyed the ascendancy in the upper house.[56]

What sort of settlement did this balance of forces achieve? The most radical act of 1689 was the break in the succession, and this can unquestionably be seen as a victory for the Whigs.[57] Throughout the crucial weeks of the winter of 1688–9, Tory Anglicans had done their best to prevent a transfer of the Crown. The bishops wanted to keep James as King, by 'binding him to the Church by Laws'. The Bishop of Ely, Francis Turner, suggested that James should surrender for his life all powers of war and peace, and his ecclesiastical and civil patronage, although such a proposal met with little support in the Convention. Most Tories favoured the establishment of a regency, with Mary exercising the regal powers on James's behalf, but this was defeated in the House of Lords on 29 January by the narrow vote of fifty-one to forty-eight. If James had to go, some Tories would have preferred to make Mary Queen, on the argument that the Crown had demised with James's flight and therefore passed to the next in line of succession. (Such a theory involved denying the claims of James's son, but doubts had been raised as to whether the Queen had really conceived the child, it being widely believed that the baby had been smuggled into the bed-chamber in a warming-pan.) This proposal was defeated largely by William, who insisted that he would not be his wife's 'gentleman usher'.[58]

The Declaration of Rights itself was couched in the language of political conservatism. It accused James of endeavouring 'to Subvert and extirpate the Protestant Religion, and the Lawes and Liberties of this Kingdome', and simply asserted that a number of things recently done by the King had been illegal: such as dispensing with and suspending laws, erecting a Court of Commissioners for Ecclesiastical Causes, prosecuting subjects for petitioning the Crown, and keeping a standing army in peace time. It also made a number of exhortations, for example that Parliaments ought to be held frequently, elections ought to be free, and that free speech ought to be guaranteed. But the authors insisted that they were doing no more than 'vindicating and asserting . . . antient rights and liberties'. This was not strictly speaking true. The Declaration undoubtedly broke new constitutional ground when it stated that 'the raising or keeping of a standing army within this kingdom in time of peace unless it be with the consent of Parliament is against the law'; the Militia Acts of 1661 and 1662 had invested control of the armed forces in the hands of the monarch alone with no suggestion that Parliamentary consent was needed to maintain an army in peace time. In other respects, the Declaration settled a number of issues which had been points of contention between the Crown and Parliament, and settled them in Parliament's favour. The first two clauses asserted the illegality of the suspending power and the dispensing power 'as it has been assumed and exercised of late', when used without the consent of Parliament. In fact, it is highly questionable whether the royal use of these powers had been illegal. Indeed, James had won legal recognition for the way he used the dispensing power in the test case of Godden *v.* Hales of 1686. The question of the suspending power was more complicated, since the House of Commons had resolved in 1673 'that penal statutes in matters ecclesiastical cannot be suspended but by act of Parliament'. Yet resolutions of the lower House do not make law, and arguably the royal supremacy established over the Church by Act of Parliament during the Reformation had vested the monarch with the power to suspend penal statutes.[59] In short, the Declaration of Rights can be said to have confirmed the legal sovereignty of Parliament.

Nevertheless, most of the Crown's powers were left intact in 1689. The monarch remained the chief executive in the state: he alone continued to determine all matters of policy (foreign and domestic); he had the right to choose his own ministers; he retained the right to veto legislation; and he was left with the power to determine the summoning, proroguing and dissolution of Parliament. It used to be thought that the Revolution assured regular Parliaments, and it is certainly true that since 1689 there has not been one year without the meeting of Parliament. Yet the Declaration of Rights made no provision for regular Parliaments; it merely stated that 'Parliaments ought to be held frequently', and even then it was the last demand made in the document, suggesting that it was not a particularly high priority. During the crisis which preceded the Civil War, an attempt had been made to tie the Crown to regular Parliaments with the Triennial Act of 1641, but this Act had been repealed in 1664 and it was not until 1694 that an Act guaranteeing triennial Parliaments was passed. What ensured regular Parliaments after 1689 was not any legal constraints imposed by the Declaration of Rights, but rather the Crown's chronic shortage of money and its dependence upon Parliament for taxation. In this, the makers of the Revolution can be said to have played some part. From the opening of the Convention a number of MPs were determined to restrict the Crown's revenue as a way of keeping the monarchy more dependent upon Parliament, and the fact that the revenue eventually settled on the Crown in 1690 was deliberately kept well short of anticipated peace-time expenditure has led one historian to conclude that the financial settlement 'created a new type of monarchy'. If so, we should not assume this was a Whig victory; the policy of using the powers of the purse to restrict the Crown's independence was pursued not only by radical Whigs, such as Colonel John Birch and William Sacheverell, but also by a significant number of Tories, led by Clarges and Seymour.[60] However, the crucial factor in the Crown's becoming financially dependent upon Parliament was England's involvement in foreign war after 1689. To raise the enormous sums required, the government learned to float long-term loans, which Parliament agreed to underwrite by appropriating the yield of specific taxes for the payment of interest. The establishment of the Bank of England in 1694 meant that the government was now assured of loans at favourable rates, but always on a Parliamentary basis, since the Bank was forbidden to lend without Parliament's approval. It was the financial revolution, and the establishment of the national debt, rather than the Glorious Revolution, which guaranteed the frequent meetings of Parliament.[61]

Some perspective on just how limited the reforms laid down in the Declaration of Rights were is provided by comparing them with the proposals for reform which had been made by opponents of the government since Charles II's reign. For example, the Whigs of the Exclusion Crisis, those involved in the Rye House Plot of 1683, and the Monmouth rebels of 1685 had all demanded annual Parliaments and that Parliaments should not be prorogued, dissolved or discontinued before petitions were first answered and grievances redressed. Radical Whigs in the early 1680s had challenged the Crown's control of the armed forces and of appointment to office: the Rye House Plotters wanted the militia placed 'in the hands of the people'; Monmouth had insisted that judges should not hold their commissions at the King's pleasure but rather 'during good behaviour'.[62] In 1688–9 a number of radical Whigs took the line that James's flight had brought about a dissolution of the kingship and a suspension of the constitution, and therefore the people (through their representatives in the Convention) were free to restructure the constitution as they thought fit. John Wildman, who sat in the Convention as member for Great Bedwin, produced a tract in which he argued that the King's legislative veto and power to dismiss Parliament be removed and that control over the militia, the declaration of war and the appointment of judges should be transferred to Parliament.[63] The initial committee appointed to consider the terms on which to offer William and Mary the Crown, which contained a Whig majority of twenty-eight to twelve, drew up a list of twenty-eight Heads of Grievances which, if all remedied, would have gone some way to satisfying the radicals' desires. These included the resolutions that Parliaments not only 'ought to sit frequently', but that 'their frequent sitting be secured', that there should be 'no interrupting of any sessions of Parliament till the affairs that are necessary to be dispatched at that time are determined', that the militia acts were 'grievous to the subject', and that judges should hold their commissions 'during good behaviour'. However, William made it clear that he was opposed to limitations, and not only was it doubtful whether such far-reaching reforms could have passed the Lords (where the Tories held the ascendancy), but even the moderate Whigs showed themselves unprepared to support them. A second committee, headed by the Williamite Whig, John Somers, and which contained sixteen Whigs to only six Tories, deliberately removed the radical proposals found in the Heads of Grievances, reducing it to the much more conservative document which became known as the Declaration of Rights.[64]

In fact, assessing the degree to which the powers of the Crown were limited at the Revolution may not be the most appropriate way of measuring the extent to which 1689 was a victory for Whig principles. In a debate in the Convention on 29 January it was a Whig, Thomas Wharton (the son of the Puritan peer), who moved that the throne be filled by making William and Mary joint sovereigns, without demanding that the rights of the people be secured first, and he was seconded by a Tory, Sir Duncombe Colchester. They were opposed by Anthony Cary, Lord Falkland, a Tory, who argued that the throne should not be filled until Parliament had decided what powers to give the Crown, so that 'we may secure ourselves from Arbitrary Government', although in this he was supported by radical Whigs such as Wildman.[65] Falkland's intervention can in part be seen as a delaying tactic, in the hope that by forestalling the offer of the Crown to William and Mary some arrangement more in accord with Tory principles might still be able to be worked out. But in part it reflected a genuine belief on the part of many Tory Anglicans that the Church was still inadequately protected against possible attacks from a non-Anglican monarch, and needed better legal securities. Anxiety here was generated by the fact that William was a Calvinist, hardly more attractive as head of the Anglican Church than a Catholic. If the Tory Anglicans were going to lose the argument about the transfer of the Crown, they were determined to ensure that the Church would be safe under a Calvinist successor.

In many respects, the Declaration of Rights satisfied Tory-Anglican anxieties very well. As we have already seen, none of the demands of the radical Whigs found their way into the Declaration. On the other hand, virtually all the demands which the Anglicans had been pressing for in their attempts to come to terms with James, such as those made by the bishops in their meeting with the King on 3 October, did. Thus the Declaration confirmed the illegality of the suspending power and dispensing power, it abolished the Commission for Ecclesiastical Causes, and it defended the right of subjects to petition the Crown (a defence of the bishops' action in opposition to the second Declaration of Indulgence). Even the most innovatory feature of the Declaration – the proviso against keeping a standing army in peace-time without Parliamentary consent – can be seen to have been a Tory concern in James's reign.

This is not to suggest that the Declaration of Rights should be seen purely as a vindication of Tory principles. From the time of James's second Indulgence, most Whigs and Nonconformists had come out against the suspending power, on the promise that if they stuck by the Church, they would be given some measure of toleration. A few of the clauses in the Declaration appear to have referred to what could only be Whig grievances. These were the clause condemning the im-panelling of partial, corrupt and unqualified jurors (a reference to the Rye House Plot trials of 1683), the clause condemning excessive fines (a reference to the crippling fines levied on Whig dissidents during the Tory Reaction), and the clause condemning 'Grants and promises made of fines and forfeitures before any Conviction and Judgment of the same against the persons upon whom the same were to be levied' (a reference to James's dealings with the Monmouth rebels).[66] Yet these were minor victories compared to the more sweeping demands for reform made by the more radical Whigs which did not find their way into the Declaration.

If the Declaration of Rights gave the Tories the sort of legal assur-ances they wanted, to what extent were they able to accommodate themselves to the break in the hereditary succession? What mattered here was how contemporaries chose to describe the events that happened in 1688–9. Many Whigs took the line that James had been deposed because he had broken his original contract with the people. Of 139 pamphlets which were published between 1689 and 1694 to vindicate the transference of allegiance from James to William, half of them defended the position of contractual resistance, and all without exception were Whig pamphlets.[67] Several Whigs in the Convention also took such a line. However, the Convention eventually eschewed any notion of deposition, and settled on the view that James had abdicated, a decision that met with approval from Whigs as well as Tories. It is true that the House of Commons agreed on a resolution on 29 January that linked James's abdication with his breaking of the original contract, but the Lords objected to this. As a result, no hints of James having broken a contractual obligation found its way into the Declaration of Rights, which simply concluded that James had 'abdicated the Government' and that the throne was 'thereby vacant'.[68]

The question was, whether the presumption of James's abdication was enough to allow the scrupulous to transfer their allegiance to William and Mary. Many Tories and Anglicans were worried about whether their oaths to James could be abrogated, and whether they were free to swear new oaths not just to Mary, who possessed an hereditary claim, but also to William. Those who had greatest scruples were precisely those High Anglican clergy who had led the opposition to James, and especially the bishops. Yet by the end of 1690 most prominent laymen and clergy had come to take the oaths to the new regime, and only a tiny minority persisted as Jacobites or Nonjurors.[69] How had this been achieved?

Many took comfort in the fact that the oaths to the new rulers made no reference to their right or title. It was therefore possible to swear allegiance to William and Mary as *de facto* rulers, whilst still recognising James II as King *de jure*. Some saw the Revolution in providentialist terms. Others had recourse to the *ius gentium* tradition associated with Hugo Grotius. Thus it was argued that William had a legitimate title to the throne because he won it by right of conquest in a just war. Such a theory could enable Tories not only to by-pass James, but also the next heir, Mary, whilst maintaining all along that they had never broken their principles of non-resistance. And the reason why the war was just, was because James had attempted to defraud William of his hereditary property rights, by presenting the supposititious heir to the throne – so the theory was thus compatible with hereditary succession. Such an argument proved powerfully attractive;

both the Whiggish Burnet and the Williamite Tory, Edmund Bohun, believed that arguments from conquest had the greatest effect in bringing people over to the new government. But people fought over their interpretation of the Revolution – and this became an issue of party strife in the next reigns.[70]

Perhaps the most difficult problem that had to be sorted out in 1689 concerned the settlement in the Church. Sherlock wrote at the time of the calling of the Convention, 'there are no Contentions so fierce as those about Religion . . . . Those of the Church of England are very glad to get rid of Popery, but they will not be contented to Part with their Church into the bargain . . . . The several sects of Dissenters are glad to be rid of Popery also; but now they expect glorious days for themselves'.[71] Some of the more extreme Whigs in the Convention pressed for the removal of the sacramental tests for office-holders as provided for under the Corporation Act and Test Acts. The repeal of these measures was opposed not only by the Tories, however, but also by moderate and staunchly Anglican Whigs such as Lord Devonshire.[72] Something had to be done to help the Dissenters, since the bishops had promised them 'a due liberty of conscience'. The scheme proposed by the Earl of Nottingham was to broaden the basis of the national Church by comprehending the more moderate Dissenters, whilst conceding a very limited toleration to those who remained outside. Nottingham believed that once Nonconformists realised how easy it would be to conform to the established Church, few would wish to suffer the inconveniences that Dissent still brought with it, so that the integrity of the Anglican Church would be preserved, without running the risk of a perpetual Protestant schism.[73]

Things did not work out as planned. A Toleration Bill went through Parliament fairly quickly, being backed by William and Mary, and agreed to as a necessary concession to the Nonconformists. Even then the provisions under the Act were fairly limited: the penal laws were not repealed, but Protestant Dissenters were merely given immunity from prosecution if they held their own religious services, provided their meeting-houses were licensed and the doors were left open when they met. When comprehension came to be discussed by Convocation, the High Anglican clergy proved unwilling to make the sort of concessions needed to comprehend the more moderate Dissenters. What was achieved in 1689 was certainly not what Anglicans such as Nottingham wanted, toleration without comprehension. This would encourage separatism, and thereby undermine the whole integrity of the Church of England, which it had been the aim of the Tories all along to protect. The Nonconformists also had reason to feel disappointed, since the relief granted was considerably less than the civil and religious liberty which they had enjoyed towards the end of James's reign.

CONCLUSION

The Glorious Revolution in England was a compromise between the two parties. Its moderate nature is further highlighted by a comparison with events in Scotland, where the Revolution was a much more radical affair. The Scottish Jacobites withdrew themselves from the Scottish Convention which met on 14 March 1689, and as a result the settlement north of the border was worked out predominantly by Whigs. The Convention scorned the suggestion that James had abdicated, and instead maintained that he had 'forefaulted' the Crown through misgovernment, implying that the King of Scotland held his throne contractually. It presented William and Mary not only with a Claim of Right – a statement of basic constitutional principles akin to the English Declaration of Rights – but also with various Articles of Grievances demanding changes in the law, and clearly intended the transfer of the Crown to be conditional upon the acceptance of the terms of these documents. The Claim of Right also condemned prelacy as 'a great and insupportable grievance and trouble to this Nation', and the following year, with the Scottish bishops refusing to acknowledge the new rulers, episcopacy was overthrown and Presbyterianism established.[74] It was a settlement which was to have significant ramifications for British politics, as we shall see later when we come to consider the issue of Jacobitism.

If the changes wrought by the Glorious Revolution in England seem, by contrast, much more limited, it would be wrong to react too far and suggest that very little of significance was achieved by the events of 1688–9. The Revolution certainly marked a belated victory for the policy of Exclusion, and finally established the legislative sovereignty of Parliament. However, it is difficult to agree with those historians who see 1688–9 as a major watershed in early modern English history, which altered the basic issues of political life at both the national and local level.[75] In many respects the Revolution did little to settle the issues which had caused such bitter political division in Restoration England. The fact that so few of the Crown's powers were redefined in 1688–9 meant that neither the old conflicts between Court and Country, nor those between advocates of limited versus strong, autocratic monarchy, had reached any satisfactory resolution. The parameters of the religious issue might have been changed somewhat by the grudging toleration granted to Protestant Nonconformists in 1689, but the religious settlement can scarcely be said to have provided a satisfactory solution to the issue of Dissent which had been such a source of tension in Restoration society. Even the compromises that were worked out in 1689 became a source of partisan divide, as rival groups came into conflict over just how to interpret what had happened at the Glorious Revolution.

Party strife continued after 1689 precisely because the Revolution did not witness a victory for any one party. It was certainly not a victory, in any clear sense, for Whig principles. In fact, James II fell only because of the opposition he met from the Tory-Anglican interest, and although most Tory Anglicans were determined to prevent the Revolution from running the full course that it did, the eventual constitutional settlement was in much greater concordance with their principles than historians have usually recognised. Indeed, it is notable that many contemporaries saw the Revolution as being mainly a Tory achievement. It is true that the High Anglican cleric, Charles Leslie, wrote in 1694 that 'the Presbyterians and Common-wealth-men, (with some Atheists and Latitudinarians . . .) were at the bottom of the whole Contrivance of the Revolution'.[76] Yet Leslie was a Nonjuror and a Jacobite, and this way of thinking was peculiar to that group. Besides, even Leslie, writing in happier days under Queen Anne, repeatedly denied that the Revolution could be seen as a victory for Whig principles.[77] And although Whigs under Anne liked to claim that James had been deposed for breaking his original contract with the people, they found it a credible way of embarrassing their political opponents to argue that it was the Tories who had been responsible for James's downfall. A Whig tract of 1711 argued that 'The Revolution was almost entirely owing to them [Tories]', whilst the Nonconformist Daniel Defoe repeatedly replied to the charge made by High Churchmen in Anne's reign that the Dissenters had been responsible for the murder of Charles, by reminding them what they 'did to his Son': 'if they will go back to 48, and provoke us to Recriminate, by telling us of Killing the Father; let us bring them back to 88, and tell them of Deposing the Son, and sending him Abroad to beg his Bread'.[78] Whilst we should be sceptical of rhetorical strategies adopted for tactical reasons, the opinions of prominent Tories expressed at the time of the Revolution itself deserve to be given more weight. Thus

Sir Thomas Clarges argued in the House of Commons in December 1689 that William 'came in by the Church of England, their pens, sermons, and sufferings'.[79] Likewise Danby, in a debate in the House of Lords over Comprehension and Toleration in the spring of 1689, said 'That at the beginning of this Revolution only Church of England men were Ingaged in it', although 'now he perceived other persons fell in with it'.[80]

The second half of Danby's remarks alludes to the revived party tensions which were already becoming apparent in the early months of 1689, especially over the religious issue. By early 1690 such tensions had again come to a head. The Parliamentary elections of the spring proved to be bitterly contentious, and were fought largely on the old party lines, centring around the issues of Dissent and/or loyalty to the new regime.[81] The Anglican clergy campaigned actively on behalf of Tory candidates, denouncing their Whig rivals as enemies to the Church and State. The Whigs responded in predictable fashion. In Suffolk, for example, the Tory gentry were called 'papists' or 'church papists', whilst the clergy were termed 'black-coated Rogues'. One Whig voter, after 'running violently against a clergyman', said 'stand out of the way passive obedience'.[82] An examination of electoral propaganda shows how little had changed since the Exclusion Crisis. Roger L'Estrange produced a pamphlet condemning the Whigs and Nonconformists as republicans, accusing them of wanting to 'pursue their Revenge on us [the Church of England]', and he asked 'Whether the Clergy of the C. of E. are not concern'd to be as diligent against Phanaticism now, as of late against Popery'.[83] A typical Whig piece accused the Tories of seeking to promote popery and arbitrary government: despite 'a pretence of Zeal, for the Church of England by Law Established, and the Monarchy', they 'have shewn that their Church is that which was Established by Magna Carta before the Reformation, and their Monarchy, the French Tyranny, or King James his suppos'd Divine Right'.[84] The perpetuation of the old sources of strife goes a long way towards explaining why party conflict continued after the Glorious Revolution, which will be the theme of the following chapter.

REFERENCES

1.   T. B. Macaulay, *The History of England from the Accession of James II*, C. H. Firth (ed.) (6 vols, 1913–15), **III**, pp. 1310–11.

2.   Jennifer Carter, 'The Revolution and the Constitution', in Geoffrey

Holmes (ed.), *Britain after the Glorious Revolution, 1689–1714* (1969), pp. 39–58; Western, *Monarchy and Revolution: The English State in the 1680s.*

3. Lois G. Schwoerer, *The Declaration of Rights, 1689* (Baltimore, 1981).
4. W. A. Speck, *Reluctant Revolutionaries: Englishmen and the Revolution of 1688* (Oxford, 1988), ch. 7 (quote on p. 141). See also Robert Beddard, 'The Unexpected Whig Revolution of 1688', in Beddard (ed.), *The Revolutions of 1688* (Oxford, 1991), pp. 11–101.
5. Henning, *The House of Commons, 1660–1690*, **I**, p. 66; Speck, *Reluctant Revolutionaries*, pp. 44–6.
6. Library of Congress, MS 18,124, IX, fol. 164; Speck, *Reluctant Revolutionaries*, p. 42.
7. BL, Add. MSS 34,508, fol. 11.
8. Library of Congress, MS 18,124, IX, fols 194, 195; *Lyme Letters*, pp. 127–8. Cf. Jenkins, *The Foundations of Modern Wales: Wales 1642–1780*, p. 144; Child, 'Prelude to Revolution', p. 99.
9. Bodl. Lib., MS Tanner 31, fols 215, 217; Evans, *Seventeenth-Century Norwich: Politics, Religion and Government*, p. 306.
10. Kenyon, *Stuart Constitution*, doc. 135, pp. 471–4.
11. John Allen, *Of Perjury: A Sermon Preach'd at the Assizes held at Chester, April the 4th 1682* (1682), p. 28.
12. *State Trials*, **X**, cols. 105–24.
13. John Standish, *A Sermon Preached at the Assizes at Hertford 9 March 1682/3* (1683), p. 28.
14. Speck, *Reluctant Revolutionaries*, pp. 39–40; Robert J. Sinner, 'Charles II and Local Government: The Quo Warranto Proceedings, 1681–1685', unpub. Rutgers PhD thesis (1976); R. E. Pickavance, 'The English Boroughs and the King's Government: A Study of the Tory Reaction, 1681–85', unpub. Oxford DPhil thesis (1976); John Miller, 'The Crown and the Borough Charters in the Reign of Charles II', *EHR*, **100** (1985), pp. 53–84.
15. Richard Pearson, *Providence Bringing Good out of Evil* (1684), p. 24.
16. Edward Pelling, *A Sermon Preached on the Anniversary of that Most Execrable Murder of K. Charles the First* (1683), pp. 12–14.
17. Jones, *Charles II: Royal Politician*, pp. 162, 187.
18. Cited in Feiling, *A History of the Tory Party 1640–1714*, p. 186.
19. Harris, 'Was the Tory Reaction Popular?': *Attitudes of Londoners towards the Persecution of Dissent, 1681–6*, Coleby, *Central Government and the Localities: Hampshire 1649–1689*, p. 203.
20. Thomas Ashenden, *No Penalty, No Peace. In a Sermon Preached at the Assizes held at Leicester, August the 10th, 1682* (1682), p. 20.
21. William Sherlock, *A Sermon Preached at St. Margarets Westminster, Before the Honourable House of Commons* (1685), p. 31.
22. Grey, *Debates*, **VIII**, p. 344.
23. Grey, *Debates*, **VIII**, pp. 347, 356, 357–8.
24. Burnet, *History*, p. 430.
25. [Robert Ferguson], *A Representation of the Threatening Dangers* (1689), p. 46.

26. Feiling, *Tory Party*, p. 221.
27. G. V. Bennett, 'Loyalist Oxford and the Revolution', in L. S. Sutherland and L. G. Mitchell (eds), *The History of the University of Oxford. V: The Eighteenth Century* (Oxford, 1986), p. 18.
28. Folger Library, Newdigate MS L.c. 1654, 1 May 1686; BL, Add. MSS 34, 508, fols 113, 117–18.
29. Tim Harris, 'London Crowds and the Revolution of 1688', in Eveline Cruickshanks, (ed.), *By Force or By Default? The Revolution of 1688–1689* (Edinburgh, 1989), pp. 47–8.
30. Kenyon, *Stuart Constitution*, doc. 115, pp. 410–13.
31. Watts, *The Dissenters: From the Reformation to the French Revolution*, p. 258; Lacey, *Dissent and Parliamentary Politics in England, 1661–1689*, pp. 181, 341.
32. Bodl. Lib., MS Tanner 29, fol. 10.
33. J. R. Jones, 'James II's Whig Collaborators', *HJ*, **3** (1960), pp. 65–73; Western, *Monarchy and Revolution*, p. 223; Mark Goldie, 'James II and the Dissenters' Revenge: The Commission of Enquiry of 1688', *Historical Research* (forthcoming); *Idem*, 'Roots of True Whiggism', p. 207; Eveline Cruickshanks, 'Religion and the Royal Succession: The Rage of Party', in Jones (ed.), *Britain in the First Age of Party, 1680–1750: Essays presented to Geoffrey Holmes* p. 23; Geraint Jenkins, *Foundations of Modern Wales*, p. 138; Philip Jenkins, *The Making of a Ruling Class: The Glamorgan Gentry 1640–1790*, p. 132.
34. Laurence Echard, *The History of England* (3 vols, 1707–18), **III**, p. 821.
35. Bodl. Lib., MS Tanner 29, fol. 13.
36. *An Address of Thanks On Behalf of the Church of England to Mrs James* (1687), p. 1.
37. Sir George Duckett, *Penal Laws and Test Act* (2 vols, Oxford, 1882–3); Western, *Monarchy and Revolution*, pp. 210–22; Jones, *The Revolution of 1688 in England*, ch. 6.
38. *Publick Occurrences*, no. 4, 13 Mar. 1687/8, no. 7, 3 Apr. 1688, no. 9, 17 Apr. 1688.
39. Harris, 'London Crowds and the Revolution of 1688', pp. 49–50.
40. Kenyon, *Stuart Constitution*, doc. 126, pp. 441–2; Western, *Monarchy and Revolution*, p. 233.
41. Schwoerer, *Declaration of Rights*, pp. 109–11.
42. 'The Clerical Cabal' (1688), in *POAS*, **IV**, p. 221.
43. John Okes, *A Sermon Preached at the Assizes held at Reading* (1681), pp. 8, 14.
44. *The True Character of a Church-man, Shewing The False Pretences to that Name* [168–?].
45. Bodl. Lib., MS Tanner 29, fols 86–7.
46. Bodl. Lib., MS Ballard 12, fol. 25. For further insights into the Anglican position, see Mark Goldie, 'The Political Thought of the Anglican Revolution', in Beddard (ed.), *Revolutions of 1688*, pp. 102–36.
47. Bodl. Lib, MS Tanner 28, fol. 187; John Miller, 'James II and Toleration', in Cruickshanks (ed.), *By Force or By Default?*, p. 22.

48. J. P. Kenyon, *The Nobility in the Revolution of 1688* (Hull, 1963); David H. Hosford, *Nottingham, Nobles and the North: Aspects of the Revolution of 1688* (Hamden, Conn., 1976); Key, 'Politics beyond Parliament', p. 574.

49. Henry Horwitz, *Revolution Politicks: The Career of Daniel Finch, Second Earl of Nottingham* (Cambridge, 1968), p. 52.

50. Eveline Cruickshanks, 'The Revolution and the Localities: Examples of Loyalty to James II', in her *By Force or By Default?*, pp. 28–43.

51. *The Parliamentary History of England*, William Cobbett (ed.) (1806–20), **VI**, p. 847.

52. William L. Sachse, 'The Mob and the Revolution of 1688', *JBS*, **4** (1964), pp. 23–40; Harris, 'London Crowds and the Revolution', pp. 51–6.

53. Sir John Bramston, *Autobiography*, P. Braybrooke (ed.) (1845), p. 340.

54. Robert Beddard, *A Kingdom Without a King: The Journal of the Provisional Government in the Revolution of 1688* (Oxford, 1988), pp. 63–5; Beddard, 'The Unexpected Whig Revolution'.

55. Henry Horwitz, 'Parliament and the Glorious Revolution', *BIHR*, **47** (1974), pp. 36–52.

56. Schwoerer, *Declaration of Rights*, chs 2, 3; Speck, *Reluctant Revolutionaries*, pp. 92–5.

57. Beddard, 'Unexpected Whig Revolution', pp. 96–7.

58. BL, Add. MSS 40,621, fol. 5; Feiling, *Tory Party*, pp. 240, 247–54; Eveline Cruickshanks, David Hayton and Clyve Jones, 'Divisions in the House of Lords on the Transfer of the Crown and Other Issues, 1689–94', in Clyve Jones and David Lewis Jones (eds), *Peers, Politics and Power: The House of Lords, 1603–1911* (1986), pp. 82–8; Howard Nenner, *By Colour of Law: Legal Culture and Constitutional Politics in England, 1660–1689* (Chicago, 1977); Beddard, *Kingdom without a King*; Idem, 'The Guildhall Declaration of 11 December 1688 and the Counter-Revolution of the Loyalists', *HJ*, **11** (1968), pp. 403–20.

59. Speck, *Reluctant Revolutionaries*, pp. 149–51.

60. Clayton Roberts, 'The Constitutional Significance of the Financial Settlement of 1690', *HJ*, **20** (1977), pp. 59–76; E. A. Reitan, 'From Revenue to Civil List, 1689–1702: The Revolution Settlement and the "Mixed and Balanced" Constitution', *HJ*, **13** (1970), pp. 571–88; Hill, *The Growth of Parliamentary Parties 1689–1742*, p. 38.

61. P. G. M. Dickson, *The Financial Revolution in England, 1688–1756: A Study in the Development of Public Credit* (1967)

62. State Trials, **IX**, col. 416; *The Declaration of James, Duke of Monmouth* (1685).

63. [John Wildman], *Some Remarks Upon Government, and Particularly upon the Establishment of the English Monarchy Relating to this Present Juncture* (1689).

64. Goldie, 'Roots of True Whiggism', pp. 195–236; Barbara Taft, 'Return of a Regicide: Edmund Ludlow and the Glorious Revolution', *History*, **76** (1991), pp. 212–13.

65. Grey, *Debates*, **IX**, pp. 29–30; Goldie, 'Roots of True Whiggism', p. 219; Schwoerer, *Declaration of Rights*, pp. 184–92.

66. Speck, *Reluctant Revolutionaries*, pp. 147–8.

67. Mark Goldie, 'The Revolution of 1689 and the Structure of Political Argument', *Bulletin of Research in the Humanities*, **83** (1980), pp. 473–564.

68. Kenyon, *Revolution Principles*, ch. 2.

69. For the Jacobites and Nonjurors, see ch. 8.

70. Mark Goldie, 'Edmund Bohun and *Ius Gentium* in the Revolution Debate, 1689–1693', *HJ*, **20** (1977), pp. 569–86.

71. [William Sherlock], *Letter to a Member of the Convention* (Edinburgh, 1689), p. 3.

72. Hill, *Growth of Parliamentary Parties*, p. 39.

73. Horwitz, *Revolution Politicks*, pp. 87–93.

74. Western, *Monarchy and Revolution*, pp. 376–9; William Ferguson, *Scotland 1689 to the Present* (1968), pp. 1–15; Bruce Lenman, *The Jacobite Risings in Britain 1689–1746* (1980), pp. 34–5; Rosalind Mitchison, *A History of Scotland* (2nd edn, 1982), pp. 278–84.

75. Jenkins, *Making of a Ruling Class*, pp. 133–4; Scott, *Algernon Sidney and the English Republic*, pp. 165–7.

76. [Charles Leslie], *Querela Temporum: Or, The Danger of the Church of England* (1694), p. 2.

77. Charles Leslie, *The Rehearsal*, **I**, no. 86, 16 Feb. 1705/6.

78. *The Whigs Appeal to the Tories* (1711), p. 7; [Daniel Defoe], *More Short Ways with the Dissenters* (1704), p. 15; [Daniel Defoe], *A New Test of the Church of England's Honesty* (1704), p. 24.

79. Grey, *Debates*, **IX**, p. 483.

80. Bodl. Lib., MS Ballard 45, fol. 58.

81. Henry Horwitz, 'The General Election of 1690', *JBS*, **11** (1971), pp. 77–91.

82. Patricia E. Murrell, 'Suffolk: The Political Behaviour of the County and its Parliamentary Boroughs from the Exclusion Crisis to the Accession of the House of Hanover', unpub. Newcastle-upon-Tyne PhD thesis (1982), p. 64.

83. [Sir Roger L'Estrange/James Harrington the Younger], *Some Queries Concerning the Election of Members for the Ensuing Parliament. Together with a Reply by Way of Query to the Same* (1690), pp. 3–5.

84. *Advice to the Citizens of London* (1690).

CHAPTER SIX

High Politics and Party Ideology under William and Anne

We have seen that there were two main forms of political alignment in Restoration England: the Whig–Tory one, which came to the fore during the Exclusion Crisis, and an earlier tradition of strife between Country and Court, which fed into, but did not directly overlap with, the subsequent party divide. The nature of this partisan strife, and the precise relationship between Whig, Tory, Country and Court, was bound to be transformed to some extent as a result of the Glorious Revolution. If many of the key issues which had divided the Whigs and the Tories during Charles II's reign had not been resolved by the events of 1688–9, their context had certainly been altered. As one contemporary, writing at the end of William's reign, put it, 'One would have thought that the Distinction of Parties was quite worn out, when the Church had quitted the Doctrines of Passive Obedience and Non-resistance', and had joined with the Whigs and Dissenters to call James to account for his maladministration and establish a liberty of conscience.[1] The Revolution also changed the earlier status of the Whigs as a party of opposition and the Tories as the party of government, as some Whigs found themselves increasingly drawn into the new royal administration, and as Tories became more and more alienated from the new regime.

Party alignments were further affected by the fact that the executive powers of the Crown were not significantly limited by the Glorious Revolution, which meant that the monarch continued to play a crucial role in shaping the pattern of politics after 1689. Neither William nor Anne wanted to become the prisoner of party, and both used 'political managers' who were prepared to work with men of either party in order to further the interests of the royal government. William, in his early years, experimented with mixed administrations, and even after the rise to political predominance of the Whig Junto in 1694, a number of Tories continued to serve in the government (notably the followers of the Duke of Leeds, the erstwhile Earl of Danby). Although Anne's sympathies lay strongly with the Tories, she too was determined to maintain the political independence of the Crown. Her administrations were headed first by the 'duumvirs', Godolphin and Marlborough, and from 1710 by Robert Harley (soon to be Earl of Oxford), none of whom were conventional party men (although Harley, a former Whig, can essentially be regarded as a Tory by Anne's reign), and her governments often contained men from both sides of the party divide.

As a result, there were two important cross-currents which could influence the political stance taken by any particular member of Parliament under William and Anne. An individual's allegiance could be shaped by questions of party principle and party loyalty, but it could also be shaped by one's relationship to the central government, or Court, and one's attitude towards the power of the executive. Contemporaries often appear to have been uncertain as to how best to describe the political structure of their day. It is true that they frequently spoke in terms of a division between Whigs and Tories, especially in Anne's reign; yet there were times when they rejected this language in favour of a distinction between Court and Country parties or even some multi-party formulation.[2] For a long time historians were happy to talk in terms of a basic struggle between Whigs and Tories during the reigns of William and Anne, whilst recognising that this occasionally broke down, and that for certain periods political battles were fought out along Court–Country lines. Such a view was challenged in the middle of this century by Robert Walcott, who argued for a more sophisticated understanding of the nature of the party structure under William and Anne. Walcott suggested there was a three-fold division in the House of Commons at this time: the government interest, which comprised placemen, pensioners and those who in other ways were dependent upon the Court for their position; a large body of independent back-bench MPs; and a middle group of professional politicians, which could be divided into seven 'connections', each tied together by family and personal relationships and electoral interests, and which were caught in a struggle for power between the 'ins' and 'outs'. Walcott admitted that the middle group of professional politicians tended to be Whig or Tory in general, but he insisted on the need to add a Court–Country axis to the traditional frame of reference. Thus at times one of the Whig connections might work together with a Tory connection in the service of the administration, and they would be opposed by a combination of Whigs and Tories who were out of office and who sought to mobilise the independent back-benchers to put pressure on the government.[3]

Since the mid–1960s Walcott's views have come under fierce attack.[4] He has been accused of misinterpreting the data and of generalising from untypical examples, whilst new evidence brought to light by subsequent research suggests that he was wrong in denying the existence of a two-party system, at least under Anne. William's reign remains more problematic; here scholars are prepared to concede a more significant role to Court–Country tensions, although it seems to be the case that at least from 1696 political strife can be understood essentially in terms of a struggle between Whigs and Tories.[5] It will be the argument of this chapter that a two-party system did exist under William and Anne, although there was a temporary blurring and realignment in the early years of William's reign. The key political battles in Parliament centred around issues on which there were distinctive Whig and Tory positions, such as the question of the security of the Church, the nature of England's role in the European wars, and diverging attitudes towards the Glorious Revolution itself. There was also a highly partisan press, which flourished after the final lapsing of the Licensing Act in 1695, and an examination of the war of words between the two parties suggests significant continuities with the party conflict of the Exclusion Crisis. Nevertheless, the parties did undergo some transformation as they adapted to a changing political climate. In particular, we shall see that with time the Whigs became increasingly identified as a party of the Court and the royal executive, whilst the Tories, by the end of Anne's reign, had essentially become a Country party.

THE STRUCTURE OF POLITICS

The obvious way to start testing the pattern of political allegiances under William and Anne is by examining how MPs voted in Parliamentary sessions. A number of division lists proper survive, which record how MPs voted on specific issues. To these can be added management lists, or forecasts of how people were likely to vote on a particular measure, and marked election return lists, which record gains and losses for a party. All of these lists have their problems. Neither forecasts nor election return lists record how people actually voted; indeed, part of their purpose was to identify possible waverers who might change sides if the right type of persuasion were applied. Often Parliamentary lists record only one side of the division, some of them contain errors, and because division lists were often published for propaganda purposes, sometimes errors were deliberately introduced in order to mislead the people about how a particular member had voted. Careful analysis of these lists, however, suggests that party allegiance was the most crucial determinant of political identity at this time. For example, W. A. Speck's work on division lists for Queen Anne's reign shows that the vast majority of MPs voted consistently either Whig or Tory, with a mere 12.2 per cent wavering in their allegiance, whilst in a similar analysis of division lists for William's reign, usually regarded as a period when party conflict was less clearly defined, Henry Horwitz found that only 14 per cent of MPs voted across party lines. Nor was it only on the great party issues of the day that Whig–Tory divisions emerged in the House; the same was true even on more mundane matters, where no great issue of party principle was at stake. Unfortunately no division lists survive for the Commons for the years 1691–5,[6] and there are strong grounds for believing (as will be discussed later) that it was precisely in this period when party lines became most blurred. Nevertheless, an extensive analysis of the surviving evidence concerning Parliamentary divisions suggests that voting behaviour after 1696 and up to 1714 was governed almost entirely by party allegiance.[7]

Division lists for the Lords suggest that definable parties existed in the upper chamber, although the pattern here was slightly less pronounced than for the Commons. In his study of Parliamentary politics under William, Horwitz examined four Lords' divisions lists – from 1689, 1696, and two from 1701 – and found that 76 per cent of those peers voting twice or more voted consistently Whig or Tory.[8] However, recently ten new Parliamentary lists have been discovered among Lord Ailesbury's papers, and they reveal the existence of more extensive cross-party voting on certain issues in the early 1690s.[9] Six division lists and two detailed forecasts enable us to assess the consistency of voting patterns in the Lords in Anne's reign. On six of the eight issues there was a recognised Whig and Tory position, to which the majority (some 77 per cent) of the peers conformed.[10] The remaining two divisions did involve a significant breach of party lines – the division over the disqualification of the Duke of Queensberry from voting in the election of Scottish representative peers in 1709, and the division on the motion disabling the Duke of Hamilton as an hereditary British peer in 1711. Both these divisions, however, appear to have been exceptions to the normal pattern, since they raised issues concerning the Union with Scotland, complex legal technicalities, as well as personal questions of sympathy for or antipathy towards the individuals concerned, all of which placed strains on the normal political sympathies of the different peers.[11]

An analysis of the Lords' Proxy Book, a study of the tellers in divisions in the Commons, or a consideration of the way the Commons dealt with cases of disputed elections, all reinforce the conclusion that most Parliamentary business – with the exception of purely private legislation, local economic issues, or social and moral questions[12] – was conducted along party lines. Although certain qualifications will need to be made to this picture, it seems best to think in terms of a basic two-party system, with certain exceptions, rather than seek another explanatory model for political conflict under William and Anne. 'Connection' does not help explain those occasions when the normal party alignment broke down. It is, of course, true that politicians sought to exploit their family and territorial ties for political ends, Godolphin and Marlborough being two important cases in point. However, many of those connections which Walcott thought he had identified appear to have been tied together by little more than familial relationship; he was not able to show that they acted together as a cohesive political force. In fact, politicians who deviated from the party norm were seldom able to carry many of their relatives with them.[13]

Both parties had their own organisations to co-ordinate the activities of their followers and ensure party unity. This was particularly true of the Whigs, under the leadership of the Junto lords: John Somers, Edward Russell (who became Earl of Orford), Thomas Wharton, Charles Montagu (who became the Earl of Halifax), and later also Charles Spencer, the third Earl of Sunderland. The Junto was a group of moderate Whigs, who had first come together in 1693–4 in the service of the central administration to support William's war effort. From the autumn of 1696 at the latest, the Junto held almost daily meetings during Parliamentary sessions, usually at a cabinet minister's house. Other leading Whigs were invited to these meetings as necessary, whilst larger meetings were convened at the Rose Tavern when tactics needed to be communicated to the party faithful prior to activity in Parliament. When Parliament was in recess, the Whig leaders continued to keep in close touch, usually by gathering at their country houses, though occasionally holding more formal councils at Newmar-

ket. Then there was the Kit-Cat Club, founded by Jacob Tonson in
1700, which became a place where Whig politicians and men of letters
met together on a regular basis. The Tory party was more loosely
structured: there were tensions between the Highflyers and the more
moderate wing that emerged under Anne, and which came to be led
by Robert Harley, whilst even the High Church chieftains – the Earl
of Rochester, the Earl of Nottingham, and Sir Edward Seymour –
worked much less closely together than the Whig Junto. Nevertheless
the Tories did have established methods for ensuring co-ordination
between the high command and the rank and file. From the late 1690s
and during the reign of Queen Anne it was common for leading Tory
commoners to hold briefing sessions for backbenchers, normally immediately before or just after the beginning of a new session. For
many years the Fountain Tavern in the Strand was the favourite venue
for these 'general meetings', which at times would witness the gathering of some 150 to 200 members. Both sides used a system of circular
letters and regional whips to co-ordinate the activity of their rank and
file, and both possessed fairly well-developed electoral organisations in
the localities, responsible for selecting candidates and planning tactics.[14]

THE ISSUES

The chief reason for the perpetuation of party strife was the fact that
politics continued to be dominated by issues which divided members
of Parliament along Whig–Tory lines. The issue of Dissent survived as
a major source of conflict. Although the so-called Toleration Act of
1689 meant that Dissenters were no longer being persecuted for their
beliefs, they were still denied full civil rights, since the continued existence of the Test and Corporation Acts technically banned them
from holding political office. The Tories, however, were convinced
that the Toleration Act had encouraged not only the growth of Dissent, but also of heresies such as Deism and Socinianism, and of irreli-
gion in general. A newsletter writer of August 1692 complained that it
was impossible to distinguish between those who did not come to
church because they were attending conventicles and those who did
not worship God at all, and he predicted the result would be the
downfall of the Church of England followed by the triumph of
popery.[15] There was also alarm about the practice of 'occasional conformity' (whereby Nonconformists were able to evade the provisions

of the Test and Corporation Acts and qualify themselves for civil office through the occasional attendance at Anglican communion) and the growth of Dissenting academies (which trained future generations of Nonconformist ministers and thus helped to perpetuate the religious schism).

From the mid-1690s, High Anglicans began to rally around the cry of the 'Church in Danger'. In 1696 the Whig cleric, William Stephens, observed that in the 'sermons Preached at Visitations, and the constant ordinary Discourses of the Clergy . . . the Church of England is always represented, as at this time, in greater danger than ever it was'.[16] Debate over the security of the Church found a focus in the Convocation controversy, largely triggered by Francis Atterbury's famous tract, *Letter to a Convocation Man* of late 1696, where he argued that the only way to stem the growth of heresy and blasphemy was through Convocation, the Church's own deliberative and legislative body.[17] Traditionally Convocation had met whenever Parliament assembled, but the institution had been largely dormant after 1664, when the clergy relinquished their right to tax themselves in return for the vote in Parliamentary elections, and had met only once since then, namely in 1689. The controversy hinged around whether Convocation could be summoned only by the King or had to be convened as of right when Parliament sat, and thus raised questions concerning the autonomy of the Church and the extent of the Crown's ecclesiastical prerogatives. When the Junto ministry collapsed in 1700, and William was forced to admit into office the Tory Earl of Rochester and his High Church followers, they were able to demand that Convocation be allowed to sit.

Under Anne, High Churchmen became preoccupied with trying to eradicate the practice of occasional conformity. Three unsuccessful bills against occasional conformity were introduced during the early years of Anne's reign, culminating in the famous attempt in 1704 to tack the third bill on to a Land Tax Bill.[18] The 'Church in Danger' became a recurrent theme in pamphlets and Parliamentary speeches. Sir John Packington, speaking in the Commons on 8 December 1705, identified a number of causes of this danger: the liberty allowed to pamphleteers to attack the Church and the clergy, the growth of Dissent and of Dissenting academies, and the practice of occasional conformity. Packington believed that the 'greatest cause of the Church's danger', however, came from the Presbyterian establishment in Scotland, reflecting the fact that many Anglicans felt deeply disturbed by the overthrow of episcopalianism north of the border after the Glorious Revolution.[19] Indeed, concern about the security of the Church was a major reason why High Tories were opposed to the Union with Scotland, which the Whigs eventually brought to fruition in 1707. A treaty of union which required the English monarch and Parliament to guarantee the security of the Presbyterian Church of Scotland, many felt, would serve only to encourage Dissent and undermine further the integrity of the Anglican Church.[20]

It was the Sacheverell affair which brought the conflict over the Church to a head. Dr Henry Sacheverell was a High Anglican cleric who had been delivering violent attacks on Dissenters, occasional conformists and Low Churchmen for several years. When he sought to do this from the pulpit of St Paul's on 5 November 1709 (the anniversary of the gunpowder treason plot, when preachers usually reserved their invective for Catholics), and combined it with a defence of the doctrines of passive-obedience and non-resistance, the Whig ministry of the day decided to use the opportunity to try to discredit the Church in Danger platform. The sermon was regarded as an attack on the Revolution, since it implied that James II should not have been overthrown, and Sacheverell was impeached for a 'malicious, scandalous and seditious libel'. But the Whigs had miscalculated how much sympathy there was for the High Church position. Sacheverell's trial the next spring sparked off widespread rioting in London, and although Sacheverell was eventually found guilty, he received the mild sentence of three years' suspension from preaching. A fierce reaction followed, which resulted in the downfall of the Whig ministry, and a massive victory for the Tories at the subsequent general election. The High Church backlash which followed in the wake of the Sacheverell affair eventually enabled the Tories to pass the Occasional Conformity Bill in 1711 and Schism Bill (against Dissenting academies) in 1714.[21]

In contrast, the Whigs were the 'Low Church' party, as they now came to be called: they continued to be critical of High Anglican religious intolerance, and in general remained consistent to their beliefs in liberty of conscience and religious toleration for all Protestants. They championed measures for the relief of Quakers in 1696 and after 1710, and vigorously opposed the Occasional Conformity Bills of 1702–4 and the Schism Bill of 1714. They were also the party of international Protestantism, believing that England should open its arms to foreign protestants who had fled their own country on account of their religion, and were prepared to allow them not only complete freedom of worship but also the advantages of naturalisation. The Tories stringently opposed the Whigs on this front, partly on the grounds that foreign immigrants posed a threat to national security and took away jobs from native workers, but also because they were concerned that a great influx of non-Anglicans would further undermine the Church of England. In March 1704, when the Whig House of Lords proposed a Naturalisation Bill for subjects of the principality of Orange, it was strongly opposed by the Tory-dominated House of Commons, and eventually dropped. A greater furore developed over the bill to naturalise the Palatines in 1709. The bill passed what was now a Whig-dominated Commons, although the Tories did try to introduce an amendment to make the foreigners take the sacrament in accordance with the rites of the Church of England, and when the Tories gained power after the 1710 General Election they repealed the Act.[22]

There were limits, however, to what the Whigs were prepared to do on behalf of Protestant Dissenters. Few wanted to see the repeal of the Test Acts, which required that all office holders take the sacrament in accordance with the rites of the Church of England, since these measures had in part been designed against Catholics (an important consideration when many Whigs still feared the possibility of a Stuart restoration). After their success in the General Election of 1708 there was speculation that the Whigs would try to abolish the sacramental test, but such plans, if they were ever made, were soon shelved. Indeed, in January 1709, when the Commons were discussing a recently published Nonconformist tract calling for the repeal of the Test, it was a Whig, Sir James Montagu (brother of the Junto chief), who moved the House to vote it a seditious and pernicious libel.[23] A more startling development occurred in 1711, when in order to win Nottingham's support against the peace policy of the new Tory ministry, the Whigs abandoned the Nonconformists and supported the Occasional Conformity Bill. This can be seen as an example when the Whigs compromised one party principle in pursuit of another (the Whig hostility to the Tory peace proposals are discussed below); moreover, the Junto were worried that the ministry was about to bring in a far tougher Occasional Conformity Bill to appease its High Church supporters in the Commons, and therefore thought it better to let a less stern one pass, especially if other political advantages could be reaped thereby. Yet many party supporters were outraged by this betrayal of the Whig tradition, and the very fact that the issue of liberty of conscience could now be given a low priority in the party agenda is perhaps indicative of the beginnings of the process whereby Whiggery was to divorce itself from the cause of Dissent. Although the Whigs repealed the Occasional Conformity and Schism Acts after the Hanoverian Succession, they took their time in doing so, and the party became bitterly divided on the issue.[24]

The Whigs also modified their stance on episcopacy, for the basic reason that they managed to capture a number of key positions within the Church hierarchy. There were an unprecedented number of vacancies following the Revolution, and many of the new appointments went to Low Churchmen who tended to be Whig in sympathy.[25] John Tillotson became Archbishop of Canterbury, to be succeeded by Thomas Tenison from 1695, whilst other latitudinarians such as Gilbert Burnet, Edward Fowler, Richard Kidder, Simon Patrick and Edward Stillingfleet also received bishoprics. The Low Church bishops proved to be valuable Parliamentary allies to the Whigs. Tenison and thirteen of the bishops voted against the Occasional Conformity Bill in the Lords in December 1702, playing a crucial role in defeating a measure which was lost by seventy-one votes to fifty-nine.[26]

As a result of this new alliance with the bishops, we see little of the anti-episcopalian rhetoric which had been such a prominent feature of the Whig platform during the Exclusion Crisis. John Tutchin, himself a Nonconformist and someone who had been involved in Monmouth's rebellion, frequently attacked the High Church lower clergy in his Whig periodical, *The Observator*, but was prepared to defend the Church hierarchy, saying that we had 'the best set of Bishops that ever England yet knew'.[27] Likewise the Whig Junto chief, John Somers, defended 'The Archbishop, and those of his worthy Brethren' against those who would 'traduce the Governors of the Church, as Enemies and Betrayers of it, and to make zealous Churchmen and others believe, that there are some men who are better Pastors, and truer Friends of the Church than the Bishops are'.[28] In contrast we find the Church party attacking the Church hierarchy. In 1694 the High Tory journalist Charles Leslie complained that 'we see among the newmade Bishops those who were formerly Fanatical Preachers; and those who, of all our Number, are least Zealous for the Church, and most Latitudinarian, for a Comprehension of Dissenters, and a Dispensation with our Liturgy and Discipline'.[29] The role of defending the Church was assumed by the lower clergy, their chief spokesman being Francis Atterbury. In February 1704 the Lower House of Convocation presented the Upper House with a representation of the grievances of the clergy, which was fiercely critical of the way the bishops were running the Church: canons were being disobeyed, discipline unenforced, whilst everywhere episcopal administration was inefficient and corrupt.[30] However, it must be stressed that the High Anglicans reserved their contempt for the Whig bishops; they recognised that there were some sound bishops (though not as many as they would like), and they remained committed to the defence of the institution of episcopacy. Indeed, in traditional High Church fashion, they were not ashamed to announce their belief in the divine-right nature of bishops. Thus in 1702 the Lower House of Convocation issued a declaration in which they denied that they were 'in Opposition to Episcopacy', asserting 'that we acknowledge the Order of Bishops . . . to be of Divine Apostolical Institution'.[31]

It is often suggested that the succession issue was a major source of controversy between Whigs and Tories. Such a statement is misleading, because it seems to imply that the Tories were Jacobites at heart; in fact, most Tories were able to accommodate themselves to the break in the succession which had taken place in 1688–9.[32] It is true that the Whigs did their best to exploit the Jacobite 'bogey', and their demands for an oath requiring peers, MPs and office-holders to abjure allegiance to James II and then the Old Pretender caused some embarrassment to those Tories who had only been prepared to recognise William as *de facto* King. Yet most Tories were as concerned as Whigs to protect the Protestant succession, and virtually all supported the Act of Settlement of 1701, which guaranteed the security of the Protestant monarchy in England by passing the descent of the Crown to the House of Hanover after the deaths of William and Anne.[33] The crisis over the succession which emerged at the end of Anne's reign did not so much divide the parties, but split the Tories. Nevertheless, Tories did remain committed to the principles of passive obedience, non-resistance and indefeasible hereditary right, but they were to argue that none of these had been compromised by the Glorious Revolution. A main source of disagreement between the parties, therefore, was over their interpretation of Revolution principles.[34]

For most Whigs, it was axiomatic that resistance had taken place at the Revolution; the logic of their position at Sacheverell's trial rested on this basic belief. Although few adopted a fully-fledged Lockeian position, most believed in the idea of a contract between rulers and ruled, the breaking of which had cost James II the throne. Thus in 1702 Daniel Defoe wrote of a 'mutual Compact between King and People', and defended the right to alter the succession 'in case of Tyranny and Illegal Governing'.[35] Whig writers frequently upheld the right to depose tyrants; as one author argued, Kings 'receive their Kingdoms upon Conditions from the Hands of the People' and 'one who has broke thro' all Laws . . . forfeits his Right to the Crown [and] releases his Subjects from their Obligation'.[36] It is true that the establishment Whigs found it increasingly necessary to downplay the original contract and the right of resistance, and came to argue that resistance was only allowable in exceptional circumstances, such as

those of 1688. Yet essentially Whigs agreed that the hereditary succession had been broken by the Glorious Revolution and that henceforth
the monarch had a Parliamentary title to the throne.

Most Tories denied that resistance had taken place in 1688. A few
did this by appealing to a providentialist explanation.[37] The majority,
however, did so by appealing to the view of the Revolution offered
by the Convention, that James had abdicated the throne. Charles
Leslie condemned the Whig identification of the deposing power with
'Revolution-Principles'; the actual Revolution Principle, that is, the
principle upon which the Convention proceeded, 'was the Vacancy of
the Throne, and Abdication, And not the Deposing Doctrine'.[38] The
Tory clergy repeatedly reasserted this doctrine in their sermons. For
example, six of the nine sermons delivered before the House of Commons on 30 January (the anniversary of Charles I's execution) between
1688 and 1700 explicitly condemned the deposition of kings.[39] Such
arguments enabled Tories to continue to pose as defenders of hereditary succession. According to one author, James II's abdication involved no abdication of his children's right, and therefore Anne
inherited the Crown 'as Queen of the Royal Succession, and not of
the Revolution'.[40] Passive obedience was still the rule, and rebellion
was directly contrary to the laws of the gospel.[41]

A minority of Tories were prepared to concede that there could be
exceptions to the theory of non-resistance *in extremis*, and in this they
admittedly came close to the doctrine of some of the more conservative Whigs. But there was an important difference, not only in the
primacy of stress placed on the doctrine of non-resistance, but also in
the fact that the concept of resistance upon breach of contract nowhere entered the language of Tory limited non-resistance. This is
well illustrated by a Tory tract of 1710. The author states that 'the
church-men hold an absolute passive obedience to be the duty of the
subjects', though he concluded that 'at the same time they allow, that
in cases where the ruin of the nation must otherwise ensure, the
necessity dispenses with the duty, and self-preservation takes place before any other law'. But this was different from the doctrine of resistance, which was not only Whiggish, but popish. For 'the modern
Whigs . . . make the bonds of allegiance so uncertain, press the
people so hard to resistance, and pass so lightly over the doctrine of
obedience, that they seem to make . . . the exception the rule'.
Moreover, the 'Modern Whigs' say that whenever 'the original contract is broken (which breach the Junto of Whigs pretend to be only
capable to give notice of) it becomes the indispensable duty to resist'.[42]

A third main cause of contention between the two parties was foreign policy. After the Glorious Revolution William was able to commit England to a continental alliance designed to contain the expansionism of Louis XIV's France, and to preserve the balance of power in Europe between the Bourbons and the Habsburgs. As a result, England became involved in major European warfare, first with the War of the League of Augsburg (1689–97), and then with the War of Spanish Succession (1702–13). The Whigs were firmly committed to the European alliance, and thought the best way to prosecute the war effort was through a full continental campaign. They supported the maintenance of a large army in Flanders, to which William and later Marlborough (Anne's commander-in-chief until 1711) gave priority. The Tories in general were more isolationist than the Whigs, although it would be wrong to suggest that they were not sympathetic to the desire to contain France after 1689. Thus most Tories supported the war with France in William's reign as both necessary and desirable, whilst it was a House of Commons with a Tory majority which committed England to war in defence of a balance of power in 1701. The Tories, however, were deeply critical of William and Marlborough's continental strategy, and instead favoured a blue-water policy, with emphasis on maritime and colonial operations. Few Tories were quite as extreme as the Earl of Rochester, who at the renewal of hostilities in 1702 argued for a strictly limited naval war as the best way to check the power of France, and most recognised the need for some form of combined operations. Yet all were critical of the commitment to the Flanders theatre, would have preferred to see some land forces redeployed in Spain, and saw the blue-water policy as central. Thus the Earl of Nottingham, Secretary of State from 1702 to 1704, and a chief advocate of such a strategy, wrote in 1703 that 'we shall never have any decisive success nor be able to hold out a war against France but by making it a sea War, and such a sea War as accompanies and supports attempts on land'.[43] From as early as 1708 most Tories were pushing for peace, so long as suitable terms could be reached with France. The Whigs, however, remained insistent that there should be no peace until the Bourbons had been driven out of Spain.[44]

A major ground of Tory opposition to Whig war strategy was expense. High wartime taxation was placing a heavy strain on the nation, and the Tories repeatedly claimed that they could 'manage the War with more Frugality than you Whigs'.[45] The Whigs, however, accused the Tories of being soft on France. One typical Whig satire of 1710 had Louis XIV thanking the Tories for coming to his rescue just as he was losing the war, saying 'your very Principles are agreeable to absolute Monarchy, and Designs of Tyranny; and your Practices are . . .

such as have often reliev'd and supported me'.[46] Eventually, the Tory ministry elected after 1710 was able to secure peace with the Treaty of Utrecht of 1713.

There seems to be much evidence for believing, therefore, that the bi-partisan model of political conflict holds good for much of the reigns of William and Anne. Party strife undoubtedly reached a peak of intensity under Anne; the death of Anne's sole-surviving child, the Duke of Gloucester, in 1700 raised once more questions about the security of the Protestant succession; religious tensions achieved a new height with the sitting of Convocation in 1701 and the campaign against occasional conformity; and England's re-entry into war that year renewed conflict on that front. Yet it is only really for a period in the early 1690s, as will be shown below, that the usefulness of the two-party model can be called into question. Moreover, the struggle between the Whigs and Tories suggests a large degree of continuity with the period before the Glorious Revolution: the Whigs are still the party of the Low Church and Dissent, of resistance theory, and committed to the need for an aggressive stance against France, whilst the Tories remain the party of the Church, of non-resistance, and more isolationist in foreign affairs.

The war of words between the two parties often reflected this sense of historical continuity, the roots of the divide frequently being traced back to the 1640s. Charles Davenant observed in 1710, 'what near Resemblance there was between the Old Rumper, and the Modern Whig (for a Child will be like his true Father) and how much they agreed in their Insolence to the Throne, Notions in Religion, Principles as to Government'.[47] The Whigs drew comparisons between the Tories and the Cavaliers of Charles I's reign, a heritage which the Tories were often not coy about acknowledging.[48] Much of the rhetoric used by both sides was couched in the language of no-popery, and bore a striking similarity to the arguments used during the Exclusion Crisis. The Whigs saw a dual popish threat: one external (from France), the other internal (from crypto-Catholics within England). According to a pamphlet of 1704, the present war was about whether England should be a popish or a Protestant country, since Louis XIV was advancing the cause of a popish prince to the throne of Great Britain, whilst at home the strength of the papists was increased 'by the Non-Jurors and Disaffected Persons of all sorts', who were zealous for a popish prince.[49] By contrast, High Anglican polemicists repeatedly sought to discredit the Whigs and Nonconformists by comparing them to Catholics and Jesuits. Leslie thought the Presbyterians were Protestant Jesuits: 'all the Mobb and Republican Principles, of Power in the People, etc. were taken from the Jesuits and Popish Doctors'.[50] Or as he put it elsewhere: 'the Deposing Doctrine, and placing the Power in the People, is but the Spittle of the Papists and Jesuits, which our Whigs and Dissenters have Lick't up'.[51] In a sermon of August 1710, Dr South accused the separatists and Dissenters of being 'the Pope's journeymen' who 'carry on his work' and 'do that for him which he cannot do for himself. . . . 'Tis their weakening the Church of England by their separation from it and their Invectives against it, that makes the Pope presume he may attack it . . . with Victory and Success'.[52]

COURT VERSUS COUNTRY AND THE TRANSFORMATION OF PARTY

If we accept the essence of the bi-partisan structure, we must recognise that political reality was not quite that simple. In the first place, divisions existed within the parties. Throughout Anne's reign we can see splits amongst the Tories, for example, with regard to their attitude towards occasional conformity.[53] From late 1710 we see the emergence of a distinct faction amongst the Tories, known as the October Club. The club, which met weekly every Wednesday evening throughout the Parliamentary session (usually at the Bell Tavern, Westminster), was composed of about 150 Tory backbenchers, and its main aim was to function as a pressure group to urge a more Tory policy on the Harley ministry.[54] Tory unity broke down seriously in the last years of Anne's reign with regard to the Hanoverian Succession. At either extreme there were committed minorities of Jacobites and pro-Hanoverians, with a majority in the middle whose attitudes were rather ambivalent. The Whigs, on the whole, were much more cohesive than the Tories, but even here we can make a distinction between Junto Whigs, Court Whigs and Country Whigs.[55] Nevertheless, the existence of such divisions does not mean that we have to talk of a multi-party system; rather, it seems better to talk of two parties, both representing a broad spectrum of political viewpoints which nevertheless remain recognisable as either Whig or Tory.

In the second place, it is important to appreciate that with time both parties underwent some degree of ideological transformation. This transformation represented a consistent outgrowth of existing Whig or Tory principles, but the fact that it occurred to a greater or lesser extent with different individuals helps explain why such a broad spectrum of opinion existed within the two parties. The most striking change that occurred was with regard to the parties' respective attitudes towards Court–Country issues. Over time the Country platform became increasingly identified with the Tory party, whilst the Whigs in turn essentially became a Court party. This transformation started in the early years of William's reign, and was largely complete by 1696.

England's involvement in European warfare after 1689 brought with it a massive expansion of the work of government, as more and more men had to be employed by the executive to meet the demands of war – in the Treasury office, and its dependent bodies the Customs, Excise, Mint and Tax Office, in the Army and Navy, and in the diplomatic service. Moreover, the establishment of the Bank of England in 1694, and the emergence of public deficit financing, led to the appearance of a new force in politics, that of the 'monied interest', men who had made huge fortunes as a result of investing in the national debt.[56] These developments greatly expanded the opportunities for political patronage, enabling the government to reward an increasing number of its followers both outside and inside Parliament with offices, pensions, or just straightforward bribes. Contemporary estimates for the period 1692–98 put the number of placemen at between 97 and 136 (to which would have to be added receivers of unreported Crown pensions or bribes), a figure which may have risen to 200 by 1714.[57] Although placemen never formed a majority in the Commons, attendance at the House was often low – the average attendance per session during William's reign was 238 – so their significance could be immense if they consistently and unanimously backed the government. The government interest was even stronger in the upper chamber, where by the end of Anne's reign between 40 per cent to 50 per cent of those peers active in the house held places or pensions from the Court.[58]

Concern about the growth of the executive led to the pursuit of a number of measures designed to limit the power of the Court and to preserve the independence of Parliament. One way contemporaries sought to curtail the influence of the Court was by securing free and frequent Parliamentary elections, and therefore electoral reform became a key element to the Country platform. Although proposals for secret ballots and annual elections came to nothing, a Triennial Bill was passed into law in 1694, whilst in 1696 Acts were passed to prevent electoral charges and expenses (to keep the price of a contest within the gentry's means) and to prevent local changes in the established franchise (which were generally thought to be made to the

Court's advantage). Between 1695 and 1705 four attempts were made to restrict membership of Parliament to men of landed wealth, in the belief that men of such independent means would be less susceptible to Court bribery, until eventually a Land Qualification Bill was passed in 1711. Bills seeking to exclude various categories of placemen from Parliament were introduced on average once every session between 1692 and 1714, and a general measure banning all placemen from the Commons found its way into the Act of Settlement of 1701 (which laid down the conditions on which the Hanoverians would succeed to the throne), although this provision was subsequently modified before the Act came into effect. The fact that William's style of governing tended to be rather autocratic also provoked opposition to the Court. William's suspension of habeas corpus in the early years of the war, his use of the royal veto, and his attempt to retain a standing army in peacetime after the Treaty of Ryswick in 1697, further aroused Country suspicions about the strength of the executive.[59]

It cannot be denied that Court–Country tensions did exist; the question to consider is the extent to which they cut across party, and served to undermine the pattern of political allegiances mapped out above. In fact, there was only a small nucleus of non-party men who were prepared to support the Court on all occasions – men such as the Secretary of War, William Blathwayt, or Treasury Secretary, William Lowndes, who were essentially civil servants. There were larger numbers of Whig and Tories who found the pull of Court strong enough to override party loyalty. The Leeds Tories (the followers of the former Earl of Danby, now Duke of Leeds), stayed in office after the rise of the Junto in 1694, whilst the moderate Whig Dukes of Shrewsbury, Somerset and Newcastle worked with the Tories after the fall of the Whig ministry in 1710.[60] Yet it is a testimony to the strength of party during this period that the Court, despite the resources of patronage at its disposal, largely failed to establish itself as an independent interest. Time and again Court politicians found themselves becoming tied to one party as the only way to pursue their policies effectively. Political disputes between his Whig and Tory ministers forced William to abandon his experiment with mixed administrations and work through the Junto. During Anne's reign, Godolphin and Marlborough – two old Tories of the pre-Revolution type – found themselves becoming increasingly dependent upon the Whigs, because the Tories were unwilling to back their wartime policies, so that by 1708–10 they were heading a Whig ministry. Placemen were seldom independent of party, since the bestowal of government favours or jobs became a way through which the governing party of the day was able to reward its

followers. Thus placemen tended to take their cue from party chieftains rather than from the sovereign or Court, and when a party fell
from power there usually followed a purge of its placemen.[61]

The only time it makes sense to talk of a distinctive Country party
in Parliament, in the sense of a genuine coalition of dissident Whigs
and Tories who were united in their opposition to the government, is
for the years 1691–5. During this period a group of Country Whigs,
led by Robert Harley and Paul Foley, separated from their former
allies who were in office, and united with Country and out-of-office
Tories to promote place bills, triennial bills, and measures against corruption. An illustration of the complex pattern of cross-party allegiances in the early 1690s is provided by the stance taken on the abortive
Triennial Bill of 1693. The measure was supported by dissident Tories
(such as Sir Thomas Clarges and Sir Christopher Musgrave), Country
Whigs (such as Robert Harley, Paul Foley, John Howe and Sir
Thomas Pelham), as well as some Court Whigs (such as the Earl of
Shrewsbury, Thomas Wharton, Sir John Trenchard and Edward Russell).
On the other hand the measure was opposed by some Whig ministers
(such as Lord Somers and Charles Montagu), Tory ministers (such as
Sir John Lowther, Sir Richard Temple and Sir Edward Seymour), and
by some rank and file Tories (such as Sir Gilbert Dolben, Sir Joseph
Tredenham and Heneage Finch, the son of the Earl of Nottingham).
What we have, it seems, is a Court–Country division cutting across
party, but one that is blurred by the fact that some old Tories (even
though backbenchers) opposed a measure which they thought was an
encroachment on the royal prerogative, whilst some Whigs (even
those close to the Court) felt obliged to support a measure which
reflected old Whig principles.[62] The fusion of a Country coalition in
opposition to the Court in the early 1690s was assisted by the common experience of working on the Commission of Public Accounts,
which led a number of Tories and Whigs to realise they had more in
common with each other than with their supposed party allies at
Court.[63] Yet by 1696, when we can test the voting behaviour through
division lists, it appears that the struggle between Court and Country
had become largely submerged within the conflict between Whigs and
Tories. Of those Whigs who were elected to serve in the new Parliament of 1690, by April 1691, according to Harley, about 125 were in
opposition, and some 85 supported the Court. In contrast, by the time
we get to the division over the standing army in 1699 – normally
thought to have been a Court–Country rather than a party issue –
there were only 36 Whigs out of a total of 221 on the Country side.
During Anne's reign the number of genuinely Country Whigs grew

even smaller; the vast majority of those who supported Country positions were Tories.[64]

The Country platform came to be supported mainly by Tories for
the simple reason that the logic of the anti-executive position as it
developed in William's reign was essentially Tory. It was the war
which had led to the great increase in government patronage and
hence also the potential for Court influence, and this was by and large
a Whig war. The Country opposition were also deeply suspicious of
the influence of the new financial interest, and a significant number of
those who had benefited from the financial revolution of the 1690s
were Whigs, many of them Dissenters.[65] The Country was suspicious
of an executive headed by a King who not only lacked an hereditary
title, but who was also Dutch, employed Dutch favourites (notably
William Bentinck, who became the Earl of Portland), and who was a
Calvinist. The death of Mary in 1694, which left William as sole ruling monarch, had the effect of furthering the Tory commitment to a
Country platform, whilst at the same time increasing the reluctance of
those who normally supported the Whigs from engaging in any criticism of the Crown. Harley thought that it was from 1694 that the
Dissenters acted 'against all their principles and the liberties of the nation' by adhering to the ministerial section of the Whig party.[66] It was
the Jacobite conspiracy of February 1696 and the subsequent demand
by the Junto that MPs sign an Association asserting that William was
'rightful and lawful King of these realms' which most seriously under-
mined the bi-partisan nature of the Country platform. Whilst Whigs
of all complexions signed with no hesitation, the Country Tories were
much more reluctant to swear allegiance in such unqualified terms,
although many eventually complied when signing was made compul-
sory.[67]

A group of Country Whigs certainly remained important 'out-of-
doors', in carrying on the propaganda war against the Court. The
anti-standing army campaign was led by radical Whigs such as John
Trenchard, Walter Moyle and Andrew Fletcher of Saltoun, who held
their own club at the Grecian Coffee House in Devereux Court off
Essex Street, London. Of about forty tracts on the standing army issue,
only one was written by an identifiable Tory. These tracts did in part
reflect a radical Whig philosophy: for example, the connection was
made between a standing army in peacetime and absolutism, and it
was also suggested that the right to resist would be nullified by a
standing army. But the anti-army writers also showed a need to appeal
to the sensibilities of their Tory allies in Parliament. Thus when
Fletcher argued that England was in no danger from France at this

time, or Trenchard reasoned that, should war occur, England's role should be 'to undertake the Sea', both were making what were essentially Tory points.[68] From the end of William's reign, when contemporaries talked of a struggle between Court and Country, they were describing what we would more readily recognise as a clash between Whigs and Tories. Thus when James Drake published his tract of 1702 attacking the strength of the Court interest, he was essentially attacking the Whigs who constituted that Court interest, and developed a 'Country' argument which was basically Tory in nature, with a heavy emphasis on the need to defend the interest of the Church of England.[69] Likewise in January 1702, James Craggs referred to 'the Church (or Country) Party'.[70]

The changing positions of the two parties *vis-à-vis* the Court caused a certain realignment in their respective constitutional positions. Some Tories came to develop the view that the combined legislative of Crown, Lords and Commons was the sovereign authority in the state. In the House of Lords on 30 January 1700, when the Tory Archbishop of York, John Sharp, defended traditional Anglican doctrines of non-resistance and passive obedience, he made it clear that the authority which must be obeyed was the law of the land.[71] In 1701 Sir Humphrey Mackworth maintained that 'Absolute Supreme, and Legislative Authority in England . . . [was] Lodg'd in the King, the Lords and the Commons'.[72] Sacheverell's defence counsel in 1710 did not deny that their client had defended non-resistance, but tried to define non-resistance as applying only to the Crown-in-Parliament, rather than the monarchy itself.[73] This seems a far cry from the Toryism of the Exclusion Crisis: the Oxford Decree of 1683 had condemned the doctrine that the Crown was one of the three estates. Some Tories even employed the Whig exclusionist language of the ancient constitution, and suggested that Parliaments predated the Norman Conquest.[74] In contrast, government Whigs can be found defending the prerogative rights of the Crown – notably *vis-à-vis* the Church in the Convocation controversy, but also on a number of other issues – and in so doing invoked a vision of England's feudal past similar to that employed by Tories during the Exclusion Crisis.[75] Contemporaries frequently commented upon this ideological transformation, accusing modern Whigs of acting on old Tory principles, and new Tories of practising the opposite of what they had formerly professed.[76] In May 1711, Jonathan Swift wrote that the two parties had so shifted their principles since Charles II's time, 'that those two fantastick Names of Whig and Tory, have at present very little Relation to those Opinions, which were at first thought to distinguish them'.[77]

The extent of this transformation must not be exaggerated, however. More extreme Tories continued to attack the theory of co-ordination (maintaining that the monarch was not one of the three estates, which instead comprised the Lords Spiritual, Lords Temporal and the Commons) and to uphold the view that 'our Kings and Queens are above the Law'.[78] Likewise, we can still find examples of Tories attacking the theory of the ancient constitution and Whigs defending it.[79] We also have to recognise that certain rhetorical strategies might be adopted for tactical reasons, especially the ploy of using one's opponents' arguments against them in order to discredit their position. In his tract justifying the activities of the Commons in the Parliament of 1701, when the Tories had made a number of attacks on the policies of the Court Whigs, culminating in the attempted impeachment of some of the Junto Lords, the High Anglican Tory, James Drake, found it plausible in one place to quote Algernon Sidney in support of his argument about the rights of the lower House; the tract as a whole, however, makes it clear that Drake can in no way be considered a convert to Sidney's particular brand of radical Whiggery.[80] Moreover, the ideological shifts that did occur can be seen to be consistent outgrowths of earlier party positions; they did not represent, as contemporary propagandists liked to suggest, an abandonment of previous principles. Tory legal-constitutionalism was nothing new in the early eighteenth century – it is in evidence during the years of the Exclusion Crisis and Tory reaction, and its roots can be traced back to the Clarendonian position at the Restoration. It is merely that after the Glorious Revolution this element within Tory ideology became increasingly dominant, gradually supplanting the more absolutist tendency within Tory political thought. But throughout our period the Tories retained an essentially authoritarian ideology. They denied that subjects possessed inalienable natural rights which would allow them to question the legitimacy of duly constituted authority, and those who maintained that sovereignty was vested in the Crown-in-Parliament did so in order to undermine Whig populist notions that the people could call their rulers to account. Typical in this respect are the views of Offspring Blackall, who became Bishop of Exeter in 1708. Blackall rejected the Filmerian claim that only absolute monarchy was legitimate, and acknowledged that God had allowed different forms of government to develop in different places at different times. Nevertheless he continued to insist that all government was of divine institution, and that political authority was conferred by God, so that resistance to the 'powers-that-be' was always a sin, regardless of what form that political authority took. For the magistrate was God's servant, Blackall maintained, and was 'subject only to God, and [was] not . . . accountable to the people'. Subjects therefore had to obey the laws of their earthly governors, in whatever they commanded that was not contrary to divine law.[81]

On the other side, the Whig defence of the executive was not totally new after 1689. Whigs and Dissenters had in the past shown themselves prepared to defend the prerogative powers of the Crown, especially in the ecclesiastical sphere, as we have seen with regard to the Declarations of Indulgence in 1672 and 1687, and Danby's proposals for limitations on a popish successor in 1677. Even during the Exclusion Crisis there were many conservative Whigs who saw Exclusion as the only way to preserve strong monarchy in England. Throughout our period, however, we see that Whigs were prepared to hold up an independent standard by which to assess the legitimacy of authority, that of fundamental law or natural law, and they were willing to challenge the legitimacy of established authority (whether royal or Parliamentary) if power was exercised in violation of people's natural rights. Magna Carta was frequently appealed to as a fundamental law which imposed limits on the sovereignty of the legislature. Gilbert Burnet was repeating an old Whig commonplace when he wrote: 'It was a maxim among our lawyers, that even an Act of Parliament against Magna Carta was null of itself'.[82] Some insight into the Whig perspective is provided by the controversy over the Kentish petition towards the end of William's reign. In May 1701 five Kentish gentlemen, probably with the encouragement of the Whig Junto, had presented the Tory House of Commons with a petition from the freeholders and grand jury at the Maidstone Quarter Sessions demanding war against France. The peace party in the Commons condemned the petition as 'scandalous, insolent and seditious', and ordered the promoters of the petition into custody. In a tract written in defence of the petitioners, Lord Somers, the Junto chief, bitterly inveighed against the House of Commons, accusing it of encroaching upon the executive powers of the Crown by seeking to impose punishments without the King's authority. In a deliberate attempt to embarrass Tories and High Anglicans, he cited Charles II's Declaration of April 1681, which had condemned the then Whig-dominated House of Commons for arresting people for matters not relating to Parliamentary privilege, whilst in defence of the right of petitioning he cited the case of the seven bishops of 1688. But he also used more populist arguments with a distinctly radical Whig heritage, arguing that the House, by imprisoning the petitioners, had violated both positive law and natural law (citing John Locke's *Two Treatises of Government*), and had invaded people's rights contrary to Magna Carta.[83] The Whigs were concerned that the arbitrary power of a prince was being replaced by the arbitrary power of the legislature. As John Tutchin was later to ask, 'Did our Fore-Fathers struggle so hard to curb the Ambition of their Kings who Invaded their Birth-Rights', only for us to be 'Oppress'd by that very Power with which our Ancestors Defended their Liberties?'[84] For both Somers and Tutchin, our representatives were the 'Trustees and Guardians of the People's Liberties'; if 'instead of Executing this Trust, they do make a Forcible Attempt upon our Liberties. . . . They have Betray'd their Trust'.[85]

CONCLUSION

The party conflict which had been in the process of emerging in England since 1660, and which had led to the clash between Whigs and Tories during the Exclusion Crisis, continued to develop after the Glorious Revolution, and reached a new height of intensity in the reign of Queen Anne. The evidence of division lists, voting patterns of peers and MPs, organisational structure, and ideological dispute, all serve to confirm the impression of a basic Whig–Tory conflict in England at this time, at least for the period after 1696; indeed, we can even talk about a two-party system. Saying this does not mean that the parties were monolithic; there were differences of opinion between moderate and extreme wings then as there are today with our major parties. Nor should we assume that the parties were static. Indeed, one of the hallmarks of a living party system is that the parties develop or even modify their positions over time, as they seek to adapt to changing political circumstances. By the end of Anne's reign we can detect some clear ideological shifts; nevertheless, there are many ways in which the Whigs and Tories were still the recognisable heirs of their earlier namesakes. In this respect, our longer chronological perspective has been vital to our understanding of the significance of these developments in party ideology. For example, the stress many Tories came to place on the sovereignty of the law under Queen Anne is easy to comprehend given what we discovered earlier about the profound attachment many Tory Anglicans had to the rule of law even prior to the Glorious Revolution. What might be called a conservative legal-constitutionalism is a consistent theme within Tory-Anglican thought throughout our period, even though not all Tory Anglicans would have argued such a position at all times with the same degree of commitment. Likewise, our earlier analysis of the roots of Whiggery make it possible to appreciate why a Court Whig position developed after the Glorious Revolution; there always existed such a potential for such a development, but it required the right political circumstances to enable it to come to fruition. By concentra-ting, as we have been, on high politics at the centre, we have so far omitted an important dimension of the story. Our understanding of what was happening to party politics under William and Anne can only be complete when we consider the wider world outside Westminster, which will be the subject of the following chapter.

REFERENCES

1.   *A Letter to a Modern Dissenting Whig* (1701), p. 5.
2.   Holmes, *British Politics in the Age of Anne*, pp. 13–20; David Hayton, 'The "Country" Interest and the Party System, 1689–c.1720', in Jones (ed.), *Party and Management in Parliament 1660–1784*, p. 37; Kenyon, *Revolution Principles The Politics of Party 1689–1720*, p. 55.
3.   Robert Walcott, 'English Party Politics (1688–1714)', in *Essays in Modern History in Honor of Wilbur Cortez Abbott* (Cambridge, Mass., 1941), pp. 81–131; *Idem.*, *English Politics in the Early Eighteenth Century* (Oxford, 1956).
4.   Plumb, *The Growth of Political Stability in England 1675–1725*; W. A. Speck, 'The House of Commons 1702–1714: A Study in Political Organization', unpub. Oxford DPhil thesis (1965); W. A. Speck, 'Whigs and Tories Dim their Glories: English Political Parties under the First Two Georges', in John Cannon (ed.), *The Whig Ascendancy: Colloquies on Hanoverian England* (1981), pp. 51–76; Holmes, *British Politics*; Henry Horwitz, 'The Structure of Parliamentary Politics', in Holmes (ed.), *Britain after the Glorious Revolution, 1689–1714*, pp. 96–114.
5.   The attempt by Denis Rubini, *Court and Country, 1688–1702* (1967), to define politics during William's reign primarily in Court–Country terms, is unconvincing. See Henry Horwitz, *Parliament, Policy and Politics in the Reign of William III* (1977).
6.   There are lists of placemen, however: Harley's list of c. 1691 and Grascome's list of the Court party from 1693.
7.   Speck, 'Whigs and Tories', p. 54; *Idem, Tory and Whig: The Struggle in the Constituencies, 1701–1715*, pp. 111–12; Horwitz, *Parliament, Policy and Politics*, p. 319. Cf. appendix C; Holmes, *British Politics*, pp. 34–40; I. F. Burton, P. W. J. Riley and E. Rowlands, *Political Parties in the Reigns of William and Anne: The Evidence of Division Lists* (*BIHR*, Spe-

cial Supplement 7, 1968); p. 37; J. G. Sperling, 'The Division of 25 May 1711, on an Amendment to the South Sea Bill: A Note on the Reality of Parties in the Age of Anne', *HJ*, **4** (1961), pp. 191–217; Henry L. Snyder, 'Party Configurations in the Early Eighteenth-Century House of Commons', *BIHR*, **45** (1972), pp. 38–72; Aubrey Newman (ed.), *The Parliamentary Lists of the Early Eighteenth Century: Their Compilation and Use* (1973); David Hayton and Clyve Jones (eds), *A Register of Parliamentary Lists 1660–1761* (University of Leicester History Department Occasional Publication, no. 1, 1979).

8. Horwitz, *Parliament, Policy and Politics*, appendix B.
9. Cruickshanks, Hayton and Jones, 'Divisions in the House of Lords', in Clyve Jones and David Lewis Jones (eds), *Peers, Politics and Power: The House of Lords, 1603–1911*.
10. Holmes, *British Politics*, pp. 36–7, appendix A.
11. Clyve Jones, 'Godolphin, the Whig Junto and the Scots: A New Division List from 1709', in Jones and Jones (eds), *Peers, Politics and Power*, pp. 133–49; Geoffrey Holmes, 'The Hamilton Affair of 1711–1712: A Crisis in Anglo-Scottish Relations', in *ibid.*, pp. 151–76.
12. David Hayton, 'Moral Reform and Country Politics in the Late Seventeenth-Century House of Commons', *PP*, **128** (1990), pp. 48–91.
13. Holmes, *British Politics*, pp. 39–46; Horwitz, 'Structure of Parliamentary Politics', pp. 101–2, 104–5; Henry L. Snyder, 'The Contribution and Limitations of Division Lists to the Study of Parliamentary Parties', in Newman (ed.), *Parliamentary Lists*, pp. 63–7.
14. Margaret, Lady Verney (ed.), *Verney Letters of the Eighteenth Century* (2 vols, 1930), **I**, p. 305; Huntington Library, Stowe MSS 26 (1–2), James Brydges's Diary, 1697–1702: 21 Jan. 1699, 13 Feb. 1699, 27 Feb. 1699; Holmes and Speck, *Divided Society*, pp. 160–1, 163, 166; Horwitz, *Parliament, Policy and Politics*, pp. 208–9; Hill, The *Growth of Parliamentary Parties 1689–1742*, p. 71; Holmes, *British Politics*, chs 7–9; Speck, *Tory and Whig*, chs 3, 4; Snyder, 'Party Configurations', p. 39; E. L. Ellis, 'The Whig Junto, in Relation to the Development of Party Politics and Party Organization, from its inception to 1714', unpub. Oxford DPhil thesis (1967), pp. 499–500; Clyve Jones, 'The Parliamentary Organization of the Whig Junto in the Reign of Queen Anne: The Evidence of Lord Ossulston's Diary', *Parliamentary History*, **10** (1991), pp. 164–82.
15. *HMC, 5th Report*, p. 376.
16. [William Stephens], *An Account of the Growth of Deism in England* (1696), p. 8.
17. Mark Goldie, 'The Nonjurors, Episcopacy, and the Origins of the Convocation Controversy', in Eveline Cruickshanks (ed.), *Ideology and Conspiracy: Aspects of Jacobitism, 1689–1759* (Edinburgh, 1982), pp. 15–35.
18. Henry L. Snyder, 'The Defeat of the Occasional Conformity Bill and the Tack: A Study in the Techniques of Parliamentary Management in the Reign of Queen Anne', in Jones and Jones (eds), *Peers, Politics and Power*, pp. 111–31; W[illiam] P[ittis], *The Proceedings of both Houses of*

Parliament, in the Years 1702, 1703, 1704, Upon the Bill to Prevent Occasional Conformity (1710).

19. W. A. Speck, 'An Anonymous Parliamentary Diary, 1705–6', *Camden Miscellany*, **23** (1969), pp. 82–4.

20. Holmes, *British Politics*, pp. 84–5, 91–2; T. C. Smout, 'The Road to Union', in Holmes (ed.), *Britain after the Glorious Revolution*, pp. 176–96; P. W. J. Riley, *The Union of England and Scotland: A Study in Anglo-Scottish Politics of the Eighteenth Century* (Manchester, 1978).

21. Geoffrey Holmes, *The Trial of Doctor Sacheverell* (1973).

22. H. T. Dickinson, 'The Tory Party's Attitude to Foreigners: A Note on Party Principles in the Age of Anne', *BIHR*, **40** (1967), pp. 153–67; H.T.Dickinson, 'The Poor Palatines and the Parties', *EHR*, **82** (1967), pp. 464 85; Daniel Statt, 'The Controversy over the Naturalization of Foreigners in England, 1660–1760', unpub. Cambridge PhD thesis (1987).

23. BL, Loan 29/320, 13 Jan. 1708/9.

24. Hill, *Growth of Parliamentary Parties*, p. 135; Holmes, *British Politics*, p. 113; Kenyon, *Revolution Principles*, pp. 178–80; G. M. Townend, 'Religious Radicalism and Conservatism in the Whig Party under George I: The Repeal of the Occasional Conformity and Schism Acts', *Parliamentary History*, **7** (1988), pp. 24–44.

25. Cf. G. V. Bennett, 'King William III and the Episcopate', in G. V. Bennett and J. D. Walsh (eds), *Essays in Modern English Church History* (1966).

26. N. Sykes, 'The Cathedral Chapter of Exeter and the General Election of 1705', *EHR*, **45** (1930), p. 261.

27. John Tutchin, *Observator*, **IV**, no. 17, 26–30 May 1705.

28. [John Somers], *Jura Populi Anglicani* (1701), p. xiii.

29. [Leslie], *Querela Temporum*, p. 16.

30. Bennett, *The Tory Crisis in Church and State, 1688–1730: The Career of Francis Atterbury, Bishop of Rochester*, p. 72.

31. James Drake, *The Memorial of the Church of England* (1711, first pub. 1705), p. 24; [Charles Leslie], *The Wolf Strip't of His Shepherd's Clothing* (1704), p. 28; *An Account of the Proceedings Between the Two Houses of Convocation which met October the 20th 1702* (1704).

32. For Jacobitism, see below, ch. 8.

33. We know for certain of only one Tory MP, Sir John Granville, who spoke against the Act of Settlement, although Sir Francis Child *may* have joined him. *Vine Tavern Queries* [1701]. I am grateful to David Hayton for this point.

34. Kenyon, *Revolution Principles*.

35. Daniel Defoe, *A New Test of the Church of England's Loyalty* (1702), pp. 24–5.

36. *An Antidote against Rebellion* (1704), pp. 40, 48.

37. Gerald M. Straka, *Anglican Reaction to the Revolution of 1688* (Madison, Wisconsin, 1962); *Idem.*, 'The Final Phase of Divine Right Theory in England, 1688–1702', *EHR*, **77** (1962), pp. 638–58.

38. Leslie, *Rehearsal*, **I**, no. 86, 16 Feb. 1705/6. Cf. [Charles Davenant], *Saul and Samuel; Or, The Common Interest of our King and Country* (1702), p. 40.

39. M. A. Goldie, 'Tory Political Thought 1689–1714', unpub. Cambridge PhD thesis (1977), pp. 11–12.

40. *The Principles of the Observator Examin'd* (1704), p. 11.

41. Henry Gandy, *Some Remarks on a Sermon . . . Or, Some Queries proposed to . . . Dr Kennet* (1704), p. 6; [Charles Leslie], *The Good Old Cause; Or, Lying in Truth* (1710), pp. 28–9 (summarising the argument of his periodical, the *Rehearsal*).

42. *The True, Genuine Modern Whig Address* (1710), in *Somers Tracts*, Walter Scott (ed.) (13 vols, 1809–15), **XII**, pp. 661–2.

43. Quoted in Feiling, *A History of the Tory Party 1640–1714*, p. 368.

44. Holmes, *British Politics*, pp. 73–80.

45. Charles Davenant, *Sir Thomas Double at Court* (1710), p. 63.

46. [Benjamin Hoadley], *The French King's Thanks to the Tories of Great-Britain* (1710), p. 2.

47. Davenant, *Sir Thomas Double at Court*, p. 35.

48. [M. Tindal], *The Nation Vindicated* (1711), p. 15.

49. *Expostulatory Letters* (1704), pp. 7, 10.

50. Leslie, *Rehearsal*, **I**, no. 25, 13–20 Jan. 1705.

51. [Leslie], *Wolf Strip't of His Shepherd's Cloathing*, p. 4.

52. Bodl. Lib., MS Carte 206, fol. 88.

53. Bennett, *Tory Crisis*, pp. 73–80.

54. H. T. Dickinson, 'The October Club', *HLQ*, **33** (1970), pp. 155–73; D. Szechi, *Jacobitism and Tory Politics 1710–14* (Edinburgh, 1984), pp. 73–84.

55. Holmes, *British Politics*, chs 7, 8; Ellis, 'Whig Junto'.

56. Plumb, *Growth of Political Stability*, ch 4; John Brewer, *The Sinews of Power: War, Money and the English State, 1688–1783* (1989).

57. Rubini, *Court and Country 1688–1702*, p. 32; Holmes and Speck, *Divided Society*, p. 5.

58. Horwitz, 'Structure of Parliamentary Politics', p. 107; Holmes, *British Politics*, p. 387. See also appendices A and B, pp. 421–39.

59. Rubini, *Court and Country*; H. T. Dickinson, *Liberty and Property: Political Ideology in Eighteenth-Century Britain* (1977), ch. 3; Schwoerer, '*No Standing Armies!': The Anti-Army Ideology in Seventeenth–Century England*, ch. 8.

60. Dickinson, *Liberty and Property*, pp. 97–8; Hayton, 'The "Country" Interest', pp. 41–2.

61. Plumb, *Growth of Political Stability*, pp. 126–7; Holmes and Speck, *Divided Society*, p. 5; Snyder, 'Party Configurations', pp. 39–40.

62. Feiling, *Tory Party*, p. 290; Kenyon, *Revolution Principles*, p. 41; Dickinson, *Liberty and Property*, pp. 44, 96–7.

63. J. A. Downie, 'The Commission of Public Accounts and the Formation of the Country Party', *EHR*, **91** (1976), pp. 33–51. Cf. Angus McInnes, *Robert Harley: Puritan Politician* (1970), pp. 41–5; B. W. Hill,

Robert Harley: Speaker, Secretary of State and Premier Minister (1988), pp. 26–33.

64. Hayton, 'The "Country" Interest', pp. 46–52; David Hayton, 'The Country Party in the House of Commons 1698–1699: A Forecast of the Opposition to a Standing Army', *Parliamentary History*, **6** (1987), pp. 141–63.

65. De Krey, *A Fractured Society: The Politics of London in the First Age of Party, 1688–1715*; Henry Horwitz, 'Party in a Civic Context: London from the Exclusion Crisis to the Fall of Walpole', in Jones (ed.), *Britain in the First Age of Party, 1680–1750: Essays Presented to Geoffrey Holmes*, p. 183.

66. Cited in Hill, *Growth of Parliamentary Parties*, p. 60.

67. McInnes, *Harley*, p. 51; Rubini, *Court and Country*, p. 52; Cruickshanks, 'Religion and Royal Succession: The Rage of Party', in Jones (ed.), *Britain in the First Age of Party*, p. 29.

68. [Andrew Fletcher], *A Discourse Concerning Militias and Standing Armies* (1697), pp. 15, 16; [John Trenchard], *A Short History of Standing Armies in England* (1698), p. 44; Schwoerer, 'No Standing Armies!', pp. 177, 180–1; Hayton, 'The "Country" Interest', pp. 56–60; Goldie, 'Tory Political Thought', p. 169, footnote 12.

69. [James Drake], *History of the Last Parliament* (1702).

70. Cited in Hayton, 'Country Party in the House of Commons', p. 161, footnote 25.

71. John Sharp, *A Sermon Preached before the Lords . . . On the Thirtieth of January 1699/1700* (1700), pp. 14, 20–1.

72. Humphrey Mackworth, *A Vindication of the Rights of the Commons of England* (1701), p. 2.

73. *State Trials*, **XV**, cols 196–7; Holmes, *Trial of Doctor Sacheverell*, pp. 182–4; Hill, *Growth of Parliamentary Parties*, p. 124; Dickinson, *Liberty and Property*, pp. 46–50.

74. Francis Atterbury, *The Rights, Powers, and Privileges of an English Convocation, Stated and Vindicated* (2nd edn, 1701), ch. 2; William Oldisworth, *A Dialogue between Timothy and Philatheus* (3 vols, 1709–11), **II**, p. 227.

75. Goldie, 'Tory Political Thought', ch. 8; R. J. Smith, *The Gothic Bequest: Medieval Institutions in British Thought, 1688–1863* (Cambridge, 1987), pp. 28–38.

76. [Charles Davenant], *The True Picture of a Modern Whig* (1701); [Somers], *Jura Populi*, pp. viii–x.

77. Jonathan Swift, *Examiner*, no. 44, 31 May 1711, in Frank H. Ellis (ed.), *Swift vs. Mainwaring: The Examiner and the Medley* (Oxford, 1985), pp. 454, 456.

78. *Principles of the Observator Examined*, pp. 13–14; Luke Milbourne, *The People not the Original of Civil Power* (1707), pp. 13–14.

79. Davenant, *Saul and Samuel*, ch. 4; *A Vindication of the Rights and Prerogatives of the Right Honourable The House of Lords* (1701), p. 5.

80 [Drake], *History of the Last Parliament*, p. 149.

81. Offspring Blackall, *The Divine Institution of Magistracy* (1709), esp. pp. 6, 12–13; Goldie, 'Tory Political Thought', pp. 179–82; Dickinson, *Liberty and Property*, pp. 48–9.
82. Cited in Dickinson, *Liberty and Property*, p. 83.
83. [Somers], *Jura Populi*.
84. Tutchin, *Observator*, **IV**, no. 2, 4–7 Apr. 1705.
85. Somers, *Jura Populi*, p. 29; Tutchin, *Observator*, **IV**, no. 5, 14–18 Apr. 1705. Cf. Kenyon, *Revolution Principles*, pp. 56–9; Anne Pallister, *Magna Carta: The Heritage of Liberty* (Oxford, 1971), pp. 49–50.

CHAPTER SEVEN

The Divided Society under William and Anne

The preceding chapter concentrated on party divisions at the level of the elite, looking at the structure of Parliamentary politics under William and Anne and the nature of the ideological disputes between Whigs and Tories. It is now necessary to consider how far down the social scale these party tensions permeated. The conventional view has been that political strife was so intense between 1689 and 1715 because party divisions cut deep into society; all elements of the population, from the gentry, through to the merchants, professionals, artisanal and trading classes, the small farmers, right down to the 'mob', were caught up in the rage of party.[1] Advocates of such an interpretation have placed particular stress on the role of the electorate in fuelling party conflict at this time. The electorate was steadily expanding during the course of the Stuart century, so that by Anne's reign perhaps as many as one in four adult males had the right to vote, whilst the passage of the Triennial Act in 1694 meant that those who were enfranchised had the opportunity to make their voice known in frequently contested elections. Scholars such as Plumb, Holmes and Speck have painted a picture of an independent and politically aware electorate whose voting behaviour was swayed by considerations of party allegiance and their attitudes towards the political issues of the day. The fact that on the whole constituencies tended to return MPs on distinct party platforms, even on occasion issuing instructions to those chosen advising them how to act once in Parliament, has led to the conclusion that the electorate played a large part in perpetuating the intensity of party strife at Westminster.[2]

Such a view has come under attack in recent years. Rather than seeing the electorate as independent and politically minded, it has been argued that they were easily susceptible to manipulation from above, and that they tended to defer to the wishes of their social superiors. Government influence, ranging from direct bribery to more subtle forms of patronage and manipulation, it has been argued, played the key role in shaping the outcome of elections, with the result that, at least under Anne, the ministry of the day never lost a General Election.[3] J. C. D. Clark has asserted that government at St James's and Westminster was conducted 'in terms which usually owed relatively little to a sense of popular pressure or wide accountability', and although he cannot deny that the electorate was growing in the period *c.* 1680–1715, he attributes this to the attempts by the party leaders to manipulate the potential electorate for their own purposes: 'The parties, in other words, created their electorate in these years (rather than vice versa)'.[4]

The survival of poll books for the reigns of William and Anne has made the analysis of electoral behaviour an attractive method of testing the political attitudes of those below the level of the elite, since a careful tabulation of voting behaviour seems to offer the possibility of a fairly scientific means of assessing swings in public opinion across the nation as a whole. Without denying the value of this approach, poll book analysis is really the wrong place to start if we are interested in determining the extent to which party tensions existed in society at large. Elections have to be seen as a product of the political culture which produced them. We need to analyse the interaction between electors, whose attitudes have already been influenced by a variety of considerations (ranging from their own sense of both national and local political issues, down to whatever perception they might have concerning their need to accommodate themselves to their social superiors), and the party electioneers, who were determined to influence the electorate in whatever way they thought fit (which invariably meant a combination of political propaganda and various forms of manipulation, bribery and intimidation). We should begin, therefore, not with the elections themselves, but by recreating the contours of the political culture in which they took place. This chapter will start by looking at the potential for politicisation in later-Stuart England, and show that most of the issues which divided the parties at this time had roots which dug deep in society. The government's policies – especially in the areas of religion and foreign policy – impinged directly on the lives of a significant proportion of the population, with the result that people could not help but be politicised to some degree. Much was done by the upper classes to cultivate the political awareness of the population at large, through various forms of propaganda ranging from tracts, newspapers, sermons, through to public celebrations and civic rituals. This context having been provided, it will be possible to reassess the significance of electoral behaviour, and although it can be seen that in some areas and in certain types of constituency manipulation and deference were key factors, on the whole the electorate could not be easily controlled from above. The final section will then examine the socio-economic configuration of support for the two parties.

THE SOCIAL CONTEXT OF PARTY STRIFE

It is a truism, but unfortunately one that needs to be reiterated, that politics does not occur in a vacuum at Westminster or the royal Court. Governments have to govern people, and not only do their policies have a direct impact on the population at large, and are likely to be shaped to some degree by an awareness of what that impact might be, but policies can also be a response to pressures or problems that emerge out of society. In later-Stuart England nowhere was this more apparent than in the area of religion. As we have seen, there were already deep religious tensions in society at the time of the Restoration, between separatists who wanted toleration, Presbyterians and moderate Anglicans who wanted a comprehensive Church settlement but no toleration, and hard-line Anglicans who wanted the re-establishment of the Church on their own lines with no concessions to either Presbyterians or separatists. Pressures for a particular settlement in the Church, in other words, emerged from within society before the establishment of the new regime; the eventual religious settlement worked out did not so much create the religious problem but rather was an attempt to deal with a religious problem that already existed, although in doing so the government inevitably created new religious tensions in the process.

The implications of the Restoration government's religious policy were wide-reaching, and touched many sections of the population. Not only did Nonconformists suffer severely under the savage penal laws, but a whole range of other people were drawn into the process of enforcing them, which meant that they could be forced to decide whether their sympathies lay with Dissent or with the intolerant Anglican establishment. During the determined drive against Dissent in the first half of the 1680s, government directives were issued to judges, magistrates, constables and churchwardens requiring them to enforce the penal laws strictly. Those who refused to do so could be removed from office or fined for neglect of duty. Even those who did not have any formal law-enforcement responsibility could be affected by the campaign against Dissent. Under English law, ordinary passers-by could be required by a constable to come to his assistance in making an arrest, failure to do so being a punishable offence. The 1670 Conventicle Act had offered financial inducements to people who were prepared to inform against Nonconformist meetings, encouraging local inhabitants to turn against their neighbours in the campaign against Dissent. Persecuting Nonconformists could have a knock-on effect in a community, hitting those who were loyal to the established Church. According to one report, some 4,000 men lost their jobs when their employer, one Mr Methuen, a wealthy clothier in Bradford, was forced to 'leave off his trade' as a result of his sufferings under the Conventicle Act.[5] In contrast, Stephen Timewell, mayor of Taunton in 1682–3, a man who prided himself as having 'tamed these stubborn Fanatics' during his term in office, nevertheless found that he too had to 'leave off my shop trade, for ever since I have done these things not one of a hundred comes near me to buy or sell and they make it their business to persuade people not to come near me'.[6] Those who suffered most were, of course, the Nonconformists themselves. Many faced heavy fines and the distraint of goods. In Southwark in December 1681 fines amounting to £9,680 were imposed on just twenty-two Nonconformist ministers.[7] In May 1685, Exchequer processes against Quakers for failure to come to church amounted to £33,300 in the county of Suffolk alone. Those who could not meet such fines could be sent to jail. At the time of James II's accession in 1685, according to a Quaker petition, there were 1,460 Friends in prison. Some were to die in jail. Over one hundred Quakers died in prison in the 1680s, most of them during the harsh winter of 1683–4, and at least 450 Quakers appear to have died for their sufferings during the Restoration period.[8]

Although the plight of the Nonconformists was eased considerably by the Toleration Act of 1689, the intensity of the persecutions under Charles II, and especially those of the 1680s, had left a bitter legacy. Many communities had become sharply divided as a result of the way the penal laws had been enforced at the local level, and understandably Nonconformists retained a deep distrust of their Anglican neighbours who until recently had been the agents of their destruction. Tensions were not eased by the grudging spirit in which toleration had been granted. Not only did the Dissenters still suffer civil disabilities, but they could still be prosecuted for worshipping outside the Church of England if they did not fulfil certain requirements at law. When, in late 1709, a Dissenting minister set up a conventicle in Monmouth without taking out a licence, he and some sixteen of his congregation were committed to prison by the mayor for failing to meet the provisions of the Toleration Act.[9] There was also anxiety that the degree of toleration allowed to Dissenters would be restricted, as indeed proved to be the case in the last years of Anne's reign with the passage of the Occasional Conformity and Schism Acts.

On the other side, the deep antipathy which many Anglicans felt towards Dissent is equally understandable. In addition to the memory of what had happened to the established Church during the 1640s and 1650s, the repeated reports of Nonconformist plots (both alleged and real) against the government in Church and State from the 1660s onwards encouraged a belief in the need for constant vigilance against a subversive Nonconformist threat. Anglican fears were heightened as a result of the revelations of the Rye House Plot in 1683 and the experience of the Monmouth Rebellion in 1685, which involved a predominant number of Nonconformists or friends to Dissent. The fact that Dissent appeared to flourish under toleration became a great cause for concern to those devout Anglicans who throughout the 1680s had been encouraged to believe that the only way to protect the Church and State was by a strict enforcement of the penal laws, and their anxieties were further reinforced by the sermons of the high-flying clergy. The cumulative effect was that by Anne's reign relations between Dissenters and Anglicans in many communities were no better than they had been in the 1680s. When Edward Mansell of Swansea and Thomas Davies of Llandaff conducted a survey into Anglican sufferings at the hands of the Puritans, their results revealed the survival of deep and widespread religious resentments in South Wales some fifty years after the Interregnum.[10] In the aftermath of the Sacheverell affair of 1710, a group of Welsh Anglicans formed 'a League to have no Commerce with Dissenters', imposing fines on those who broke the terms of this agreement. Similar trading pacts appear to have operated amongst Dissenters. Charles Lambe claimed that he knew of some Dissenters who 'will not touch either Food or Raiment, that was not bought in the Shop of a Fanatick. They'll send for the least Trifle to the other end of a long Street to one of their own Crew, when the very next Neighbour, a Church-man, has it to sell'.[11]

The depth of animosity between Churchmen and Dissenters is most famously illustrated by the passions unleashed by the Whig ministry's attempt to impeach Dr Henry Sacheverell for his provocative attack on Whigs and Nonconformists in 1709. When the trial began in late February 1710, huge crowds gathered to escort the doctor back and forth from his lodgings to Westminster Hall, shouting that they wished 'God would Bless him and send him a happy deliverance'. Serious violence first erupted on the evening of the second day of the trial (28 February), when a contingent of Sacheverell's supporters smashed the windows of Dr Burgess's meeting house in Lincoln Inn Fields, and then proceeded to do the same to his house. The greatest disorders occurred on the night of 1–2 March, as crowds chanting 'High Church and Sacheverell' proceeded to demolish a number of large meeting-houses in London's West End.[12] The rioters appear to have been drawn from a broad cross-section of London society: the majority were wage-earners, small craftsmen and tradesmen, although there was an appreciable 'white collar' or professional element, and even some gentlemen rioters. It would be wrong to suggest that the disturbances were motivated solely by hostility towards Dissent, since they reflected a complex series of political grievances against the current Whig government; yet that is precisely the point being made here, that antipathy towards Dissent had become deeply politicised.

Although Sacheverell was found guilty, the decision by the House of Lords on 21 March to impose the mild sentence of three years' suspension from preaching was widely seen as a moral victory for the doctor over the Whigs, and the news was greeted with (often violent) celebrations throughout the country. Over the next few months many places drew up loyal addresses to the Queen, defending the Church and monarchy against those they styled republicans and schismatics, and condemning 'the new Revived Doctrine of Resistance and other Republican Tenetts that gave rise to the unnatural Rebellion in 41'.[13] In June, Sacheverell started a lengthy progress through the midlands, on his way to take up a new living in Shropshire, and virtually everywhere he went he received a rapturous reception from the local inhabitants shouting 'God Bless Doctor Sacheverell'. The aggressive reaction in favour of Sacheverell at this time, however, should not obscure the fact that the whole affair merely served to fuel religious tensions which already existed in many parts of the country. Even during his triumphant progress in the summer, the doctor did not always receive a unanimous reception. For example, when he was invited to visit Bridgnorth (Shropshire) in early July, rival crowds made alternative bonfires, 'where about one they drank Dr Sacheverell's health and the other his confusion', with the inevitable result that the two groups eventually fell to blows.[14] A number of communities drew up counter-addresses in opposition to the High Church ones. The Gloucestershire Whigs, for example, drew up an address against those who had 'showed respect' to Sacheverell on his progress, and although it was eventually rejected by the grand jury, which was dominated by Tory JPs, a number of subscriptions were procured, especially by the local Nonconformist ministers amongst the 'spinners and weavers and other mean people under their teaching'.[15]

Religion was the political issue which aroused the most passionate emotions amongst the population at large. Nevertheless, many of the other sources of conflict between the two parties under William and Anne reached beyond the walls of Westminster, and in their different ways had a significant impact on society. The wars against France aroused questions of national security and economic interest as well as more jingoistic sentiments. William's return to London in September 1690, after securing victory over the French-backed Jacobite forces in Ireland, was greeted with bonfires and fireworks throughout the metropolis. In Covent Garden, Luttrell tells us, 'the image of the French king was made and drawn in a chariot, and over his head in capital letters was wrott, Lewis the greatest tyrant of fourteen', which they eventually committed to the flames.[16] The government did its best to rally public opinion behind the war effort by encouraging public celebrations to commemorate war victories. News of victory over the French and the Bavarians at Blenheim was announced to Londoners in early August 1704 by the discharging of guns from the Tower, and in the evening there were bonfires and celebrations not just in the City but, according to Evelyn, 'everywhere'. The official thanksgiving, held on 7 September, saw an elaborate civic ritual in London, with the Queen, the Court, and the great officers of state processing through the streets from St James to Temple Bar in great pomp and splendour, where they were met by the Lord Mayor and Aldermen who then escorted the royal cavalcade to St Paul's. Again the evening concluded with bonfires and illuminations.[17]

Many people were directly affected by the implications of the French wars. The negative impact is easiest to demonstrate: the high burden of taxation, billeting of troops, and the press-gang generated increasing resentment over time. The Tory decision to end the war proved very popular, and it was clearly a decision that was, at least to some extent, predicated upon their appreciation of the general war weariness in the nation in the later years of Anne's reign. Indeed, there was much celebration throughout the country when the peace of Utrecht was officially proclaimed in May 1713.[18] Yet there were certain groups who saw either their own or the nation's interests as being intimately bound up with an aggressive anti-French foreign policy. In the 1670s and 1680s commercial interests in London had pressed for war on the grounds that French expansionism, if left unchecked, would jeopardise England's trading interests. There seems to have been much genuine enthusiasm for the renewal of war with France in the early eighteenth century. For example, after the second election of 1701, the freeholders of Sussex sent instructions to their two newly elected Whig MPs urging them to vote William a sufficient supply so that he could renew the war against the French, arguing that 'the power of France' had grown 'so formidable' that it posed a threat not just to 'our trade and commerce abroad in the world', but also to 'our religion, laws, liberties, properties'.[19] The Treaty of Utrecht provoked considerable opposition from certain vested interests who were worried about the economic implications of the peace terms agreed with France. In May and June 1713 various trading and manufacturing groups throughout the country – cloth merchants, woollen and silk weavers, distillers, and gold and silver wire-drawers – petitioned Parliament against the legislation needed to ratify the commercial clauses of the Treaty. It was the woollen weavers who were most alarmed, fearing that the proposed reduction of import duties on French wines to the same level as those on Portuguese wines would provoke the Portuguese to lay a high duty on English woollen goods, or even prohibit their import altogether, which would be the 'Utter Ruin of that Trade'. (The Portuguese had removed the prohibition on the import of English woollen goods, under the terms of the Methuen Treaty of 1703, only on condition that England admitted their wines at preferential rates.) The petitioners eventually got their wish; enough Tories deserted the government to enable the Whigs to defeat the Commerce Bill of 1713.[20]

Religion and war are two obvious areas where government policy could have a direct impact on the population at large, and these were the two major sources of party conflict at this time. Yet the same could be true of other political issues of the day, even if the impact was less universal and more limited to specific sectional interests. The Whig desire to promote the naturalisation of foreign immigrants, most of whom were petty tradesmen or artisans, was seen as a direct threat to the economic welfare of domestic producers. A good example of this is provided by the reaction provoked by the influx of the Palatines, fleeing religious persecution in Germany, and the Whig ministry's decision to allow them the benefit of naturalisation in 1709. The government found it very difficult to persuade communities to help settle the Palatines. When the Junto leader, the Earl of Sunderland, suggested that some be settled in Canterbury, the mayor refused point blank, arguing that as a result of the recession in the silk-weaving and wool-carding trades, there was not enough work to employ the poor families already living in the city. The parish of Sundridge in Kent grudgingly decided to accept two Palatine families, up to a maximum of ten people, but their arrival produced angry demonstrations from the local inhabitants, who forced the Palatines to leave the parish.[21] The public reaction to the German refugees was exploited by the Tory ministry in their efforts to repeal the Naturalisation Act in 1711–12. The fact that they arranged for a petition from the inhabitants of Southwark, complaining about those who had welcomed the Palatines, to be presented to the Commons on the same day that they brought in the bill of repeal,[22] suggests that contemporary politicians (unlike some modern-day historians) did believe that popular pressure could have a powerful impact on events at Westminster.

Although only a few of the sources of political controversy of the time have been touched upon, enough has been said to demonstrate that people could not be immune from the implications of political decisions taken at Westminster or St James's. Merely the experience of being governed was enough to provide a political education. This political education was reinforced in a number of ways. Two have already been hinted at, namely sermons and public rituals. The anniversary of the regicide (30 January), of the Restoration (29 May), and of the deliverance from the Gunpowder Plot (5 November), were official days of thanksgiving in the Church calendar, and the sermons delivered on these occasions typically carried pointed political messages, either about the sins of regicide or the evils of popery. In 1694 Jean Gailhard wrote a pamphlet urging that the annual commemoration of 30 January and 29 May be stopped, arguing that the sermons delivered on that day helped perpetuate the country's political divisions, though it is clear that what he objected to was the fact that these days helped promote a Tory vision of government in Church and State, since he himself did not believe anything done during the reigns of Charles I or Charles II was worth commemorating.[23] November 5, on the other hand, became the occasion for commemorating the Glorious Revolution, since it was also the anniversary of William's landing at Torbay. From 1689 a new form of service was established for that day, thanking God for discovering 'the snares of death that were laid for us' in 1605, 'and likewise upon this day' for bringing King William 'safely into this Kingdom, to preserve us from the late attempts of our enemies to bereave us of our religion and laws'.[24]

Gunpowder Treason Day normally concluded in the evening with more informal festivities in the streets around a bonfire to celebrate the deliverance from popery. On 5 November 1692, for example, a crowd in Westminster burnt effigies of the Pope and of James II's Jesuit confessor, Father Petre.[25] Restoration Day, the anniversary of Elizabeth's accession (17 November), royal birthdays (4 November for William III, 6 February for Queen Anne, 30 April for Queen Mary), as well as a number of other commemorative days, provided further opportunities for public display and popular rejoicing. On 18 December 1689 the anniversary of William's first entrance into London was celebrated with a huge procession through the City, as crowds carried effigies of James's chief ministers through the streets to Temple Bar, where they ritualistically hanged them at a 'triple galloes' set up next to a great bonfire.[26] All of these anniversaries, however, were politically charged, with the pro-William and anti-popish celebrations of November being Whiggish occasions, and the pro-Stuart commemorations of the spring being more pro-Tory. In this way, the great ideological divide between the two parties over their interpretation of 'Revolution Principles' was acted out annually in public rituals throughout the country.

There was a great intensification of the partisan use of the festive calendar in the final years of Anne's reign. In 1711 the Whig Kit-Cat Club spent £200 on planning an elaborate procession in London for 17 November, along the lines of those staged by the Green Ribbon Club during the Exclusion Crisis, culminating in burning effigies of the Pope, the devil, and the Pretender. Fearing disorder, the Tory Secretary of State, Lord Dartmouth, had the effigies confiscated on the night of the 16th, but the Whigs still managed to improvise a makeshift procession and pope-burning.[27] In contrast, Queen Anne's birthday in 1712 was celebrated 'with Bonefires, illuminations and Prosperity to her Ministers and to the Loyal House of Commons' in many parts of the country, notably in Plymouth and Gloucester, and led one newsletter writer to conclude that 'there was a fresh spring of Loyalty in the Kingdom after its long discountenances by crying up Revolution Principles'.[28] The highly-charged atmosphere in the aftermath of the Sacheverell affair meant that the partisan use of public anniversaries often resulted in violent clashes between rival groups. This was particularly true for the capital. In London on 4 November 1710, a number of people had their windows smashed by Tory groups 'for Illuminating them on K. William's Birth-Day'.[29] The following year, William's birthday was celebrated with great rejoicings throughout London and Westminster. In particular, a group of peers, gentlemen and citizens organised an elaborate festival at a bonfire outside the 'Three Tuns and Rummer' in Gracechurch Street, giving beer 'to the Mobb' to pledge healths to 'the Queen, the House of Hanover, and the memory of King William'. Some Tories 'rais'd an Opposite Mobb, who offering to disturb the Rejoycings round the Bonfire, a Scuffle ensu'd, in which the Aggressors were repuls'd with some broken Heads and bloody Noses'.[30]

Political awareness was further heightened by the press. The expiry of the Licensing Act in 1695 led to a massive output of printed propaganda, in the form of pamphlets, broadsides and newspapers, and the press proved to be highly partisan in nature. By 1705 there were twelve newspapers appearing regularly in London, whilst by the end of Anne's reign Bristol, Liverpool, Newcastle-upon-Tyne, Norwich, Nottingham, Stamford and Worcester each had their own press.[31] Some writers worked as independent agents, such as the High Tory, Charles Leslie, who produced his *Rehearsal* at first weekly, and then bi-weekly, between 1704 and 1709. Others were in the employ of leading politicians. John Tutchin, who produced his *Observator* twice a week from 1702 until his death in 1707, worked for the Junto Whigs, as did for a while that indefatigable pamphleteer, Daniel Defoe. At various times, Robert Harley employed Charles Davenant, Jonathan Swift, and even Whigs like Defoe and John Toland as part of his government propaganda machine. The political leaders themselves were often active propagandists; both Somers and Harley, for example, wrote their own tracts.[32] This literature had a reasonably wide circulation. It has been estimated that the nine London newspapers in existence in 1704 between them published 44,000 copies per week.[33] Care was taken to ensure that party propaganda had an impact not just in the capital, but also reached the provinces. At the time of the second General Election of 1701 we hear of a club of Tory MPs who subscribed a guinea a head for batches of Davenant's papers to be given away among acquaintances 'as antidotes against the poison that is spread by the other side, who spare no cost to scatter their libels . . . round the kingdom'.[34] The Earl of Jersey noted that in Kent, towards the end of Anne's reign, 'Postboys, Examiners, etc. [both Tory periodicals] are the usual entertainments of the country gentry'. According to John Oldmixon, Swift's *Examiner* was 'distributed . . . gratis to the poorer Vicars and Curates' across the country.[35]

Journalists believed that their message could reach even the lower orders. Swift said of his *Examiner* that he was writing 'to the Vulgar, more than the Learned', whilst Leslie saw his *Rehearsal* as intended for the 'common people' who had been poisoned by the pernicious principles of the Whigs. Leslie was aware that most people 'cannot Read at all', but said he had seen them in the streets 'Gather together about one that can Read' and listen to a newspaper being read aloud. Every week the Tory MP for Scarborough, John Hungerford, sent a copy of Swift's *Examiner* home, which the parson used to carry about with him 'to read to such of his parishioners as are weak in the faith'. And every Sunday after service he invited 'a good number of his friends to his house, where he first reads over the paper, and then comments upon the text'.[36] There were numerous illustrated broadsides and woodcuts which carried their message in visual form. Even the more sophisticated tracts, which would have been beyond the comprehension of those on the margins of literacy and were unsuitable for reading aloud, could have had a wider impact than their style might suggest, since their purpose was to furnish people who could read them with arguments which would enable them to go away and convince others of the merits of their party's cause. As the Tory pamphleteer of the Exclusion Crisis, John Nalson, had advised his readers: 'If you think, and find I have told you a plain Truth . . . inform the Ignorant, confront the Impudent, satisfie the Doubtful and Staggering, and unite the Loyal'.[37]

The impression the above evidence leaves is of a fairly sophisticated mass political culture in England under the later Stuarts. Certainly more research is needed in this area, especially in the provincial context, before we can make confident generalisations. Yet it is probably fair to suggest that few people could have been immune from the implications of the party struggle at Westminster, since decisions taken by the central government often had a direct affect on ordinary people's lives, and few people could have avoided being exposed to the political controversies of the day through the various media of propaganda. The potential for political expression was not restricted to those who had the right to vote at General Elections every two or three years, since people of all classes could let their feelings be known through petitions, demonstrations, and riots.

Moreover, the struggles between the two parties were often fought out in the local arena, at the annual elections of town magistrates, sheriffs and parish officials. In the corporation of London, for example, the fact that local elections were spread across the year (with those for the sheriffs being in midsummer, for the lord mayor in September, and for the common councilmen in December), and were invariably fought out along party lines, meant that political passions seldom had a chance to cool down. In some towns, party rivalries during Anne's reign become so intense that they resulted in the setting-up of rival Whig and Tory corporations, as was the case for example at Brackley,

Buckingham, Camelford, Marlborough and Portsmouth.[38] The corporation of Devizes swore in two mayors in 1706, both of whom set up their own common councils, with the Whig one meeting at the Guildhall, and the Tories at Weavers' Hall. The existence of competing bodies claiming to exercise jurisdiction in the town inevitably provoked violent confrontation. In April 1707, when the Whig mayor and his officers attempted to levy a toll at the cornmarket after the Tories had already done so, they were set upon by an angry crowd egged on by the Tory mayor. On another occasion a mob smashed the windows of the Guildhall whilst the Whig common council was in session. The following autumn, rival mayors were again set up, and on the Sunday following the mayor-making, both sought to validate their claim to office by securing occupancy of the mayor's pew in the two local churches. In the morning, the Whig mayor, John Eyles, arrived at St Mary's at 10 a.m. to find the Tory mayor, Richard Bundy Franklin, had turned up two hours early and was installed in the mayor's pew. Eyles managed to get his officers to eject his rival, with the result that Franklin stood directly in front of Eyles for the duration of the service. For the afternoon service at St John's, it was Franklin who arrived late and found the door of the church locked, but he forced an entry, and in a rather childish fracas, 'put his legs between [Eyles's] legs, lifted him up', and attempted to throw him into the next seat.[39] Party strife also permeated many other levels of local life, such as the enforcement of the law, the administration of parish poor relief, and even the running of charitable institutions.[40]

THE DRAMA OF ELECTIONS

Elections were not the only occasions when those below the level of the elite could give voice to their political inclinations, nor were they the only points of contact between the world 'out-of-doors' and that of Westminster. Nevertheless, they were one of the more important points of contact, since they were responsible for determining the political complexion of the House of Commons. The reigns of William and Anne saw an unprecedented amount of electoral activity. Between 1689 and 1715 there were twelve General Elections – in 1689, 1690, 1695, 1698, 1701 (two), 1702, 1705, 1708, 1710, 1713, 1715 – that is, virtually one every two years. Not all of the 269 constituencies in England and Wales went to the polls every time: indeed, the average number of contests at each general election was a little under 100. Sometimes local arrangements were made to share representation between the two parties. Yet if we take all elections held under the Triennial Act in the twenty year period from 1695, including by-elections, we find that only nineteen constituencies avoided a contest altogether.[41]

A study of electoral propaganda conveys the impression that many of the General Elections were fought out on the great party issues of the day: religion, the war, and the security of the protestant succession.[42] The most notable exception is the General Election of 1698, when Court–Country issues, centring around the grievances of placemen and high taxation, came to the fore.[43] Looked at from the ground, however, a rather different picture emerges, since it is clear that in many constituencies local issues were of greater importance, and even where national issues played a role, they were often distinctively shaped by peculiar local circumstances. The difficult task for the historian is to get the balance right for each General Election, and to assess the various ways in which local and national issues interacted at different times in different constituencies. Even in the 'Court–Country' Election of 1698 the partisan rivalries of Church politics came to the fore in some areas. In Berkshire and Oxfordshire, for example, the cry of the 'Church in Danger' was raised by some 'hot heads' who feared the recent attempts by Nonconformists to set up a nationwide 'correspondence' to pursue 'the reformation of manners' was a plot against the Anglican establishment. In the 1695 Election support for the war was the major national issue, but most election contests appear to have been dominated by local rivalries and concerns, and in fact there was relatively little controversial pamphleteering at this time, despite the recent expiry of the Licensing Act. This Election provides a stark contrast with the one of 1690, when there had been a great deal of controversial pamphleteering, and where a significant number of contests had been fought over the issues of the Church and the security of the Protestant Succession.[44]

Partisan considerations generated considerable passion at several of the General Elections of Anne's reign. The Election of 1705, for example, which occurred shortly after the unsuccessful attempt to tack the Occasional Conformity Bill to the Land Tax Bill, was fought largely over the issue of the Church in Danger, and produced a series of bitter contests throughout the country. One Scottish observer noted that 'both parties are angry to a higher degree than ever I saw them even in the Exclusion time'.[45] In Suffolk, supporters of the Whigs shouted 'No Tackers, No French Shoos; Hear the Queen', whilst the

Tories replied with the chant of 'No Forty Eight. No Presbyterian. Save the Queens White Neck'. At Worcester, the High Church Tory Sir John Packington paraded through the streets carrying a banner which showed a steeple crumbling and falling, indicating what the electors could expect if they returned his Whig rival. At the Middlesex election, held at Brentford, 'the Tacking Party cry'd out, No Reformation, no Presbyterian', whilst at Chester, the Whigs allegedly shouted 'Down with the Church!'.[46] Similar passions can be detected at the Election of 1710, which occurred in the aftermath of the Sacheverell affair.[47] The slogans of the electors at Westminster typify how the two sides saw each other, with the Whigs shouting 'no Pretender' and the Tories 'no Managers' and 'for the Queen and Church'.[48] At the Norfolk election, where Robert Walpole, one of the manager's at Sacheverell's trial, was standing for re-election, the Tories' supporters marched behind a picture of Dr Sacheverell shouting 'No Manager', and even 'pelted Mr Walpole with Dirt and Stones . . . Spoiling his fine Lace Coat, which they told him came out of the Treasury'.[49] The 1713 Election, by contrast, was fought mainly over the issue of ending the war. At Norwich, where the weavers were upset by the provisions in the commercial treaty with France, the Whigs 'adorned their outsides with wool' and drove a flock of sheep through the centre of the city. Nevertheless, the general war-weariness of most of the electors still ensured a Tory victory.[50] At the Buckinghamshire contest, the Whigs' supporters put wool in their hats, 'saying 'twas all going into France, and they were resolved to keep some on't, before 'twas all gone'. The Tories, on the other hand, put oaken boughs in their hats, claiming they did this not merely to commemorate Charles II's famous escape at Worcester in 1651 (where he had hidden in an oak tree to avoid the Parliamentary forces), but also to show 'that with hearts of oak at the bottom, they will stand fast to the old English constitution both in church and state, in opposition to the miscellaneous tribe of atheists, deists, republicans . . . who triumph in their stolen wool'.[51]

It would be wrong to assume that only those who were privileged with the franchise were concerned with the outcome of electoral contests, since those without the right to vote were often able to make their feelings known through demonstrations or riots, which became increasingly common features of electoral contests at this time. Fierce party rivalry at Devizes, where the electorate numbered less than sixty, led to a double return of two Whigs and two Tories in 1710. When the Tory-dominated House of Commons predictably decided in favour of the two Tories, 'the Mobile' celebrated the news by carrying an effigy of one of the Whig candidates 'round the Towne, shouting and huzzaing, and at last threw him into a Bonefire, and burnt him as a Martyr to the dying Whigg Cause'.[52] In 1713, at the election for the City of London (where the franchise was vested in the liverymen), 'a great Mob of Weavers and such people' (who were presumably not enfranchised) turned up at the Guildhall in support of the Whigs, and 'made a disturbance and caus'd much fighting and quarrelling', although the four Tory candidates eventually carried the day, 'notwithstanding the Rabble'.[53] At Bristol that year, party tensions were so fierce that 'the ruder sort went to Blows, breaking one anothers Heads'.[54] Women were often active at election demonstrations, even though they could not vote. At Southwark in 1705, the women took exception to the candidacy of a local Tory JP, a bachelor and renowned misogynist, who had once said 'that he had rather see a Sow and Pigs, than a Woman and her Children'. At the election, the women of the borough turned up in large numbers shouting 'No Sow and Pigs'.[55] At Coventry in that year, when the two sitting MPs (both of whom were 'eminent Tackers') returned to contest the election, they were greeted by a huge crowd of local supporters, lay and clerical, who marched in a ritualistic procession carrying a maypole and a banner with a picture of a church on both sides. The crowd included a sizeable female contingent, headed by someone called 'Captain Kate'. When the cavalcade finally reached the market cross, Captain Kate made a speech to the crowd and presented one of the Tory MPs with 'a Sprig of Gilded Rosemary, stuck into an Orange', and, slapping him on the back, exhorted 'Now, Boys, or Never, for the Church'.[56]

The party elite and the local activists certainly tried their utmost to influence the outcome of elections. One of the main ways in which they did this was by seeking to rally people behind their cause by appealing to the issues of the day, through the press, pulpit, and the speeches given by the candidates at the hustings. In the large county constituencies, where some people would have to travel large distances to exercise the right to vote, transport was often laid on to help known supporters get to the poll.[57] Yet the party leaders also used various forms of manipulation and intimidation in their efforts to secure a victory. Contemporaries believed that the riots which occurred at elections were frequently caused by 'hired gangs' employed by one of the parties to prevent their opponents' supporters from coming to the poll. Although we should be wary of taking all such accounts at face value, since party feeling often ran sufficiently high amongst local inhabitants that little encouragement was needed for them to come to blows, such practices certainly did go on. At the Westminster election of 1698, for example, 300 horsemen who were in the service of the

Court Whigs, James Vernon and Charles Montagu, charged at their opponents in Tothill fields, and cudgelled them into nearby ditches.[58] Other forms of intimidation were widespread. Landlords might try to coerce their tenants into voting for their favoured candidates, threatening them with eviction if they failed to comply. Local magistrates also abused their authority in order to influence voters. At Coventry in 1701, to give one typical example, one Whig alderman threatened to deprive a couple of local alehousekeepers of their licences if they refused to give both their votes to the Whig candidates.[59] When Admiralty Lord, Sir Robert Rich, stood for Dunwich in 1695, he arranged for three 'men-of-war' to anchor off the small Suffolk port during the time of the election, to hold out the threat of the press-gang to any who voted against the Whig candidates.[60] Bribery, in the form of financial inducements and electoral treats, was another common method employed to 'persuade' voters to opt for certain candidates.

The parties also sought to manipulate the structure and workings of the electoral system to their own advantage. Control over the position of returning officer was crucial, since he was able to determine not only who was eligible to vote, but also how long to keep the poll open. Following their defeat at the Wiltshire election of 1713, the Whig candidates petitioned the House of Commons, complaining that the under-sheriff, in collusion with the two Tory candidates, had delayed opening the poll until the afternoon, 'when many freeholders, who would have voted for the petitioners, were necessitated, by reason of the harvest, to go away without voting', and also that he had 'refused those who voted for the petitioners, and had a right; and polled others amongst them, who had no right'.[61] Votes were often manufactured by the splitting of freeholds or the creation of new freemen to augment the size of a party's following amongst the electorate. At Ipswich the fact that both sides were engaged in the practice of manufacturing freemen meant that the number of voters rose from 271 in 1698 to nearly 600 by 1715.[62] In 1701–2, the Whig mayor of the small corporation of Wilton, Wiltshire, created nineteen new burgesses, all of whom were Dissenters who did not even qualify under the terms of the Corporation Act, with the result that in 1702 he was able to reverse the defeat suffered by the Whigs in the election of the previous year.[63] At Hertford in 1705, according to Tutchin, when it became clear that the Tackers 'could not carry it there by Legal Votes', the town magistrates created between 100 and 150 'Honorary Freemen, all of the Tackers side', and managed to ensure a Tory victory.[64] Undoubtedly the greatest electoral influence was wielded by the government of the day. The remodelling of commissions of the peace, and the careful disposal of government offices, had the effect of greatly increasing the ability of the government-backed party to bring pressure to bear on electors to vote in their favour, whilst the mere fact that the Crown was making a clear statement as to where its own political sympathies lay was often by itself a powerful factor in swaying public opinion.

Trying to determine whether political conviction or influence was more important in determining how the voters behaved at the polls is no easy task. An analysis of poll books for Bedfordshire, Buckinghamshire, Hampshire, Rutland and Westmorland for the early eighteenth century has revealed a remarkable consistency of partisan loyalties amongst the electorate. In those constituencies where two Whig and two Tory candidates stood, the vast majority gave both their votes to men from the same party. Out of 2,560 freeholders voting in Bedfordshire in 1705, for example, only 313 (12.2 per cent) split their votes, whilst in 1715 a mere 142 out of 2,529 split them (5.6 per cent). In Buckinghamshire in 1710 there were 164 split votes out of 4,301 freeholders who went to the polls (3.8 per cent); in 1713, 197 out of 3,957 (5 per cent). Similar consistency has been found in urban constituencies. At Norwich in 1710 96.4 per cent of the electors voted for one or other of the party slates. When only three candidates stood, cross-party voting was inevitably more common. Nevertheless, there was a strong tendency in some constituencies for voters to 'plump' for one candidate and waste their second vote, rather than give it to someone from the opposing party. When two Whigs and one Tory stood for Hampshire in 1705, only 201 out of 3,517 freeholders voting split their votes (5.7 per cent), whilst 724 plumped for the single Tory candidate. The bulk of the electorate also remained loyal to the same party in successive elections. However, there was a significant minority of floating voters: on average about 20 per cent of the electorate. In addition, there was also a very high turnover of voters from one election to the next, with the result that the 'casual voters' normally outnumbered those who regularly took part in the poll.[65]

This data is open to a variety of interpretations, and can be used to lend weight both to the participatory model and to the deferential model of electoral behaviour. The loyal voter may have voted consistently out of party principle, or because ties of dependence persistently obliged him to defer to the wishes of committed partisans amongst the local elite. Likewise, the floating vote might be indicative of some electors making up their own minds on the issues of the day; it might equally reflect pressure brought to bear 'from above', perhaps by those attached to the Court who wanted a change in the complexion of the

House of Commons, to 'persuade' those electors to change their allegiances. Finally, the high turnover at the polls might be indicative of changes in the local population, or prudential calculations amongst particular electors as to whether it was worth one's while trying to exercise one's right to vote (on the logic that people will not bother to turn up to the poll if they believe their preferred candidates have no chance of success); it could equally well be indicative of various forms of electoral manipulation and influence, such as the artificial creation of new electors, the ability of returning officers to prevent one side's supporters from polling, or the ability of some members of the local elite to 'persuade' electors not to register a vote in opposition to their wishes.

The only way to determine which of these possible readings best explain the behaviour of voters in different localities is through an in-depth study of all the constituencies in England and Wales, such as is currently being undertaken by the History of Parliament Trust. Any confident assessment of the precise role of influence at elections, therefore, must await the publication of their findings. In the present state of research it is probably fair to suggest that although influence did have a powerful impact on the outcome of a number of elections, on the whole the electorate was not particularly easy to control, and that members of the political elite, despite all their efforts, often failed to achieve their ends. There were some constituencies where the interest of a local patron was so strong that he effectively had the power of nominating MPs. The Earl of Exeter owned so much property in Stamford (Lincolnshire) that he was able to keep its 2,500 electors firm to the Tory interest without a contest during the reign of Anne.[66] Patronage tended to be more important, however, in boroughs with smaller electorates: Lord Brooke dominated Warwick's 400 voters, the Whig Earl of Carlisle dominated Morperth's electorate of 120, whilst there were a number of proprietary boroughs with electorates of fewer than 100 where both seats remained safe for a particular party.[67] The smaller boroughs also tended to be the most vulnerable to electoral manipulation, either through 'treating', as at a number of venal boroughs, or through tampering with the composition of the franchise. But even the petty boroughs were not always easy to handle. At Bury St Edmunds the franchise was vested in the thirty-seven members of the corporation, but the complexion of the electorate could only be altered when a vacancy occurred naturally in their ranks. As a result, the Whig MP John Hervey had to work extremely hard to cultivate the corporation, and although he did use various financial incentives, he found that the best way to keep their support was by serving their interests both locally and in Parliament.[68] A recent study of Parliamentary boroughs in the south-west of England has shown that even in urban constituencies with small electorates it was never easy for a narrow elite or wealthy patrons to control elections, and that the voters remained capable of autonomous action and independent choice.[69]

The electorates in the open boroughs and in the counties were much more difficult to control. At the Bristol election in 1713, the Whig candidate, Sir William Daines, spent large sums of money 'in procuring the freedom of the city for many hundreds of poor people to vote' and gave 'many hundreds to the mob' in the form of direct bribes and alcoholic refreshment. Bristol had been dominated by the Whigs since 1695, and had fallen to the Tories only in 1710 in the Sacheverellite backlash, so Daines had good reason to believe that a careful cultivation of the electorate could pay dividends. Yet despite all his efforts, the election, which was conducted amidst scenes of almost continuous rioting, went in favour of the Tories.[70] In some counties, great landed magnates seemed able to rely on the support of the freeholders residing in the vicinity of their estates. In Buckinghamshire, for example, 60 per cent of those who lived in areas where the Whig peers Lord Wharton, the Dukes of Montagu, Bedford and Devonshire, and the Earl of Bridgewater owned lands voted Whig in the election of 1705; by 1713 this figure had risen to 66 per cent. Yet the fact that up to 40 per cent felt under no compulsion to oblige the local magnates with their votes is revealing, and makes us wonder whether those who polled for the Whigs really did so out of deference or as a result of political conviction. The Buckinghamshire freeholders who lived in the immediate neighbourhood of the Tory local landowner, Sir John Verney, in fact also tended to poll in favour of the Whigs.[71] Electoral magnates often experienced severe setbacks at the polls. When Wharton had to relinquish his seat in Buckinghamshire on his elevation to the peerage in 1696, he was unable to replace himself with a suitable man, and the by-election went in favour of a local Tory, Lord Cheyne. In the 1698 General Election, Wharton's candidates fared relatively badly in several Buckinghamshire constituencies, including the county, whilst in Oxfordshire, where Wharton was Lord Lieutenant, his candidates were defeated by two Tories.[72]

It is sometimes suggested that it was the government, rather than the electorate, which determined the outcome of elections, and that any ministry which enjoyed the full weight of the Crown behind it was unlikely to lose a general election. Certainly government influence had a powerful impact, and could normally secure the return of favoured candidates in constituencies where there were significant government installations (such as the postal service at Harwich, or the dockyards at Plymouth, Portsmouth and the Cinque Ports).[73] Yet there were limits to what the government could achieve. The Whig ministers lost the General Election of 1698, although it is true that William had not thrown his support wholeheartedly behind them. Even under Anne, when the ministry of the day never did lose a General Election, it was not always able to get the type of Parliament it wanted. The efforts of the newly established coalition ministry in 1705 to secure the election of a moderate House of Commons balanced between the two extremes proved to be largely unsuccessful. It is true that the elections resulted in a House fairly evenly balanced between the two parties, but the fact that the elections came to be fought over the issue of the Church in Danger meant that those Tories who were returned were in no mood for compromise, with the result that the new House proved extremely difficult for the ministry to manage.[74] In 1708 Godolphin hoped to obtain 'a Parliament for the Court, a Parliament that may be guided' but the public reaction to the Jacobite invasion scare of that year produced 'the most Wig Parliament . . . since the revolution'.[75] The new Tory ministry under Harley may have been successful in changing the previous Whig majority in Parliament into a Tory one in the General Election of 1710; but the furore unleashed by the Sacheverell affair meant that a Parliament dominated by High Tories was returned, which was much more extreme than a moderate like Harley would have wished. The conclusion seems inescapable that the electorate did have a significant impact in determining the composition of the Commons, and therefore the very nature of party strife at Westminster itself.

THE SOCIO-ECONOMIC CONTOURS OF THE DIVIDED SOCIETY

English society during the great rage of party under William and Anne divided primarily on religious grounds, with the Nonconformists siding overwhelmingly with the Whigs, and High Church Anglicans with the Tories. Dissenters were visibly active in support of Whig candidates at the polls, and their electoral impact was often significant, since they might have comprised one-fifth of the total electorate, whilst in some constituencies the proportion of voters who were Nonconformists was much higher.[76] The Anglican clergy, on the other hand, tended to rally behind the Tories, often marching to the polls *en masse* to give their support for the Church and Queen candidates.[77] In the small county constituency of Rutland, of forty-three beneficed clergymen who polled in the election of 1710, thirty voted for the two Tories, four split their votes, and a mere nine voted for the two Whigs.[78] At the Suffolk elections of 1705 and 1710, 80 per cent of the clergy voted for the two Tory candidates.[79] As these figures suggest, however, there was always a small minority of Low Church clergy who sided with the Whigs, whilst the Low Church bishops, of course, often used whatever influence they could to frustrate the election of Tories. In the 1702 election for Worcestershire, for example, the local Whig Bishop, William Lloyd, tried to rally his clergy and his tenants into forming an interest against the High Tory, Sir John Packington.[80] In the Sacheverellite election of 1710, we find Lloyd 'strenuously' promoting 'the Whig interest' in many parts of the south, including Surrey, Hampshire and Cornwall.[81]

The split between the Whigs and Tories is normally thought to have corresponded to a fundamental economic cleavage amongst the English upper classes, between the monied and the landed interests. A fall in the price of land and in the value of rents meant that the reigns of William and Anne were difficult times for the landed classes, and their plight was exacerbated by the fact that they were being hit by a tax on land of four shillings in the pound to finance the wars against France. By contrast, those who were involved in the new machinery of public credit which had been set up as a result of the financial revolution were doing remarkably well, through their investments in institutions such as the Bank of England and the New East India Company, and from the interest they received on loans to the government. Tory propagandists repeatedly alleged that the war policies of the Whigs were designed to promote the interests of the new monied men at the expense of the gentry. In a satire of 1710, Charles Davenant had his character of a Court Whig say to a country squire: 'Let us eat out all your Lands and Tenements with Taxes of our devising; let us have the sole Management of a long protracted War, and gather our wonted Fruits from it'.[82] Likewise in 1711 Jonathan Swift complained that 'we have been fighting . . . to enrich usurers and stockjobbers; and to cultivate the pernicious designs of a faction, by destroying the landed interest'.[83]

Although party polemicists (especially the Tories) frequently referred to the existence of a fundamental conflict between a Whig monied and a Tory landed interest, recent research has warned us to be cautious of accepting such remarks as an accurate description of social and political realities. There were Tory monied men; indeed, before the financial revolution, the monied interest in the City of London had been predominantly Tory. Tories opposed the new credit system set up in the 1690s not because they objected to this type of economic enterprise, but because the benefits to be accrued from it largely passed them by. The new financial institutions, established by the Whig Junto in William's reign, came to be dominated by Whigs. Only three Tories served as directors of the Bank of England between 1694 and 1715, compared to a total of thirty Whigs, whilst of the known directors of the New East India Company in the period 1698–1708, again only three were Tories, as opposed to thirteen Whigs.[84] Yet Tory directors of the Old East India Company and the Royal African Company continued to outnumber Whigs directors by two to one during this same period, and Tories rushed to invest in the South Sea Bubble Company, set up by Harley in 1711.

Likewise it would be wrong to assume that economic difficulties worked to push the gentry increasingly into the Tory camp. In the first place, we should not paint too pessimistic a view of what was happening to the landed classes, since the experiences of this group varied considerably from region to region. In some counties, the land tax was relatively lightly assessed; in Cumberland and Westmorland, for example, landowners might have been paying less than 5 per cent of the true value of their rents. Secondly, if gentry support for the Whigs had really begun to disintegrate, then they would have soon collapsed as a political force, since the bulk of the political nation comprised the landed interest. In many areas, Whigs clearly continued to hold their own amongst the squirearchy. Philip Jenkins has shown that in South Wales at the turn of the century Whig and Tory gentry were equal in terms of wealth and numbers, and further that a number of once firm Tory gentlemen converted to Whiggery after the Glorious Revolution.[85]

We should not go too far and argue that the alleged conflict between the monied and landed interests was nothing more than a propagandist's fiction. Propaganda, if it is to have any effect at all, must have some basis in truth. The conflict of interests was certainly a significant factor in the south-east, where the land tax was relatively highly assessed and where the new monied men had made a noticeable intrusion into local economic life, though it could also possess some degree of reality in more remote parts, such as South Wales.[86] Moreover, the economic cleavage that was perceived to be developing in this society did appear to correspond to the religious tensions that were generating party strife, and to anxious High Church Tories seemed to be yet another part of the process whereby Dissenters were thriving in the changed political climate after the Revolution at the expense of the Anglican interest. The fact that Nonconformists were so prominent in the new financial institutions became a source of deep concern, both for the landed classes, who had by now largely severed any ties they had once had with Dissent, and also for the old Tory financial interests in the City, who saw their former economic ascendancy being eclipsed. At least 43 per cent of those who served as directors of the Bank of England between 1694 and 1715 were either Dissenters or from Dissenting backgrounds, whilst persons from the Dissenting interest also figured prominently as holders of Bank stock and as directors of the New East India Company.[87]

To judge from election results, the Tories appear to have become the more popular party by the early eighteenth century. Tory success in the elections to Anne's first Parliament in 1702 led Dr Henry Sacheverell to boast that 'the Majority of the People are for the Church of England'.[88] The Whigs had recovered somewhat by 1705, giving the Tories a good run for their money, and they actually won the Election in 1708, although this was to be the only General Election they were to win under Anne. The Election of 1710 gave the Tories a majority of 151 in the Commons; after the Election of 1713 it was increased to 213. Other evidence, such as the demonstrations in favour of Sacheverell in 1710, or in favour of peace in 1713, seems to reinforce the view that by the end of Anne's reign public opinion was overwhelmingly behind the Tories. This is in stark contrast with the Exclusion Crisis, when both the electorate and, at least initially, 'the crowd', appear to have been largely in favour of the Whigs.

The reasons for this shift in public opinion from the Whigs to the Tories are not hard to discern. A general war weariness, grievances over high taxation, and a deep fear amongst the Anglican majority of the population that the Church was now in greater danger from Protestant Nonconformists than it was from popery, all worked to the Tories' advantage. Under Anne, it was only in 1708, which saw an attempted Jacobite invasion of Scotland, that the Whigs were able to play the 'no popery' card with any success. The fact that by the early eighteenth century the Whigs had become to all intents and purposes a Court party, whilst the Tories were increasingly associated with Country concerns, also helps explain the relative shift in the support base for the two parties. Several contemporaries suggested that the reason why the modern Whigs were losing support was because they had deserted old Whig principles.[89] As the Whigs gradually began to retreat from their erstwhile espousal of populist causes, the Tories increasingly appeared to be the party with more to offer ordinary people.

This process of transformation can be seen most dramatically in London. Whereas during the 1670s and 1680s the City Whigs had argued for an extension of democratic rights within the Corporation, they abandoned this position after the Glorious Revolution and instead became increasingly identified as defenders of the oligarchical forces within the City's government. The old Whig platform for constitutional reform was slowly taken up by the London Tories, with the result that by the last years of Anne's reign they had largely absorbed their opponents' former libertarian rhetoric. The Tories had also come to steal the Whigs' former following amongst the petty craftsmen and mechanic tradesmen. In the early 1680s, although the liverymen of the substantial City companies had not noticeably favoured one party, the Whigs had attracted more support from the lesser companies than the Tories. By the end of Anne's reign, in contrast, the majority of the substantial companies were Whig in sympathy, whilst the lesser companies were predominantly Tory.[90]

Whilst there is much truth in the view that the Tories were gaining popular support at the expense of the Whigs, care must be taken not to exaggerate the shift in public opinion that was occurring during this time. Lower-class support for the Whigs did not evaporate completely during Anne's reign, even in London, and in particular there were many poor Nonconformists who remained loyal to the party of Low Church and Dissent. Thus the London weavers, an economically depressed group, but one which nevertheless contained a high preponderance of Nonconformists, rallied behind the Whig government at the time of the Sacheverell affair and helped the trained bands suppress High Church crowds in the City.[91] The transformation of political sympathies identified for London might be exceptional, being directly linked to particular developments within the Corporation, and therefore a poor indicator of shifts in public opinion in the nation as a whole. A recent analysis of voting behaviour in Norwich in 1710, for example, has shown that the Tories were strongest amongst the more well-to-do types: the gentry and professional classes, retailers and merchants. The craftsmen, however, were more evenly divided, even at the high point of Tory fortunes in the City, with the majority still favouring the Whigs. Whiggery was strongest in those parishes which had a heavy concentration of weavers, and virtually unassailable wherever weaving was combined with Nonconformity.[92] Moreover, an exaggerated impression of the growth of popular support for the Tories is conveyed by comparing Anne's reign with the period of the

Parliamentary Exclusion Crisis. The years between the calling of the first Exclusion Parliament in the spring of 1679 and the meeting of the Oxford Parliament in March 1681 was the time when the Whigs were at the peak of their popularity, but this was a rather untypical situation, even for the Restoration era. At the time of the Restoration itself Anglican-Royalist sentiment was strong not only amongst the gentry but also amongst the population at large, whilst there was a marked reaction against the Whigs and in favour of the Tories following the defeat of the Parliamentary Exclusion movement. It is by no means clear that the Church and Queen position of 1710–14 was any more popular in the nation at large than had been the Church and King position of either 1660–2 or 1681–5.

We also need to be cautious before asserting that the Tories became a populist party, in the sense of championing the interests of the less privileged classes within society. Again, we should not assume that developments amongst the London Tories, at the level of corporation politics, were typical of developments amongst Tories as a whole. Most Tory propagandists continued to hold a rather contemptuous view of the populace. No-one was more anti-populist than Charles Leslie, admittedly a rather extreme Tory, but whose *Rehearsal* was nevertheless a powerful vehicle for the propagation of Tory ideology for the middle years of Anne's reign. Leslie thought the voice of the people was the 'Voice of the Devil', and that the people were 'Always in the Wrong'.[93] His elitism is well brought out in his description of the elections of 1705, where he claimed that 'the Principal Gentry, both for Estates and Reputation', supported the Tory candidates, and 'the Refuse and Scum, the Beasts of the People', supported the Whigs; he went on to recommend changing the franchise qualification from forty shillings worth of freehold land to '10 Pounds at least'.[94] Even in the aftermath of the Sacheverell affair, Francis Atterbury could still maintain that 'the Voice of the People is the Cry of Hell', and that 'The People are by the Voice of Heaven declared Foolish, Sottish, void of Understanding, wise for Wickedness; and senseless for Good'.[95] Indeed, most Tories sought to distance themselves from the actions of their own supporters amongst the rank and file. Charles Lambe denied that the Tories had been responsible for raising the Sacheverell mobs, and blamed the Whigs for instilling into people the idea that 'they are the original of government'. It was no surprise, Lambe maintained, that the people acted in accordance with the doctrines they had been taught, though it happened 'that this Mob rose with Inclinations perfectly different from what was expected from them'. Lambe concluded by saying that 'All tumultuous Assemblies are against my Principle', and that he hated 'Mobs and Insurrections, though they favour my side'.[96]

Tory propagandists were certainly prepared to argue that the people's interests were not being protected by the Whigs. In a tract written shortly before the 1715 General Election, Atterbury maintained that 'the People' had been 'fleec'd so often' by the heavy taxes imposed by the Whigs to fight their wars, that 'they have scarce enough to keep them from Perishing'.[97] But if we are to generalise, it is better to characterise the Tory position as paternalist, rather than populist. Tories remained fiercely critical of Whig arguments about popular sovereignty, and tended to argue that the people would be better off if they accepted their place in society and allowed the Tory elite to attend to their welfare. As Leslie put it, 'No Evils' were 'of such Hurtful Consequences to the People, as those of Anarchy and Confusion', which were the inevitable consequences of 'Mobb Principles'; the 'Miserably Deluded People' should 'Recover their Senses', and 'Adhere to the Laws and Constitution' (which for Leslie meant divine-right monarchy).[98]

CONCLUSION

Party rivalry was so intense in England under the later Stuarts because it affected not just the political elite at the centre, but cut deep into society. A wide range of people throughout much of the country – from the local gentry, through to the professional and mercantile classes, down to the middling and lower sorts of town and countryside – were actively caught up in the partisan controversies of the time. People became politicised because many of the issues of the day affected them directly, and they often had the chance to give expression to their political feelings through petitions, demonstrations, riots and, for those with the right to vote, at the polls. More still needs to be learned about politics 'out-of-doors' for the reigns of William and Anne; in particular, we need to find out more about the ways local and national issues interacted in specific localities, and we are still in the process of discovering about the dynamics of electoral politics. It is clear, however, that political historians cannot afford to confine their attention to the goings-on at Westminster or St James's, and that the history of party under the later Stuarts is as much about the divisions that emerged in society at large as it is about what happened in Parliament or at the royal Court. Not only did the existence of a divided society help fuel party tensions under William and Anne, but taking the longer perspective covered by this book as a whole, it might even be fair to suggest that the emergence of the party divide amongst the political elite was itself a symptom of the bitter divisions that already existed in this society, divisions which we have traced back to the Restoration in 1660. A wide range of factors shaped how people aligned themselves politically – from personal considerations or considerations of economic self-interest through to political or religious conviction – and the way these factors interrelated could differ over time to produce shifting patterns of popular allegiance. One theme that has emerged throughout this book, however, and which has been reinforced by the analysis presented in this chapter, is the importance of religion in determining people's political identity. Throughout the first age of party, Nonconformists (together with those sympathetic to Dissent) tended to identify strongly with the Whigs, whilst High Anglicans identified overwhelmingly with the Tories. The party struggle, whether in- or out-of-doors, was never solely about the conflict between the Church and Dissent; nevertheless, this conflict was a powerful and central feature of that struggle, which we see present throughout most of the period.

REFERENCES

1   Holmes and Speck, *The Divided Society: Parties and Politics in England 1694–1716.*
2   Plumb, 'The Growth of the Electorate in England from 1600 to 1715'; Holmes, *The Electorate and the National Will in the First Age of Party*; Speck, *Tory and Whig: The Struggle in the Constituencies, 1701–1715*
3.   Norma Landau, 'Independence, Deference and Voter Participation: The Behaviour of the Electorate in Early Eighteenth-Century Kent', *HJ*, **22** (1979), pp. 561–83.
4.   J. C. D. Clark, *English Society 1688–1832* (Cambridge, 1985), pp. 19–20.
5.   John Oldmixon, *The Critical History of England, Ecclesiastical and Civil* (2 vols, 2nd edn, 1728–30), **II**, p. 395.
6.   *CSPD, July–Sept. 1683,* p. 358.
7.   *CSPD, 1680–1,* p. 613.
8.   J. Besse, *A Collection of the Sufferings of the People Called Quakers* (2 vols, 1753), **I**, p. 687; Craig W. Horle, *The Quakers and the English Legal System 1660–1688* (Philadelphia, 1988), p. 102; W. C. Braithwaite, *The Second Period of Quakerism* (Cambridge, 1961), pp. 109, 115, 119; Harris, 'Lives, Liberties and Estates', pp. 226–7.

9. BL, Loan 29/320, 3 Dec. 1709.
10. Jenkins, *The Making of a Ruling Class: The Glamorgan Gentry 1640–1790*, p. 144.
11. William Bisset, *The Modern Fanatick* (1710), p. 4; [Charles Lambe], *A Vindication of the Reverend Dr. Henry Sacheverell* [1711], pp. 38–9.
12. BL, Loan 29/321, 28 Feb., 2 Mar. 1709/10. The following account, unless otherwise stated, draws on: Geoffrey Holmes, 'The Sacheverell Riots: The Crowd and the Church in Early Eighteenth-Century London', in Paul Slack (ed.), *Rebellion, Popular Protest and the Social Order in Early Modern England* (Cambridge, 1984), pp. 232–62; *Idem, Trial of Dr Sacheverell*.
13. BL, Loan 29/321, 25 Mar., 15 Jun. 1710.
14. History of Parliament, unpub. constituency report, Bridgnorth.
15. BL, Loan 29/321, 17 Aug. 1710; Kenyon, *Revolution Principles: The Politics of Party 1689–1720*, pp. 151–3.
16. Luttrell, *Brief Historical Relation*, **II**, p. 103.
17. Evelyn, *Diary*, **V**, pp. 575, 578; Luttrell, *Brief Historical Relation*, **V**, pp. 454, 462–3.
18. Bodl. Lib., MS Gough Somerset 2, p. 147, Appendix p. 99.
19. History of Parliament, unpub. constituency report, Sussex.
20. D. A. E. Harkness, 'The Opposition to the 8th and 9th Articles of the Commercial Treaty of Utrecht', *Scottish Historical Review*, **21** (1923), pp. 219–26; Geoffrey Holmes and Clyve Jones, 'Trade, the Scots and the Parliamentary Crisis of 1713', *Parliamentary History*, **1** (1982), pp. 47–77; D. C. Coleman, 'Politics and Economics in the Age of Anne: The Case of the Anglo-French Trade Treaty of 1713', in D. C. Coleman and A. H. John (eds), *Trade, Government and Economy in Pre-Industrial England* (1976), pp. 187–211. For the petitions, see *CJ*, **XVII**, pp. 347–420.
21. Statt, 'Controversy over the Naturalization of Foreigners', pp. 258–9, 285–7.
22. Dickinson, 'The Poor Palatines and the Parties', pp. 483–5.
23. [Jean Gailhard], *Some Observations upon the Keeping the Thirtieth of January and Twenty-ninth of May* (1694).
24. Cressy, *Bonfires and Bells*, p. 185.
25. Luttrell, *Brief Historical Relation*, **II**, p. 610.
26. Luttrell, *Brief Historical Relation*, **I**, p. 612; *HMC, 5th Report*, pp. 379–80.
27. *An Account of the Mock Procession* (1711); *A True Relation of the several Facts and Circumstances of the Intended Riot and Tumult* (1711); Cressy, *Bonfires and Bells*, p. 188; Rogers, *Whigs and Cities: Popular Politics in the Age of Walpole and Pitt*, pp. 365–6.
28. *Lyme Letters*, p. 239. See below, pp. 219–23 for political demonstrations at the time of the Hanoverian Succession.
29. Bisset, *Modern Fanatick*, p. 7.
30. Abel Boyer, *The History of the Reign of Queen Anne* (11 vols, 1703–13), **XI**, p. 291; Cressy, *Bonfires and Bells*, p. 188.

31. W. A. Speck, 'Politics and the Press', in Michael Harris and Alan J. Lee (eds), *The Press in English Society from the Seventeenth to the Nineteenth Centuries* (1986), p. 47.

32. J. A. Downie, *Robert Harley and the Press: Propaganda and Public Opinion in the Age of Swift and Defoe* (Cambridge, 1979); William L. Sachse, *Lord Somers: A Political Portrait* (Manchester, 1975).

33. Henry L. Snyder, 'The Circulation of Newspapers in the Reign of Queen Anne', *The Library*, **23** (1968), pp. 206–35; James O. Richards, *Party Propaganda Under Queen Anne: The General Elections of 1702–1713* (Athens, Georgia, 1972), p. 10.

34. *HMC, Cowper*, **II**, pp. 436–7.

35. Ellis (ed.), *Swift vs Mainwaring*, pp. xl–xli; [John Oldmixon], *Remarks upon Remarks: Or, the Barrier-Treaty and the Protestant Succession Vindicated* (1711), p. 28; *HMC, Dartmouth*, **I**, p. 296; Richard I. Cook, 'The Audience of Swift's Tory Tracts, 1710–14', *Modern Language Quarterly*, **24** (1963), pp. 31–41.

36. Leslie, *Rehearsal*, **I**, preface; *HMC Portland*, **IV**, p. 641.

37. Nalson, *Complaint of Liberty and Property*, p. 6.

38. Speck, *Tory and Whig*, p. 52.

39. Edward Bradby, 'A Deadlock in Eighteenth-Century Devizes', *Wiltshire Archaeological and Natural History Magazine*, **81** (1987), pp. 100–1; History of Parliament, unpub. constituency report, Devizes.

40. Craig Rose, 'Politics, Religion and Charity in Augustan London c. 1680 – c. 1720', unpub. Cambridge PhD thesis (1989); S. M. Macfarlane, 'Studies in Poverty and Poor Relief in London at the End of the Seventeenth Century', unpub. Oxford DPhil thesis (1982); Robert B. Shoemaker, *Prosecution and Punishment: Petty Crime and the Law in London and Rural Middlesex, c. 1660–1725* (Cambridge, 1991).

41. W. A. Speck, 'The Electorate in the First Age of Party', in Jones (ed.), *Britain in the First Age of Party, 1680–1750: Essays Presented to Geoffrey Holmes*, p. 47.

42. Speck, *Tory and Whig*, pp. 86–7.

43. Ellis, 'Whig Junto', p. 356; Horwitz, *Parliament, Policy and Politics in the Reign of William III*, p. 237.

44. Horwitz, *Parliament, Policy and Politics*, pp. 51, 157, 238; Horwitz, 'The General Election of 1690'.

45. Cited in Hill, *The Growth of Parliamentary Parties, 1689–1742*, p. 103.

46. Leslie, *Rehearsal*, **I**, no. 42, 12–19 May 1705; *Ibid.*, no. 45, 2–9 June 1705; Sykes, 'Cathedral Chapter', p. 260; Geoffrey Holmes, *Religion and Party in late Stuart England* (1975), p. 18; Tutchin, *Observator*, **IV**, no. 20, 6–9 Jun. 1705; *HMC, Portland*, **IV**, p. 189; P. J. Challinor, 'The Structure of Politics in Cheshire, 1660–1715', unpub. Wolverhampton Polytechnic PhD thesis (1983), p. 219.

47. Mary Ransome, 'Church and Dissent in the Election of 1710', *EHR*, **56** (1941), pp. 76–89; *Idem*, 'The Press in the General Election of 1710', *CHJ*, **6** (1939), pp. 209–21.

48. BL, Loan 29/321, 7 Oct. 1710.

49. BL, Loan 29/321, 14 Oct. 1710.
50. History of Parliament, unpub. constituency report, Norwich.
51. History of Parliament, unpub. constituency report, Buckinghamshire. Cf. Richards, *Party Propaganda Under Queen Anne: The General Elections of 1702–1713*, pp. 145–6.
52. BL, Loan 29/321, 23 Dec. 1710.
53. BL, Loan 29/8, 20 Oct. 1713.
54. Bodl. Lib., MS Gough, Somerset 2, Appendix p. 99; Rogers, *Whigs and Cities*, p. 287.
55. Tutchin, *Observator*, **IV**, no. 13, 12–16 May 1705.
56. Tutchin, *Observator*, **IV**, no. 4, 11–14 Apr. 1705.
57. Richards, *Party Propaganda*; Speck, *Tory and Whig*, ch. 3.
58. Thomas Carew, *An Historical Account of the Rights of Elections* (1755), **II**, p. 235.
59. Carew, *Historical Account*, **I**, p. 188.
60. History of Parliament, unpub. constituency report, Dunwich.
61. Carew, *Historical Account*, **II**, pp. 252–3.
62. Murrell, 'Suffolk', pp. 143–56. Cf. Holmes, *Electorate and the National Will*, p. 17.
63. Holmes, *Religion and Party*, p. 16.
64. Tutchin, *Observator*, **IV**, no. 14, 16–19 May 1705.
65. W. A. Speck and W. A. Gray, 'Computer Analysis of Poll Books: An Interim Report', *BIHR*, **43** (1970), pp. 105–12; W. A. Speck, W. A. Gray and R. Hopkinson, 'Computer Analysis of Poll Books: A Further Report', *BIHR*, **48** (1975), pp. 64–90; Rogers, *Whigs and Cities*, p. 329.
66. Speck, *Tory and Whig*, p. 68. Stamford had seen contests in 1689 and 1695: Horwitz, *Parliament, Policy and Politics*, p. 331.
67. Speck, *Tory and Whig*, pp. 69–70.
68. Murrell, 'Suffolk', pp. 241–52.
69. Triffitt, 'Politics and the Urban Community'.
70. History of Parliament, unpub. constituency report, Bristol.
71. Speck et al., 'Poll Books . . . Further Report', pp. 74–5.
72. Ellis, 'Whig Junto', pp. 358, 361; Feiling, *Tory Party*, p. 329.
73. Speck, *Tory and Whig*, p. 72; Landau, 'Independence, Deference, and Voter Participation'.
74. Speck, *Tory and Whig*, ch. 7.
75. Holmes, *British Politics*, pp. 352–3 and footnote.
76. Holmes, *Religion and Party*, p. 21; Speck, 'Electorate', p. 41.
77. G. V. Bennett, 'The Era of Party Zeal, 1702–1714', in Sutherland and Mitchell (eds), *History of the University of Oxford*, p. 62.
78. Bennett, *The Tory Crisis in Church and State, 1688–1730: The Career of Francis Atterbury, Bishop of Rochester*, p. 140.
79. Murrell, 'Suffolk', p. 424.
80. Worcester Record Office, Packington MS 705:349 BA 5117/1 – *The Evidence Given at the Bar of the House of Commons upon the Complaint of Sir John Packington* (1702); Carew, *Historical Account*, **II**, pp. 265–71.
81. BL, Loan 29/321, [before 5th] Sept. 1710.

The Divided Society under William and Anne

82. Davenant, *Sir Thomas Double at Court*, p. 63.
83. Jonathan Swift, *The Conduct of the Allies, and of the Late Ministry, in Beginning and Carrying on the Present War* (1711), in Angus Ross and David Woolley (eds), *Jonathan Swift* (Oxford, 1984), p. 321.
84. De Krey, *A Fractured Society: The Politics of London in the First Age of Party, 1688–1715*, p. 125.
85. Colin Brooks, 'Public Finance and Political Stability: The Administration of the Land Tax, 1688–1720', *HJ*, **17** (1974), pp. 281–300; J. V. Beckett, 'Local Custom and the "New Taxation" in the Seventeenth and Eighteenth Centuries: The Example of Cumberland', *Northern History*, **12** (1976), pp. 105–26; J. V. Beckett, 'Land Tax or Excise: The Levying of Taxation in Seventeenth- and Eighteenth-Century England', *EHR*, **100** (1985), pp. 285–308; Jenkins, *Making of a Ruling Class*, pp. 136, 138; Linda Colley, *In Defiance of Oligarchy: The Tory Party 1714–60* (Cambridge, 1982), pp. 14–16; Speck, 'Conflict in Society', in Holmes (ed), *Britain after the Glorious Revolution*, pp. 135–54; Holmes, *British Politics*, pp. xliv–lxii.
86. Geoffrey Holmes, 'The Achievement of Stability: The Social Context of Politics from the 1680s to the Age of Walpole', in Cannon (ed.), *The Whig Ascendancy: Colloquies on Hanoverian England*, pp. 18–19; Jenkins, *Making of a Ruling Class*, pp. 139, 141.
87. De Krey, *Fractured Society*, p. 109.
88. [Henry Sacheverell], *The New Association of those called Moderate-Church Men* (1702), p. 14.
89. *A Letter to a Modern Dissenting Whig*, p. 23; Davenant, *Sir Thomas Double at Court*, p. 76.
90. De Krey, *Fractured Society*, pp. 165–212; *Idem*, 'Political Radicalism in London after the Glorious Revolution', *Journal of Modern History*, **55** (1983), pp. 585–617.
91. *HMC, Portland*, **IV**, p. 532.
92. Rogers, *Whigs and Cities*, pp. 332–4.
93. Leslie, *Rehearsal*, **I**, no. 201, 19 Apr. 1707.
94. Leslie, *Rehearsal*, **I**, no. 44, 26 May – 2 Jun. 1705.
95. F[rancis] A[tterbury], *The Voice of the People, No Voice of God* (1710), pp. 6, 13.
96. Lambe, *Vindication of Dr Sacheverell*, pp. 8–9.
97. [Francis Atterbury], *English Advice to the Freeholders of England* (1715), p. 16.
98. Leslie, *Rehearsal*, **I**, no. 24, 6–13 Jan. 1704/5.

CHAPTER EIGHT
Jacobitism

Not everyone was reconciled to the breach in the succession that occurred with the Glorious Revolution. There were a number of
Jacobite plots throughout the 1690s, as various attempts were made to
help James II recapture his Crown, including a plot to assassinate William
III in 1696, and in 1715 there was a rebellion in Scotland and the
north of England on behalf of his son, James Francis Stuart (the Old
Pretender). Jacobitism was a continual destabilising force in British
politics under the later Stuarts, so it is vital to consider precisely what
impact it had on partisan strife during this period, and exactly how
widespread sympathies for the exiled Stuarts were amongst the general
population. This is a subject over which there has been much controversy. Some believe that Jacobitism was a fairly significant force
both within the Tory party and in society at large (especially north of
the border), so that at the time of the Hanoverian succession there was
a realistic chance that a Jacobite coup might succeed.[1] Others see the
Jacobites as a small minority of rather cranky dissidents, who included
amongst their ranks not just extreme Tories, but also professional plotters and even some outré Whigs, and would maintain that a Jacobite
rebellion never stood any realistic chance of success.[2]

Jacobitism is not an easy subject to study, because of the problems
inherent in the sources. Since Jacobite activity was by definition trea-
sonous, every wise Jacobite presumably did his best not to leave in-
criminatory evidence behind. There is plenty of material about
Jacobite activity from those hostile to a Stuart restoration, but since
this was a time when immense political advantage was to be gained by
tarnishing one's opponents with the stigma of loyalty to the exiled

royal family, such sources must be treated with immense scepticism. Some of the correspondence sent to the Jacobite Court in St Germain-en-Laye has survived, although few original letters have come down to us, and we are heavily reliant on copies and draft translations into French.[3] The main source for the history of Jacobitism is the Stuart papers, but they have survived only in part for the period before 1715, since the Stuart papers kept at the Scots College in Paris were almost totally destroyed by fire during the French Revolution.[4]

Even without these source difficulties, identifying who the Jacobites were would be an extremely difficult task. For obvious reasons, few people were likely to admit to being Jacobites. Yet what degree of commitment should we expect from someone before we decide to label them a Jacobite? Should we include anyone who just wished James II or the Old Pretender well? Or should we limit ourselves only to those who were prepared to engage actively on behalf of the cause? A Jacobite agent writing towards the end of Queen Anne's reign thought that there were people in England who 'wish the King [i.e. 'James III'] well, who would not hazard their estates for him'.[5] The test of being an active rebel is clearly inappropriate, since it would exclude the likes of William Shippen, a notorious Jacobite MP who nevertheless avoided being implicated in the 'Fifteen.[6] On the other hand, we cannot assume that all people accused of Jacobite activity were guilty as charged; some fell victim to the false allegations of professional perjurers.[7]

The issue is further complicated by the fact that many people remained inconsistent in their Jacobitism. Some drifted towards a Jacobite position as others moved away from it. Then there was what might be-called 'fire-insurance Jacobitism': in the 1690s a number of leading politicians – amongst them Tories such as Marlborough and Godolphin and Whigs such as Shrewsbury and Edward Russell – thought it wise to maintain some contact with the exiled Stuarts so that their own political security would be guaranteed should there be another Stuart restoration.[8] There were some people who might show sympathy towards the Jacobites even though they were not Jacobites themselves. There was treachery even in the executive branch of William's government: as Paul Hopkins has shown, Jacobites received constant information from the secretaries' clerks on warrants and charges against them, and the messengers who made arrests and detained prisoners were often not reliable.[9] Non-Jacobites might have close contacts with people who were Jacobites. John Ellis, who was Under-Secretary of State to William, had one brother who was a Secretary to James and another who was a Catholic bishop. The brother of the

loyal Lord Bath joined the Court at St Germain. The Earl of Nottingham, an entirely loyal minister of state, was nevertheless subsidising
William Lloyd, the deprived Bishop of Norwich, who was in regular
contact with those who were trafficking with France.[10]

It will be the argument here that Jacobitism was not a coherent
movement. A Jacobite solution could be attractive to different people
for different reasons at different times. This chapter will begin, therefore, by examining the different dimensions of Jacobitism, and then
proceed to a consideration of how extensive Jacobite sentiment was in
British society at large. It will be suggested that those who became
Jacobites because of a deep attachment to the principles of divine-right
monarchy and Stuart legitimism were relatively few; most who turned
to Jacobitism did so because of disillusionment with developments after
the Glorious Revolution. Jacobitism became an ideology of opposition, and Jacobites tended to unite around negatives; there was much
less support for the positive alternative represented by either James II
or his son, the Old Pretender. Hostility towards the policies and corrupt practices associated with the Court Whigs might have caused
more and more people to look on the possibility of a Stuart Restoration with increasing sympathy; the fact that the Stuarts never re-
nounced their Catholicism and remained closely identified with France
explains why this growing sympathy was never translated into an effective challenge to the Protestant succession as guaranteed by the
Glorious Revolution and the Act of Settlement.

THE DIMENSIONS OF JACOBITISM

A small group of people, known as the Non-Compounders, desired an
unconditional restoration of James II. Their following was probably
quite small in England, but the Jacobite Court which was established
at St Germain-en-Laye near Paris was dominated by them, many of
whom were former Catholic servants of the King. Those at St Germain
never questioned the validity of James II's acts as King, and for them
the Revolution remained totally unjustifiable. They put their trust in a
military solution to right the wrong that had been done in 1688, and
looked to France for help. They also co-ordinated the Jacobite organisation, had spies and correspondents in England, and directed propaganda. The Court at St Germain, however, was riven with personal
rivalries and intrigues, which weakened Jacobite organisation consider-

ably. There were also religious differences between Catholics and Protestants, as well as tensions between English, Scottish and Irish factions. Those at the exiled Court became hopelessly out of touch with political realities in post-Revolutionary England; many of them were living in the world as they thought it had been in the late 1680s, and their platform increasingly appeared to have less and less relevance to the new problems facing England. By contrast, the majority of English Jacobites desired a conditional restoration of James II, with firm guarantees for the security of the Protestant religion and certain limitations placed on the power of the Crown. They therefore disagreed with St Germain over a number of fundamentals: their view of the Revolution; their view of the constitution; the advisability of an attempted military solution; their attitude towards France; and, perhaps most importantly, their attitude towards Catholicism.[11]

Many English Catholics remained deeply committed to the Stuart dynasty, for obvious reasons, although they were only a tiny minority of the population. Besides them, support for Jacobitism in England stemmed from two main sources. There were those whose attachment to the principles of divine right and hereditary succession was so strong that they felt that James and his heirs could be the only legitimate Kings of England, whilst others turned to Jacobitism out of disillusionment with political developments since the Revolution. Of the two, historians normally attach greatest significance to the former. Jacobite propaganda repeatedly rehearsed the principles of Stuart legitimism.[12] Such a belief did not necessarily entail an uncritical acceptance of everything James II had done as King. Nevertheless it was the King's ministers, the argument ran, who should be held accountable for the misdeeds of the Crown, not the King himself. As Alexander Irvine put it in 1694:

> it is a Maxim in our Law, 'That the King can do no Wrong'; the Meaning whereof is not, that nothing can be done amiss that he does in point of Government, but whatever there is amiss to it, is not to be imputed to him, but to those by whose Advice and Ministry he acts; and consequently, that not he, but they are punishable for them.

In this instance, however, Irvine believed, 'the case is quite inverted', for 'the King himself is charged with all the Faults of Government, and . . . punished for them', and his ministers 'not only suffered to escape Punishment, but . . . highly preferr'd and rewarded' – a reference, in particular, to the favour shown by William to James's former chief advisor, the second Earl of Sunderland.[13]

The group who were the most uncompromising in their attachment to divine and hereditary right were the Nonjurors. They were not numerous: only a minority of lay office-holders refused the oaths of allegiance to William and Mary (although they included ten peers and sixty-one present or former MPs), as did a little under 400 clergymen (3.5 per cent of a total clerical estate of at least 12,000). But the significance of the Nonjurors was much greater than their numbers might suggest. Nearly half of the episcopal hierarchy refused the new oaths, and as a result opened up a schism in the Anglican Church. Moreover, the Nonjurors included some of the best scholars of the day, skilful and productive polemicists who made a powerful intellectual impact: well over one hundred political pamphlets are attributable to them.[14]

In one sense, the Nonjurors were Jacobites by definition, since they refused to accept that as a result of the Revolution William and Mary were now rightful and lawful rulers instead of James. However, only a few Nonjurors became active Jacobites, in the sense of being agents or conspirators. The second Earl of Clarendon was involved in the Preston Plot of 1690, as was Bishop Turner of Ely, whilst at various times Charles Leslie and George Hickes worked for the exiled Court. Some Nonjurors, though never implicated in Jacobite intrigue, nevertheless were committed to the principle of a Stuart restoration – for example the cleric, Jeremy Collier, or the lawyer, Roger North, who had been attorney-general to the Queen in James II's reign.[15] Yet there were others who clearly did not relish James's rule, having actively opposed him when King, and who did their best to distance themselves from the Jacobite cause after the Revolution, Archbishop Sancroft being the most famous example. It was not so much Jacobite principle that led to Nonjurism, but rather a sincerely held belief about the inviolable nature of oaths. Some lay Nonjurors returned to communion with the Church of England after the death of James II, feeling that now they were relieved from the oaths, as did some of their clerical counterparts after the demise of the last Nonjuring bishop in 1710. In contrast, Jacobites often showed few scruples about taking oaths. In a pamphlet of 1693, the Nonjuror Jeremy Collier, himself a Jacobite, rebuked those Jacobites who had submitted to the oaths in order to further their cause.[16] John Lade, later to be MP for Southwark, shortly after the passage of the Abjuration Act of 1702, said 'that his friends, meaning the Jacks, were milksops for kicking at oaths, asserting they should never be able to do anything if they, his friends, did not take all the oaths that could be imposed'.[17] Those Nonjurors who remained committed to a Jacobite restoration were often at odds with St Germain, being both anti-French and anti-Catholic.

Whigs often liked to suggest that all Tories were by definition sympathetic to a restoration of the Stuarts, because of their belief in indefeasible hereditary right.[18] However, most historians would agree that, at least until the Hanoverian Succession, only a minority of Tories were Jacobites. As we have already seen, Tories were largely able to accommodate themselves to the Revolution; most could accept William at least as *de facto* ruler, and some, following Edmund Bohun, were even able to rationalise the events of 1688–9 in such a way as to conclude that William was also monarch *de jure*.[19] Most Tories supported the Act of Settlement of 1701.[20] The latest study of Jacobitism within the Tory party at the end of Anne's reign has identified only fifty-one probable and a further fifteen possible Jacobite MPs during the period 1710–14, when Parliamentary Jacobitism was at its strongest. There were at most twenty-two Jacobite peers in the House of Lords, ten of whom were Scottish representative peers, who owed their places to the Union of 1707 (under the terms of which, the Scottish peers as a whole elected sixteen of their number to sit in the upper chamber at Westminster). Moreover, unlike their counterparts at St Germain or amongst the Nonjurors, these Jacobite MPs were not 'archaic unreconstructed upholders of Divine Right', but Country Tories. They were concerned about the threat to English liberties posed by corruption, placemen and the growth of the executive, and championed not Stuart absolutism, but mixed monarchy, the ancient constitution and the liberties of Parliament.[21]

Indeed, it should not be assumed that Jacobitism was based solely – or even primarily – on the legitimist principle. Jacobitism often grew out of disillusionment with developments which had happened since the Revolution, rather than out of opposition to the Revolution itself. Jacobite literature from the early years of William's reign commonly rehearsed Country arguments, complaining about the arbitrary style of William's rule (the suspension of habeas corpus, the vetoing of Parliamentary bills), the mismanagement of the war, heavy taxation, the decay of trade, and the influence of Dutch favourites.[22] One anonymous poem from these years, for example, stated that

> . . . now we're come to count our gains
> Wee fynd wee did but shift our chains,
> The Tyrant's gon, the Tyranny remains.[23]

Country Jacobitism and legitimism were not necessarily incompatible. Propagandists could always argue that the fact that so many misfortunes had befallen England since the Revolution confirmed how wrong it had been to dethrone the rightful sovereign.[24] Country-Tory Jacobites in Parliament, whilst critical of what James II had done as King, nevertheless maintained that a restoration of the ancient constitution required a restoration of the right line.[25] Yet a number of those who became Jacobites had no particular attachment to the legitimist principle, including several former Whigs. Some MPs who had previously voted for the Exclusion Bill turned Jacobite, amongst them Sir William Whitlock (a former member of the Green Ribbon Club) and Edward Harvey (though in the process they also became High Tories). So too did a number of James II's Whig collaborators of 1687–8: the Quaker, William Penn; Penn's associate, Charlwood Lawton; the Independent divine, Stephen Lobb; and the Presbyterian lawyer, Edward Nosworthy, another erstwhile member of the Green Ribbon Club. The Quakers, in particular, had obvious reasons for continuing to support James, for the toleration they enjoyed towards the end of his reign was far more extensive than that allowed under the Toleration Act of 1689. Yet we also have the example of Robert Ferguson, the Whig plotter who had been mixed up in the Rye House intrigues and Monmouth's Rebellion. Ferguson, in fact, had been fiercely critical of those Dissenters who had taken advantage of James II's Declaration of Indulgence of 1687; by 1690, however, he had turned Jacobite.[26]

These 'Whiggish Jacobites', as they referred to themselves, produced a number of pamphlets in which they argued that William, through various acts of despotism, had broken the contract he had made with the nation in 1689, and thus forfeited his right to obedience.[27] In a tract of 1695, Ferguson complained that William had 'departed from our known Laws . . . utterly Impoverished us', and had attempted to bribe 'so many Members of both Houses to sell their Country' that it amounted to 'a direct subversion of the Constitution'. In typical Whig language, Ferguson concluded that

> the Sovereign having no other Ground of claim to any Power or
> Prerogative, save what he hath from the Constitution which hath settled
> and vested them in him, That Prince who goes about to overthrow this,
> does all he can to cancel his own Right.[28]

An anonymous tract of February 1691 started with the premise that 'Government as ordained by God, has for its End or Object the Common Good', and argued that the heavy taxes, the decay of trade, and the oppressions of war suffered under William meant that his Government was 'not an Upholder of the common good; and consequently

. . . no more a Government'.[29] Many of these Whig Jacobite tracts can be said to reflect commonwealth principles, in the sense that they argued for a monarchy which would be severely limited. One author denounced the Convention for making William King without making it 'impossible for that king to be like the kings that went before him'; another condemned the members of the Convention because

> They did not mend the Constitution . . . . Had we our Annuall Parliaments Settled, the Negative Voice Restrained, a Committee of Lords and Commons to be the Privy-Council, no Officers of the King to serve in Parliament, the Revenue Appropriated, all Eminent Offices had upon good Behaviour and Election of Members to Parliament secured, the Work might have deserved a better Character'.[30]

What the Whiggish Jacobites wanted, therefore, was a conditional restoration of James II. As Charlwood Lawton put it in 1693, there were Jacobites for reformations, 'That think it Lawful for Kings, and their Parliaments, to limit and explain the Nature of Prerogatives', and he went on to advocate certain legal reforms, reform of the militia, the frequent sitting of Parliament (Lawton was writing before the passage of the 1694 Triennial Act), and Parliament's right to scrutinise and punish ministers of state.[31]

The attempt to build a broad Jacobite alliance of disaffected Whigs and Tories around Country principles met with some degree of success in the early 1690s. When a proposed Abjuration Bill was defeated in the House in December 1692, it was reported that 'the Jacobites and Comonwealths men joyn'd together' to oppose it.[32] Some Whigs were implicated in Jacobite activities, amongst them John Wildman, Charles Mordaunt (third Earl of Monmouth), the Earls of Dorset and Shrewsbury, and the Duke of Bolton, although whether we should see their alleged intrigues as much more than fire-insurance Jacobitism is unclear.[33] Jacobite pamphlets often reflected an awareness of the mixed nature of their support. Lawton, for example, claimed to speak for the Whiggish Jacobites, the Church of England Jacobites, and the Roman Catholics.[34] James II even issued a Country Jacobite declaration in April 1693, promising to do 'more for their Constitution, than the most renowned of our Ancestors', by instituting free elections and frequent Parliaments, and by allowing Parliament to determine the limits of his dispensing power.[35] The Country Jacobite coalition, however, did not last. There were too many internal contradictions which prevented the different constituencies from working effectively together. If Country Jacobitism had for a time in the early 1690s represented an alliance of disillusioned Whigs and Tories, it nevertheless ended up as a platform which drew support almost exclusively from Tories.

JACOBITISM IN SOCIETY

Jacobite polemicists sought to target a mass audience. Much of their propaganda was produced in a popular idiom, such as poems and broadsides, clearly designed for people who might lack the sophistication to cope with the lengthier, more intellectual justifications of Jacobitism. There were even Jacobite ballads, some of them performed by itinerant singers; in this way, the Jacobite message could be transmitted even to those who could not read.[36] One way we can examine the nature and extent of Jacobite sympathies amongst the populace is by looking at those who got into trouble with the law for Jacobite disaffection. Beyond investigating who engaged in actual plotting, we can examine riots and demonstrations which seem to have had Jacobite overtones, and also look at more individual statements of Jacobite sympathy such as the uttering of seditious words.

Most cases of seditious words expressed a belief in the principle of Stuart legitimacy.[37] In November 1691, for example, Clemens Storey, a London woollendraper, expressed his belief that King James was 'the right and lawfull King', whilst in September 1695 George Dent, a Southwark glover, allegedly said that 'King James hath more right to the Crowne than King William and that King William is not Lawfull King, and that he is a Nasty Little Fellow'.[38] Sometimes the principle of legitimism was voiced in an explicitly Anglican context. Towards the end of May 1689 one Londoner said that 'the Crowne and Kingdome was King James proper right', and 'that King James had promist to settle the Church as now by law Established'.[39] After James II's death, and during the reign of Anne, Jacobites usually claimed that James Francis Stuart was the rightful heir to the throne, who should succeed his sister: it was not until after the Hanoverian succession that we find him being hailed as James III.

Yet such evidence, taken at face value, perhaps gives a misleading impression about the significance of legitimism as a determinant of Jacobite disaffection. What else should we expect to find from such a source? Jacobite seditious words, by their nature, express the belief that James should be King and not William; often the speeches recorded in the legal documents are short and cryptic, and do not offer a full explanation of how that belief came to be arrived at. There is sufficient evidence to suggest, however, that Jacobite disaffection might commonly have arisen out of dissatisfaction with William. Some of the speeches were more anti-William than pro-James. Charges that there had been no good times in England since William came in, or that William had ruined the nation, were fairly common.[40] Sometimes seditious speeches complained about the various injustices suffered under William, reflecting a Country Jacobite position. John Owen was a Bristol gentleman who, as he admitted in 1692, looked to James's return as a way of getting relief from the burdens of the customs and excise.[41] There was also resentment against the Dutch. William Pennington, a London labourer, allegedly said in December 1689 'God damne King William and Queene Mary for a Dutch Dogg and a Dutch Bitch', whilst in the summer of that year George Smith, after drinking a pot of ale in an alehouse in Coleman Street, had said 'God Damn all the Dutch Men . . . . Bake them in An Oven and Broile them on a GridIron'.[42] James Weenes, in a conversation he had with the wife of a London weaver in September 1690, expressed his opinion that William was 'a Dutch Dogg and an Usurper', who 'like a Villain came and took the Crowne from the head of his Father', and also that 'the nobility was a parcel of Rogues and all of them lived as high as Kings. And that the nobility did not vote in King William for the good of the Commonwealth nor for religion but to preserve their riches and honours' – a curious speech which combined legitimism with Country Jacobitism and even a sense of class hostility.[43]

Although the evidence of seditious words can tell us something about the range of motives which led people to Jacobitism, it can tell us little about how prevalent such sympathies were. Often, the words alleged against the accused were spoken in an alehouse, and although alcohol might help loosen one's inhibitions, we surely have to be sceptical about the depth of commitment of someone whose only Jacobite statement was made in a drunken stupor. We also have the problems of erroneous accusation and malicious prosecution. Most charges of seditious words occurred during times of Jacobite scares and tended to be levied at those groups suspected of Jacobite sympathy: Roman Catholics, the Irish, Nonjurors, and the high-flying clergy and gentry. Given the fact that less than 30 per cent of charges brought resulted in successful conviction (when the rate for most other crimes was about 50 per cent), we may wonder how much substance there was in many of the accusations, or whether at times of political anxiety certain types of people were likely to be vulnerable to false accusations because they conformed to the popular stereotype of who a Jacobite was.[44]

There are only a few isolated examples of Jacobite riots or demonstrations in England during the 1690s, perhaps suggesting that Jacobite sentiment was not particularly widespread. In Bristol there was much revelry on the occasion of Queen Mary's death in 1694, as people celebrated to refrains of 'The King shall enjoy his own again'.[45] The decision by the Whig House of Commons to overturn the election of Samuel Swift in February 1694 to serve as MP for Worcester in favour of the man he had defeated, who happened to be brother-in-law to the Junto chief, Lord Somers, provoked demonstrations in the city, with crowds shouting 'A Cheat, A Cheat, A Presbiterian Cheat. All honesty was taken away with K[ing] J[ames]'. When Swift returned to Worcester a few days later, he was greeted with the ringing of bells, illuminations and bonfires, at many of which could be heard the tune of 'The King shall have his own again'.[46] However, other Jacobite demonstrations from this time appear to have lacked much genuine support. There were disturbances in Drury Lane on 10 June 1695, when a number of people gathered at the Dog Tavern to celebrate the birthday of the Prince of Wales. In the evening they constructed a bonfire outside, where they drank the healths of James II and his son, forcing passers-by to do the same, and offering insults to those who refused. The Dog Tavern was a notorious Jacobite haunt, and the demonstration appears to have been staged by Jacobite agents as a way of testing popular sympathies. The result was disappointing, since the effect was to prompt the appearance of a Williamite crowd, who managed to drive away the Jacobites.[47] In November 1697 a group of men in Carlisle committed a riot on the day that the conclusion of the peace was announced, 'threatening to break the windows . . . being illuminated upon that occasion, causing the Candles to be put out, and offering mony to drink King James's health'.[48] Yet what seems to have upset them was the fact that many of the townsfolk were celebrating William's peace.

Although there was a flurry of Jacobite plotting and conspiracy in the period 1689–97, none of it stood much chance of success. Jacobitism as a movement was as yet too incoherent and badly organised, and lacked a firm social base. Support for the exiled King was greatest amongst Catholic recusants and immigrant Irish in the north, who played a prominent role in the plots of the 1690s.[49] There were pockets of disaffection in other parts of the country, amongst Anglicans and even Quakers, but these were thin on the ground; the memories of the 1680s were still too powerful to make many people seriously wish to see the Stuarts back on the throne again. Despite the existence of a certain amount of disaffection towards William's regime, the attempts by Jacobite agents to turn this into a more positive commitment to the Jacobite cause were largely unsuccessful. Indeed, Jacobite activity was more likely to provoke the wrath of the common people. There was a riot against suspected Jacobites in London in early August 1690, at the time of the Jacobite insurrection in Ireland, and the prospect of a French-backed invasion across the channel in May 1692 led to talk of a further rising by Londoners against those suspected of disaffection.[50] If James II were to recapture his throne, it would have to be by force, as the result of a successful foreign invasion, but William's government proved more than a match, putting down the Jacobite rebellions in Scotland and Ireland, and defeating the prospect of a French-backed invasion with victory at La Hogue in 1692.

Jacobitism seemed to be growing more widespread in England towards the end of Anne's reign. A greater distance from the events of 1680s made it easier for people to develop a nostalgic longing for the return of the exiled Stuarts as the solution to the nation's ills. War weariness was increasing the unpopularity of the Whigs, and although the Tories were happy with Queen Anne, the prospect of the succession of the House of Hanover, foreign Lutherans who were known to be sympathetic to the Whigs, was not particularly appealing to them. Jacobite candidates did well in the elections to Anne's last two Parliaments, although it must be remembered that Tory candidates in general did well, so that the absolute rise in the number of Jacobite MPs did not necessarily reflect a relative rise in the strength of Jacobitism within the Tory party as a whole. But electoral success gave the Jacobites a greater visibility at the centre of politics, and perhaps encouraged fellow travellers in the localities to become more open about their political convictions. Jacobitism was noticeably strong in parts of Wales, and seemed to develop under Anne because of the strength of the High Church there. The major bastion of Welsh Jacobitism was the north-east, where Watkin Williams Wynn (who was to be MP for Denbighshire from 1716 to 1749) established a Jacobite club called the 'Cycle of the White Rose' on 10 June 1710. Some of the gentry in South Wales also had Jacobite leanings, and looked for leadership to Lewis Pryse of Aberystwyth and the Duke of Beaufort.[51]

There was extensive Jacobite unrest throughout much of England in the years following the Hanoverian Succession. There were riots in London, throughout much of the midlands and the north-west, in parts of the west and of Wales, and also in cities such as Bristol, Oxford, Cambridge, and Norwich.[52] These disturbances typically evinced a High Church and Country Tory brand of Jacobitism. The Hanoverian succession *per se* does not appear to have been what triggered most of the unrest. It is true that cases of seditious words brought before the courts at the time of the disturbances show that disaffection was often expressed in terms of a belief in Stuart legitimism: in early 1715, Londoner Phillip Hide cursed King George and said 'he had no right to the Crowne of England', whilst on 29 May 1715, during the Jacobite demonstrations in London, John Burnoist was noticed to be wandering the streets shouting 'James the third is right and Lawfull King of England', the 'protector of the protestant religion', and 'George is a Usurper to the Crown'.[53] Yet it seems to have been the realisation of what the Hanoverian succession would mean – namely Whig supremacy – which provoked the disturbances. The proclamation of George as King in August 1714 provoked little discontent, although some observers did notice that the celebrating was not that extensive either.[54] There was unrest in some twenty-six English and Welsh towns on 20 October, the day of George's coronation, by which time the new monarch had already begun to turn out the old Tory ministers and replace them by Whigs. But the disorders really began to escalate after the spring of 1715, which saw the consolidation of the Whigs in power as a result of their success in the General Election of March, achieved with the full weight of royal patronage behind them. Whig political supremacy aroused not only High Church anxieties about the security of the established Church, but also fears about Whig warmongering and the concomitant high taxation, which were intensified when the new administration began impeachment proceedings against those responsible for the Tory peace of 1713. Even Thomas Hearne, a Nonjuring Jacobite who himself was convinced that James III was the legitimate King, nevertheless thought that the reason why people were becoming more sympathetic to a Stuart restoration was a result of the favour George I had shown to the Whigs:

> He hath turned the Tories out, and filled all places with those of the Whiggish party. This hath justly caused Abundance of Discontent, and 'tis from hence that we have heard of so many Tumults and Riots. Those that were before against K. James are now zealous in his Behalf.[55]

Most of the riots followed a similar pattern. Angry crowds would curse George I, Whigs and Dissenters, the Duke of Marlborough (a warmonger, and the man widely believed to be responsible for encouraging George I to show all his favour to the Whigs), and often even William III, whilst reserving their cheers for James III, the Duke of Ormonde (the Tory who had replaced Marlborough as Captain-

General of the Land Forces in 1712), Dr Sacheverell, and the Church of England. Public anniversaries normally provided the cue for unrest. Important days in the Jacobite calendar were 23 April (the anniversary of the coronation not only of Queen Anne, but also of Charles II and James II), 29 May (Restoration day), and 10 June (the Pretender's birthday). Days from the Whig or Hanoverian calendar of celebration – such as 28 May (George I's birthday), 1 August (George I's accession day), 20 October (George I's coronation day), 30 October (the birthday of George, Prince of Wales), and 4 and 5 November (the birthday of William III and the dual anniversary of Gunpowder Treason day and William's landing at Torbay) – could often provoke Jacobite counter-theatre of mockery and subversion. But there was also unrest on other occasions, as in the summer months of 1715 and 1716. All of the riots evinced deep hostility towards the Nonconformists (and especially the Presbyterians), and would typically reach a climax with the demolition of the local meeting-houses. One correspondent, seeking to explain the motives behind the attack on the meeting-houses in the west midlands in the summer of 1715, informed Staffordshire MP, William Ward, that the rioters

> have got a Notion, that the Ministry and Dissenters have ruined Trade, on Purpose to make the Nation out of Love with the late Peace, and Peace-makers; and because the Ministry, and secret Committee, and their Friends, will not let the Country have Peace and Trade, they resolve (if they can hinder it) the Dissenters shall not have a quiet Toleration.[56]

Some of the disturbances were triggered by the provocative actions of local Whigs and Dissenters. At Dorchester on 20 October 1714, the day of George's coronation, it was the decision of the Dissenters to burn an effigy of the Pretender that provoked the wrath of the Jacobites, who armed with clubs proceeded to set about 'those who carried him about the Town. . . . Crying out "Who dare disowne the Pretender?!" . . . drinking Dr Sacheverell's health and insulting the Meeting House'.[57] The riots in Bristol on that day were triggered by rumours that the Whigs were going to burn an effigy of Dr Sacheverell.[58] In other places we find Whig crowds retaliating to a Tory initiative. At West Bromwich in the west midlands the Dissenters defended their meeting-house with guns and swords, some of them even being mounted on horses.[59] In London Whigs and Dissenters not only organised counter-demonstrations, where they burnt effigies of the Pope, the Pretender and Tory defectors, but they also engaged in vigilante activity, as they sought to suppress the activities of the Jacobite crowds.

An analysis of those involved in the Jacobite disturbances shows that most came from the petty trading and artisanal classes of the towns and industrial villages. These were the groups which had suffered most from the dislocations of the war, and an element of class antagonism can perhaps be detected in their hatred of wealthy Whig financiers and rich local Dissenters (especially the Presbyterians). The class dimension should not be pushed too far, however. Jacobite crowds sometimes attacked poor Dissenting groups, such as the Baptists. Moreover, some of the riots were incited by local High Church clergy and gentry. There is a certain amount of evidence to suggest that local Tory leaders played a part in inciting the unrest. The Dorchester crowd that sought to rescue the Pretender's effigy from being burnt by the Dissenters on George I's coronation day were encouraged by a certain gentleman who gave them half a hogshead of beer.[60] The riot at Bristol on that day was instigated by an organisation known as 'the Loyal Society'.[61] The Jacobite riot at Newcastle-under-Lyme in July 1715 was a well-planned and carefully staged affair, and one of the patrons seems to have been Ralph Sneyd, MP for Staffordshire.[62] This is not to suggest that all the anti-Hanoverian crowds were encouraged from above; as Nicholas Rogers has shown, patrician involvement seems to have become less common after the early stages of unrest, and increasingly the riots in most areas appear to have been led from below by more lowly types.[63] And although Whig observers typically suggested that Jacobite agents had 'animated the mob', there is little evidence to suggest that this was the case. It seems that the unrest should be seen as an authentic expression of High Church hostility towards Whigs and Dissenters, shared by plebeians, gentry and clergy alike. Such an interpretation is reinforced by an analysis of the geography of protest. The riots occurred in places which were strongholds of Tory Anglicanism, but where there was a highly visible and influential Dissenting presence. There was extensive unrest in the west midlands, and in particular in Staffordshire, and these were the areas which had rapturously received Dr Sacheverell on his triumphant progress following his trial of 1710. The Jacobite unrest in Bristol, Norwich and London was symptomatic of the bitter political tensions which existed in these communities between Tories and High Church Anglicans on the one hand and Whigs and Nonconformists on the other.

Historians have been more dismissive of the evidence of Whig crowds at the Hanoverian Succession, on the grounds that these appear to have been deliberately manipulated from above. We know that in London, for example, the anti-Jacobite crowds were organised by loyal societies (or 'mug-houses', as they were known) run by Whig politicians and members of the urban elite.[64] Yet given the strength of Dissent in the capital and the depth of religious tensions, there is no reason to doubt that the rank and file who followed the leaders of the mug riots were genuinely anti-Tory.[65] The fact that several provincial towns reported pope-burnings in November 1714 and 1715 should make us question how extensive support for the Jacobite position was at this time.[66] And it should be remembered that the Whigs did much better than the Tories in the open and more popular constituencies in the elections of early 1715, largely because the Jacobite scare and the fear of popery worked to their advantage.[67] All this should remind us that it would be unwise to read the Jacobite unrest of 1714–17 as being a typical reflection of public opinion; the public were divided, and a significant number remained pro-Whig and pro-Hanoverian.

SCOTTISH JACOBITISM

Jacobite sentiment was most widespread north of the border. This is not to say that James II (or VII as he was in his northern Kingdom) was any more popular in Scotland at the time of the Revolution than he had been in England. His rule had managed to alienate most of the traditional elites in both town and countryside, and few people were prepared to stir themselves on James's behalf when the crisis came. Although there was a Jacobite rebellion in the summer of 1689, led by John Graham of Claverhouse, Viscount Dundee, and supported by some of the Highland clans, it was not joined by any of the major regional magnates. However, there was also little positive support for William, except from the Presbyterian extremists, who wanted a radical constitutional and ecclesiastical settlement. Although William would have been happy to keep bishops within the Kirk, the Scottish episcopal bench, led by Bishop Alexander Rose of Edinburgh, refused to accept the legitimacy of the new regime. As a result, episcopacy was abolished and a Presbyterian settlement established. The Church settlement was bitterly resented amongst the Scottish nobility, and also amongst many of the established clergy, more than half of whom refused to accept the abolition of episcopacy. Although more than 650 Scottish clergymen were deprived in theory, in practice it was difficult to find staunch Presbyterians to replace them, and many continued to be active. In contrast to the English Nonjurors, whose Jacobitism tended to be lukewarm at best, the Scottish episcopal clergy actively preached the divine right of the Stuarts to real power. Episcopalianism, combined with legitimism, therefore, became the major ground for Scottish Jacobitism.[68]

Support for the Jacobite cause grew further as a result of the insensitive way the new regime in England began to govern Scotland. William's attempt to achieve a pacification of the Highlands turned into a disastrous tragedy, when the dreadful massacre at Glencoe was carried out in February 1692 because MacDonald of Glencoe accidentally missed the deadline imposed by the government for swearing the oath of allegiance to William by five days. William also upset the political classes of lowland Scotland. He kept his Secretary of State for Scotland in London. He ignored the demand for frequent Parliaments in the Scottish Claim of the Right, instead keeping the Convention Parliament sitting in Scotland for nine consecutive sessions. The post-Revolution wars placed a terrible burden on the Scottish economy, exacerbated by the fact that the 1690s in Scotland saw a major crisis of subsistence. The final act of betrayal by William's ministers was committed when they failed to call Parliament within twenty days of his death (a violation of the Act of Security of 1696), so that the Privy Council would have time to declare war on France without facing opposition from the Scottish Parliament. Increasingly the Scots were coming to feel that they had benefited little from the establishment of the new regime in 1689, and as a result Jacobitism north of the border took on nationalistic overtones. To quote Bruce Lenman, 'a very substantial and apparently growing section of the Scottish ruling class was prepared to embrace Jacobitism as an expression of a complex of resentments against their English masters'.[69]

The developments of the 1690s could be as upsetting to Presbyterians who had supported the Revolution as to Episcopalians. The growing Country opposition to William's ministry in the Scottish Parliament consisted mainly of men who stood on a Revolution and Presbyterian foot, but whose exclusion from office exacerbated their disillusionment and allowed them to indulge their nationalist sentiments.[70] Although this Presbyterian nationalism did not normally lead to Jacobitism, we do see a brand of Scottish Whig Jacobitism during William's reign, centring around the person of James Montgomerie of Skelmorlie. He had been the leader of the 'Club' which had sought to impose a radical, Presbyterian settlement on William in 1689–90. Even before the final settlement was reached, Montgomerie, disillusioned by William's stalling tactics and by the fact that his own personal political ambitions had been frustrated, turned to plotting, attempting to build up an alliance of Club members and Jacobites who would be able to 'bring home King James in a Parliamentary way'. After the collapse of the plot Montgomerie fled to London, but he continued to engage in Jacobite intrigue, and in late 1691 he tried to encourage a rising of Presbyterian extremists in the south-western lowlands. In September 1692 he produced a Whiggish Jacobite tract in which he rehearsed all the traditional charges against William (adding to the list the recent massacre at Glencoe), and argued that 'If it was to preserve our Liberties from the insults of King James, we placed the Prince upon the Throne, we have certainly either mistaken the Disease or the Cure'. He was to end his days at St Germain in 1694.[71]

Whig Jacobitism, however, appears to have been of minimal significance in Scotland. Most historians see Montgomerie as a rather unstable figure, motivated more by ambition than political principle. Moreover, Presbyterian nationalism was given the kiss of death by the Act of Union of 1707, which most of the influential Presbyterian politicians and clergymen supported. The episcopalians, by contrast, strongly opposed the Union, which proved to be deeply unpopular. Politically, Scotland seemed to have sacrificed her independence by giving up her own Parliament in exchange for a very limited representation in that of England. The supposed economic benefits were slow to materialise, and the immediate consequences seemed to be a loss of trade to France and increased taxation. The Jacobites were quick to assume the leadership of nationalist sentiment in Scotland, by portraying the restoration of Scotland's ancient dynasty as the only way to undo the Union.[72]

By the end of Anne's reign, disaffection north of the border was fairly widespread. Jacobitism's main base was in the north-east lowlands, an area where it had been difficult to insert Presbyterian ministers after the Glorious Revolution, and where Stuart loyalism continued to be nurtured by an active episcopalian clergy. The political allegiances of the Highland clans present a complex picture. Some of the clans, such as the Campbells of Argyll, were staunchly Whig, others were divided amongst themselves, and many were not really committed strongly one way or the other. However, by the time of the 1715 rebellion Jacobitism seems to have been particularly strong amongst the ruling class of the Grampian highlands. The lowland south remained predominantly pro-Hanoverian, but even here Jacobite sentiment was in evidence. For example, there were riots at Edinburgh and Leith on James's birthday in 1712, with people singing 'the King shall enjoy his own again'. It was only really in the south-west (a predominantly Presbyterian area) that the Whig interest seems to have enjoyed overwhelming support.[73]

THE JACOBITE CHALLENGE OF 1714–15

The potential for a successful Jacobite restoration was probably greatest at the time of the Hanoverian Succession. In the last years of Queen Anne's reign Jacobites became hopeful – and Whigs fearful – that the Tory ministry, with the connivance of the Queen, might undo the Act of Settlement and establish the Old Pretender as the next in line to the throne. The Elector of Hanover was known to hold little sympathy for the Tories, whom he felt had betrayed the Allies at the Peace of Utrecht, and few doubted that when George I became King the Tories would lose the political ascendancy they had enjoyed since 1710. Nevertheless, the number of committed Jacobites in Parliament, although greater than at any other time in Anne's reign, was still a small minority, and most Tories appear to have been committed to the Hanoverian Succession, though with varying degrees of enthusiasm. The view that Anne was a sentimental Jacobite who secretly wished her brother-in-law to succeed her has now been debunked as myth. It is true that Robert Harley (now Earl of Oxford) and Viscount Bolingbroke seemed to flirt with Jacobitism in the period 1710–14, but they were never sincere, and their actions must be set in the context of their attempts to rally disparate groups of Tories behind them in their own personal struggle for dominance within the party. Faced with a growing number of desertions from within Tory ranks over the peace negotiations of 1711–13, Oxford needed to court the support of the Scottish Jacobite peers and Jacobite MPs to maintain his majority in Parliament. By promising the Jacobites that he would seek to get James Francis Stuart acknowledged as Anne's successor, he not only won Jacobite support at home, but was also able to neutralise the Jacobite threat abroad, by making it appear that there was no point in St Germain or the French attempting an invasion. Oxford's bluff worked for some time, but when by late 1713 the Jacobites finally realised they had been taken for a ride, they began to look to Bolingbroke for support. Bolingbroke could not resist the opportunity to control such a crucial bloc of Parliamentary votes, and decided to play them along, but primarily with the aim of strengthening his own position within the party. At the same time he was busy courting his supporters amongst the Country Tories by playing on the theme of the 'Church in Danger', and his strategy appears to have been to unite the various dissident Tories behind him in order to oust Oxford from power, and then try to ensure that Tory political dominance was so unchallengeable that when George I became King he would be forced to work with them. In fact the policy backfired disastrously; when Anne died the Tories were still bitterly divided, and in no position to offer a credible alternative to George I's own preference for a Whig ministry.[74]

The situation of 1715, however, was very different from that of 1714. Political proscription drove more Tories into the arms of the Pretender (amongst them leading figures such as Bolingbroke, Ormonde and Sir William Wyndham) as their only hope of political salvation. As seen above, the accession of George I provoked widespread unrest throughout much of England and Wales, and given the extensive discontent in Scotland, it seemed that the time might be ripe for a Jacobite rebellion. The challenge came on 6 September, when the Earl of Mar raised James III's standard at Braemar in Scotland. Yet after a few weeks, during which time only parts of the north of England and the borders had risen on the Pretender's behalf, the rebellion was put down.

In accounting for the failure of the 'Fifteen, historians sympathetic to Jacobitism tend to stress how difficult it is to launch a successful invasion, and that all the trump cards lie with the government of the day. Although this is undoubtedly true, on two occasions during the period covered by this book (1660 and 1688) an invading army (one from Scotland, the other from Holland) had been able to exploit a severe domestic political crisis and widespread popular disaffection in order to bring about a change of political regimes. That Mar failed where Monck and William of Orange had succeeded is partly related to military factors, but also reflects the fact that neither the domestic political crisis was so severe nor popular disaffection so widespread in 1714–15 as it had been in either 1659–60 or 1688–9. The government of George I and the Whigs never lost its credibility, but retained the support of a substantial proportion of the traditional ruling class and probably a higher proportion of the mass of the population than is usually realised. It never showed any sign of collapsing from within in the way that the governing regimes did in 1659–60 and 1688.

The rebels can be blamed for tactical military mistakes. Mar was initially joined by eighteen lords, bringing with them some 5,000 men, which should have been more than a match for the 1,500 regular troops stationed in Scotland. An immediate offensive might have given victory in Scotland and enabled him to march into England, where Thomas Forster and the Earl of Derwentwater were trying to raise the northern shires on behalf of the Jacobites. However, Mar delayed in an attempt to raise more men, which allowed the British government time to build up concentrations of its own troops and collect reinforcements from its foreign allies. Yet the failure of the 'Fifteen tells us much about the nature and limitations of the Jacobite position. Jacobitism was always more powerful in the negative, as an expression of disaffection; positive commitment to the restoration of the exiled Stuarts was less strong. Many Tories who had flirted with Jacobitism developed second thoughts in 1715. Thomas Forster was the only English Tory MP who actually took up arms for the Pretender. Sir William Wyndham was implicated in a design to raise the Tory-Anglican interest in the west country, but this was frustrated by the government. Some Tories were obviously nervous about converting their disaffection into active treason once it became clear that France, the Jacobites' main European ally, was in no position to back an expeditionary force. But there were others who, despite their disaffection to Hanover, had little desire to risk their necks for the positive alternative the Pretender represented. With the failure of Wyndham's efforts, the rebellion in England became essentially a movement of Catholic recusants in the north, which few Anglicans could have wanted to see succeed, especially since the Pretender had refused to renounce his religion. The Anglican gentry of Cheshire, who had allegedly been ready to rise in August, narrowly voted not to join the rebellion in the north. In many parts of the country, leading Tories were not far behind the Whigs in sending in loyal addresses deploring the threat which the rebellion posed to their religion and liberties.[75] Whereas in 1660 and 1688 the alternative to the existing regime seemed positively attractive to a wide range of people, the same simply was not the case in 1715.

CONCLUSION

Jacobitism was a complex phenomenon, and generalisations about its nature and significance are difficult. As we have seen, there were a variety of different types of Jacobitism, whilst the serious source problems involved in studying this subject will always limit our understanding and inevitably mean that there will continue to be much room for interpretative disagreements. Most scholars have tended to stress the principle of Stuart legitimism as being fundamental to Jacobitism, and certainly this was a significant element. However, this chapter has emphasised that Jacobitism was more potent as a negative force, as an ideology of opposition, a way of expressing dissatisfaction with various post-Revolution developments, rather than as a positive commitment to a Stuart restoration. Jacobitism became attractive to a variety of different groups in the 1690s, including commonwealth Whigs, although at this time it still had little support in society at large. Jacobite sentiment had become more widespread by the end of Anne's reign, and also more distinctively Tory in nature, but it was an attachment to Country ideology, and a deep hostility to the Whigs and Dissenters (and what they stood for), which was its main defining characteristic. It was precisely the power of Jacobitism as a negative ideal which explains the strength of the Jacobite challenge at the time of the Hanoverian succession, but also its ultimate failure, since there were few people who were really committed to the positive alternative which the Stuarts represented.

This analysis sheds much insight into the place of the succession issue in party politics under the later Stuarts. Undoubtedly the succession was an important issue; the terms Whig and Tory had been coined in the first place to describe different sides taken during the Exclusion controversy, whilst for a long time after the Glorious Revolution Whigs continued to be able to embarrass the Tories by alleging that their attachment to the divine-right, hereditary succession meant that deep-down they were Jacobite sympathisers. But the party conflict had always been about more than the succession. Indeed, as this book has argued, party identities were being forged before the succession issue came to the fore, and even during the Exclusion Crisis, party conflict was not solely – or even mainly – about the Catholic succession. Most Tories – whatever the Whigs might charge – were not Jacobites, and could genuinely continue to remain Tories after the Glorious Revolution without wishing to see James II or his heirs restored to the throne. That is because the deeper issues of the party divide lay elsewhere – in the political, constitutional and, in particular, the religious tensions which have been explored in this book, many of which dated back to the Restoration.

REFERENCES

1. Clark, *English Society 1688–1832*, *passim*; J. C. D. Clark, 'On Moving the Middle Ground: The Significance of Jacobitism in Historical Studies', in Eveline Cruickshanks and Jeremy Black (eds), *The Jacobite Challenge* (Edinburgh, 1988), pp. 177–88; Eveline Cruickshanks, *Political*

       Untouchables: The Tories and the '45 (1979); Lenman, *The Jacobite Risings in Britain 1689–1746*; Frank McLynn, *The Jacobites* (1985), p. 79.

2.   Colley, *In Defiance of Oligarchy: The Tory Party 1714–60;* Goldie, 'The Roots of True Whiggism 1688–94' pp. 228–9; G. V. Bennett, 'English Jacobitism, 1710–1715: Myth and Reality', *TRHS*, 5th series, **32** (1982), pp. 137–51.

3.   G. H. Jones, *The Main Stream of Jacobitism* (Cambridge, Mass., 1954), p. 40.

4.   Eveline Cruickshanks, 'Introduction', in her *Ideology and Conspiracy: Aspects of Jacobitism, 1689–1759*, p. 1; Paul Hopkins, *Glencoe and the End of the Highland War* (Edinburgh, 1986), p. 5.

5.   James Macpherson, *Original Papers Concerning the Secret History of Great Britain from the Restoration, to the Accession of the House of Hanover* (2 vols, 1775), **II**, p. 212.

6.   Speck, 'Whigs and Tories', in Cannon (ed.), *The Whig Ascendancy: Colloquies on Hanoverian England*, p. 58.

7.   Paul Hopkins, 'Sham Plots and Real Plots in the 1690s', in Cruickshanks (ed.), *Ideology and Conspiracy*, pp. 89–110.

8.   Jones, *The Main Stream of Jacobitism*, pp. 39–40; Horwitz, *Parliament, Policy and Politics in the Reign of Willaim III*, p. 99; McLynn, *Jacobites*, p. 22.

9.   Hopkins, 'Sham Plots', p. 93.

10.   Feiling, *A History of the Tory Party 1640–1714*, p. 300.

11.   Cruickshanks, *Ideology and Conspiracy*, pp. 5–6; Miller, *James II: A Study in Kingship*, p. 236; Szechi, *Jacobitism and Tory Politics 1710–14*, chs 1, 2.

12   Howard Erskine-Hill, 'Literature and the Jacobite Cause: Was There a Rhetoric of Jacobitism?', in Cruickshanks (ed.), *Ideology and Conspiracy*, pp. 49–69; Paul Monod, *Jacobitism and the English People, 1688–1788* (Cambridge, 1989), ch. 3.

13.   [Alexander Irvine], *A Dialogue Between A. and B. Two Plain Countrey-Gentlemen, Concerning the Times* (1694), p. 29.

14.   My discussion of the Nonjurors draws on: Monod, *Jacobitism,* esp. pp. 17–23, 138–45; John Charles Findon, 'The Nonjurors and the Church of England, 1689–1716', unpub. Oxford DPhil thesis (1978); Goldie, 'Tory Political Thought', ch. 6; *Idem*, 'Nonjurors, Episcopacy, and the Origins of the Convocation Controversy' in Cruickshanks (ed.), *Ideology and Conspiracy*; Henning, *The House of Commons 1660–1690*, **I**, p. 100.

15.   F. J. M. Korsten, *Roger North (1651–1734): Virtuoso and Essayist* (Amsterdam, 1981).

16.   Jeremy Collier, *Perswasive to Consideration, Tender'd to the Royalists* (1693).

17.   Cited in Holmes and Speck, *The Divided Society: Parties and Politics in England 1694–1716*, p. 102.

18.   Holmes and Speck, *Divided Society*, p. 9; BL, Add. MSS 32,095, fol. 409.

19.   See above, pp. 138–9

20. Dickinson, *Liberty and Property: Political Ideology in Eighteenth-Century Britain*, p. 39.

21. Szechi, *Jacobitism and Tory Politics*, pp. 50–4 (quote on p. 52), Appendix 1, pp. 200–3.

22. Horwitz, *Parliament, Policy and Politics*, pp. 99–100.

23. BL Add. MSS 29,497, fol. 75, 'A Familiar Epistle to K.W.'

24. Lenman, *Jacobite Risings*, p. 19.

25. Szechi, *Jacobitism and Tory Politics*, pp. 53–4.

26. Goldie, 'Roots of True Whiggism', pp. 228–9; Paul Monod, 'Jacobitism and Country Principles in the Reign of William III' *HJ*, **30** (1987), p. 300; *Idem, Jacobitism and the English People*, pp. 23–7, 154–7; Henning, *House of Commons*, **II**, p. 505, **III**, p. 712.

27. For example, [Robert Ferguson], *A Letter to Mr. Secretary Trenchard, Discovering a Conspiracy against the Laws and Ancient Constitution of England* (1694). The term 'Whiggish Jacobites' was coined by Charlwood Lawton. See his *A French Conquest Neither Desirable nor Practicable* (1693).

28. [Robert Ferguson], *Whether the Preserving the Protestant Religion was the Motive unto, or the End that was designed in the late Revolution* (1695), p. 42.

29. *The Trimming Court-Divine; Or, Reflexions on Dr Sherlock's Book* (1690), pp. 9, 15–16; CLRO, Sessions File, May 1691, ind. of Thomas Rosse, publisher, shows that it was published in Feb. 1691.

30. *The English Man's Complaint* (1690), p. 1, cited in Horwitz, *Parliament, Policy and Politics*, p. 86; *Humanum est Errare: Or, False Steps on Both Sides* [1689], p. 6.

31. [Charlwood Lawton], *The Jacobite Principles Vindicated* (1693) (quote on p. 3).

32. Rubini, *Court and Country 1688–1702*, p. 43, footnote 28.

33. Goldie, 'Roots of True Whiggism', p. 228; Horwitz, *Parliament, Policy and Politics*, p.99.

34. [Lawton], *French Conquest*.

35. James II, *His Majesties most Gracious Declaration to all his Loving Subjects* (1693).

36. Monod, *Jacobitism*, ch. 2.

37. This section draws on Monod, *Jacobitism*, ch. 8 and Nicholas Rogers 'Popular Protest in Early Hanoverian London', in Slack (ed.), *Rebellion, Popular Protest and the Social Order in Early Modern England*, pp. 263–93, but supplements their material with my own archival research.

38. CLRO, Sessions File, Jan. 1692, ind. of Storey; CLRO, Sessions File, Oct. 1695, rec. 41.

39. CLRO, Sessions Papers, 1689 (undated), information of John Collier.

40. CLRO, Sessions File, Feb. 1690, ind. of Christopher Salisbury; Sessions Papers, Feb. 1690, information of Robert Blackbourn.

41. Paul Monod, 'For the King to Enjoy His Own Again: Jacobite Political Culture in England, 1688–1788', unpub. Yale PhD thesis (1985), p. 367.

42. CLRO, Sessions File, Jan. 1690, ind. of Pennington; CLRO, Sessions File, Jul. 1689, ind. of Smith; Sessions Papers, 1689, informations of Redway et al. (23 June).

43. CLRO, Sessions File, September 1690, rec. 2 (G.D.), ind. of Weenes.
44. Monod, *Jacobitism*, pp. 241, 248.
45. Nicholas Rogers, 'Popular Jacobitism in Provincial Context: Eight-eenth-Century Bristol and Norwich', in Cruickshanks and Black (eds), *Jacobite Challenge*, p. 127.
46. Bodl. Lib., MS Rawlinson Letters 94, fol. 375.
47. GLRO, MJ/SP, Jul. 1695, nos. 45–51; Bodl. Lib., MS Carte 239, fol. 14; Hopkins, 'Aspects of Jacobite Conspiracy', p. 140; Luttrell, *Brief Historical Relation*, **III**, p. 483–4.
48. PRO, PC2/77, fol. 117.
49. Monod, *Jacobitism*, ch. 4.
50. Bodl. Lib, MS Tanner 27, fol. 176; Hopkins, 'Aspects of Jacobite Conspiracy', p. 140.
51. Szechi, *Jacobitism and Tory Politics*; Philip Jenkins, *The Making of a Ruling Class: The Glamorgan Gentry 1640–1790*, pp. 152–3; Idem, 'Jacobites and Freemasons in Eighteenth-Century Wales', *Welsh Historical Review*, **9** (1979), p. 393; Geraint Jenkins, *The Foundations of Modern Wales: Wales 1642–1780*, pp. 148–51.
52. Important discussions of these disturbances can be found in: Monod, *Jacobitism*, pp. 173–94; Rogers, 'Popular Protest in Early Hanoverian London'; Nicholas Rogers, 'Riot and Popular Jacobitism in Early Hanoverian England', in Cruickshanks (ed.), *Ideology and Conspiracy*, pp. 70–88; John Stevenson, *Popular Disturbances in England 1700–1870* (1979), pp. 20–3, 58–9; J. L. Fitts, 'Newcastle's Mob', *Albion*, **5** (1973), pp. 41–9; J. H. Y. Briggs, 'The Burning of the Meeting House, July 1715: Dissent and Faction in Late Stuart Newcastle', *North Staffordshire Journal of Field Studies*, **14** (1974), pp. 61–79; D. G. Isaacs, 'A Study of Popular Disturbances in Britain, 1714–54', unpub. Edinburgh University PhD thesis (1953), ch. 8.
53. CLRO, Sessions Papers, Jan./Feb./Apr. 1715, informations of Charles Stuart and Edward Walter; *Ibid.*, May 1715, various informations against John Burnoist.
54. Hearne, *Remarks and Collections*, **IV**, p. 389.
55. Hearne, *Remarks and Collections*, **V**, pp. 97–8; Rogers, *Whigs and Cities*, p. 366; Rogers, 'Popular Protest in Early Hanoverian London'.
56. *CJ*, **XVIII**, p. 227.
57. *Lyme Letters*, p. 264.
58. Rogers, 'Popular Jacobitism in Provincial Context', pp. 127–8; [Atterbury], *English Advice*, p. 27.
59. *CJ*, **XVIII**, p. 227.
60. *Lyme Letters*, p. 264.
61. *The Bristol Riot* (1714), p. 4; Bodl. Lib., Gough Somerset 2, p. 147; Folger Library, Newdigate MS L.c. 3826, 30 Nov. 1714.
62. Briggs, 'Burning of the Meeting House', pp. 71–3.
63. Rogers, 'Riot and Popular Jacobitism', pp. 73–7; Rogers, *Whigs and Cities*, pp. 367–71; Monod, *Jacobitism*, pp. 177, 186–7.
64. Rogers, 'Popular Protest in Early Hanoverian London', p. 271.

65. Monod, *Jacobitism*, p. 228.
66. Rogers, *Whigs and Cities*, p. 366.
67. W. A. Speck, 'The General Election of 1715', *EHR*, **90** (1975), pp. 507–22.
68. Lenman, *Jacobite Risings*, chs 2, 3; Bruce Lenman, 'The Scottish Episcopal Clergy and the Ideology of Jacobitism', in Cruickshanks (ed.), *Ideology and Conspiracy*, pp. 36–48; P. W. J. Riley, *King William and the Scottish Politicians* (Edinburgh, 1979), pp. 3–4, 8–9.
69. Lenman, *Jacobite Risings*, ch. 3 (quote on p. 78); Hopkins, *Glencoe*.
70. P. W. J. Riley, 'The Formation of the Scottish Ministry of 1703', *Scottish Historical Review*, **44** (1965), p. 112.
71. James Halliday, 'The Club and the Revolution in Scotland 1689–90', *Scottish Historical Review,* **45** (1966), p. 143–59; Riley, *King William and the Scottish Politicians*, pp. 30–1, 39–41; Goldie, 'Roots of True Whiggism', pp. 228–9; Hopkins, *Glencoe and the End of the Highland War*, pp. 208–9, 211, 219–21, 273–4, 312, 367; [James Montgomerie], *Great Britain's Just Complaint* (1692), p. 30.
72. Lenman, *Jacobite Risings*, ch. 4. For a discussion of the motives behind the Union, see also: T. C. Smout, 'The Anglo-Scottish Union of 1707', *Economic History Review*, **16** (1964), pp. 455–67; *Idem*, 'Road to Union'; C. A. Whatley, 'Salt, Coal and the Union of 1707: A Revision Article', *Scottish Historical Review*, **66** (1987), pp. 26–45; Riley, *Union of England and Scotland*.
73. Lenman, *Jacobite Risings*, p. 130; McLynn, *Jacobites*, ch. 4; Szechi, *Jacobitism and Tory Politics*, p. 36.
74. Edward Gregg, *Queen Anne* (1980), ch. 14; *Idem*, 'Was Queen Anne a Jacobite', *History*, **57** (1972), pp. 358–75; Szechi, *Jacobitism and Tory Politics*, ch. 9; Bennett, 'English Jacobitism', pp. 142–6; Hill, *Harley*, ch. 14.
75. Lenman, *Jacobite Risings*, chs 5, 6; Bennett, 'English Jacobitism', pp. 147–50; Colley, *In Defiance of Oligarchy*, pp. 29–31; W. A. Speck, *Stability and Strife. England, 1714–1760* (1977), pp. 179–82.

CHAPTER NINE
Conclusion

When considering the first age of party politics in England, it makes sense to treat the years 1660–1715 as a coherent whole. In several respects this period witnessed a working out of the legacy of the Civil War, and many of the issues which were to cause political division in English society under the later Stuarts stemmed from problems which had been left unresolved by the Restoration of 1660. Political parties themselves cannot be said to have existed before 1679. This is not just because the terms Whig and Tory were not to become current usage until the Exclusion Crisis, but because the political polarities which were emerging in the 1660s and 1670s – between Court and Country – did not predict the Whig–Tory split that was to emerge after the Popish Plot. Nevertheless, the issues which created the divide during the Exclusion Crisis were not new; concerns about the prospect of a popish successor, the growth of popery and arbitrary government, and the nature of government in both Church and State, had been creating tensions long before Titus Oates made the revelations which were to precipitate the political crisis at the end of Charles II's reign.

The degree of organisation developed by both Whigs and Tories during the Exclusion Crisis was probably sufficient to allow us to describe them as parties, although opinions on this matter will vary depending upon how strong a definition of 'party' one chooses to adopt. On the other hand, we cannot talk about a party system prior to the Glorious Revolution. The Whig and Tory groupings had come into existence over a particular crisis, and although that crisis was not about just one issue – Exclusion – it was the case that the parties polarised over how they thought the crisis could be resolved. The battle was fought out in three short Parliaments which met between 1679 and 1681, after which politics was driven out-of-doors for the rest of the reign, whilst during the period of the Tory Reaction a successful campaign of legal recriminations taken against the political enemies of the Court meant that the first Whigs as a political movement were almost destroyed. It is only after the Glorious Revolution – with the emergence of regular sessions of Parliament, when much of the ordinary business of government (as opposed to just crisis situations) came to be conducted along party lines, when Parliamentary divisions over a range of issues allow us to see the consistency of party allegiance amongst MPs, and when the parties came to develop fairly sophisticated organisational structures for the pursuit of their political goals – that it is possible to talk of a two-party system.

Throughout this period contemporaries continued to describe partisan conflicts in terms of Civil War allegiances. As late as the end of Anne's reign we still find Whigs and Tories calling each other Cavaliers and Roundheads. Even more common was the language of religious rivalry, with the Tories being styled the High Church or episcopalian party, and the Whigs Presbyterians or fanatics – rivalries which, as protagonists on both sides were quick to point out, had their origins in the religious upheavals of the 1640s and 1650s. Indeed, religious tensions appear to have been at the root of the party divide – not the sole cause, it should be stressed (indeed, much of this book has been concerned with documenting the complex ways constitutional and religious issues interacted), but perhaps the most potent source of conflict, with attitudes towards Dissent (whether one was sympathetic or hostile to Protestant Nonconformists) being one of the strongest predictors of partisan allegiance. These religious tensions go a long way towards explaining why the party divide cut so deep into society: political strife during the first age of party did not just affect the political elite at the centre and a minority of the more affluent and better-educated classes in the localities, but all sorts of people, including those of fairly humble backgrounds, women as well as men, were caught up in the party divide. Once more, in searching for the roots of this divided society we are forced to go back to 1660, and to start with the legacy left by the Civil War and republican experiments.

Stressing these elements of continuity is not to imply that nothing changed. Certainly there were new developments after 1660 which created new sources of political tension and which fed into the emergence of party, whilst over time the parties modified and adapted their positions to cope with new problems, issues and contingencies. The context of the partisan struggle was altered as a result of the Glorious

Revolution of 1688, which modified the relationship between the Crown and Parliament, created new issues for the government as England became involved in major European warfare, and transformed the relationship of the two parties towards the Court as the Whigs came to hold political power for the first time and the Tories discovered what it was like to be in opposition. Under William and Anne a certain degree of ideological adjustment can be detected for both parties, as the Whigs shed their Country wing and became to all intents and purposes a Court party, whilst the Country platform came to be absorbed within Toryism. Nevertheless such changes can be seen as consistent outgrowths of earlier party positions; the Whigs and Tories of Anne's reign remained the recognisable heirs of their namesakes of the Exclusion Crisis.

If it makes sense to see the period 1660–1715 as a coherent whole, what was it that changed with the Hanoverian Succession and the failure of the Jacobite rebellion? It used to be argued that party strife declined rapidly under the first two Georges; that political stability was finally established under Sir Robert Walpole during the 1720s, and by 1733, as Plumb once put it, 'the two-party system was at an end'.[1] Such a view can no longer be so confidently held. Much of the latest research points to the survival of party rivalries well into the 1740s, and even to the survival of an organised Tory party.[2] It would be foolish here to enter the debate over the survival of party under the early Hanoverians: such a subject would require extensive treatment in a separate book. Nevertheless, a number of factors can be briefly identified which explain why it makes sense to stop our account of the first age of party in 1715.

Tory proscription following the Hanoverian Succession and the failure of the 'Fifteen fundamentally changed the context in which political strife was fought out. Although Toryism might have survived as a distinctive ideology, and although a Tory party with its own organisation might have continued to exist, the fact of the matter is that single-party government was established under George I and George II, and there was no swinging back and forth between Tory- and Whig-dominated administrations such as had happened under William and Anne. Moreover, political supremacy and the absence of a strong Tory challenge led to a breakdown in Whig unity; as a result, many of the Parliamentary struggles under the first two Georges saw Court Whigs being opposed by a combination of out-of-office Whigs, Country Whigs, and Tories, to an extent that had never been the norm during the rage of party under the later Stuarts. In such a situation, it was inevitable that political disputes tended to be expressed in the language of Court versus Country rather than in terms of the old party ideologies – even if the use of such rhetoric was forced on people for tactical reasons, and a Tory who espoused Country arguments in order to make common cause with opposition Whigs still remained recognisably Tory at heart.

After 1715 we see a sudden and dramatic shift in the leadership of both parties. The Tories were in some disarray after the association of some of their leaders with Jacobite intrigue: Oxford was impeached and sent to the Tower in 1715, and although eventually acquitted in 1717, his political power was effectively destroyed; Bolingbroke fled abroad, and although he returned in the 1720s to play a leading role in the propaganda campaign against Walpole, he was not allowed to resume his seat in the House of Lords. The Tories did not really begin to recover as a party until Sir William Wyndham's accession to the leadership from about 1724. The Whigs, likewise, lost their great Junto leaders shortly after achieving political ascendancy: Halifax and Wharton died in the spring of 1715, Somers in the spring of the following year. Control of the party passed to a new generation – the third Earl of Sunderland (the most experienced, but somewhat erratic), James Stanhope, Charles Viscount Townshend, and Sir Robert Walpole – who soon fell to competing amongst themselves for political dominance. These new men showed they had neither the time nor the political inclination to instigate a programme of Whig reform; indeed, partly reacting against the Jacobite challenge of 1715, they introduced a number of measures designed to ensure their and the new dynasty's political security which seemed to represent an abandonment of what Whiggery had traditionally stood for. The passage of the Riot Act of 1715, which made assembling for political (as well as other) purposes potentially a capital offence, reveals how far the Whigs had come from the early days when they had actively promoted political demonstrations and deliberately sought an alliance with 'the crowd'. In the following year they passed the Septennial Act, which extended the life of Parliament (including the present one elected under the terms of the Triennial Act) to seven years, a deliberate attempt to shield themselves from the electorate. Again this provides a strong contrast with the first Whigs, who had pressed for frequent Parliamentary elections. Hanoverian Whiggery also became more divorced from association with the cause of Dissent. The Occasional Conformity and Schism Acts, it is true, were repealed in 1719 (although there was some division in the party over this), but the sacramental test for office-holders remained, and the new Whig leadership developed a strong alliance with the Church establishment, which they ensured would be dominated by Whig clergy. We should be careful not to exaggerate the suddenness of the change within Whiggery after 1715; some of these developments – such as the decline of Whig populism, or the association of the Whigs with the Low Church bishops, did have earlier roots. It nevertheless seems clear that the brand of Whiggery we associate with the Walpolean ascendancy of the 1720s and 1730s was very different from that which had been predominant for much of the later-Stuart period.[3]

The argument of this book has forced us to question the appropriateness of seeing either 1660 or 1688 as significant watersheds in English history. Does this mean that we should instead see 1715 – or perhaps 1725 – as the key divide? This search for watersheds is to a large extent misguided; where we place the transformation will depend on the precise question we are asking and what we are seeking to explain. When tracing the various political, constitutional and religious developments which made the age of Walpole very different from the Restoration, we shall discover not one watershed when everything changed at once, but rather a series of discrete chronologies of change. In many respects the Glorious Revolution was a significant landmark: it did alter in certain ways the relationship between the Crown and Parliament, it did guarantee the legislative sovereignty of Parliament, it did establish some limited degree of religious toleration for Protestant Dissenters, and the fact that after 1689 Parliament came to meet on a regular basis each year did significantly alter the context in which politics operated. On the other hand it is difficult to argue that the Revolution resolved the major issues that had been sources of political tension since the Restoration, and it certainly did not restore the political consensus that had eluded the nation in 1660. If we are asking when the issue of who were England's legitimate rulers was resolved, then the answer can clearly not be 1660 or 1688; 1715, with the failure of the Jacobite rebellion might have a strong claim, although there are some scholars who would maintain that Jacobitism continued to be a significant threat thereafter, so that the succession did not finally disappear as a political issue until after the failure of the rebellion in 1745. If we are asking about the growth of political stability in England, and how and when it was established, a multi-layered explanation of different factors – each with their own chronologies – would be required. As Geoffrey Holmes has suggested, the demographic and economic underpinnings of stability were emerging in the second half of the seventeenth century – a stagnant population, years of agricultural plenty and a more buoyant economy meant that there was not the same pressure on resources and scarcity of food and employment which had caused such social distress and serious unrest in the late-Elizabethan and early-Stuart period.[4] The fiscal and institutional roots of stability might be traced back to the 1690s, with the financial revolution (which meant that England's ruling elite finally worked how to finance government effectively) and the growth of bureaucracy (which laid the foundations for firm executive control by the central government which emerged in the eighteenth century). An account of the decline of partisan and religious strife, by contrast, would take us past the Hanoverian Succession – indeed, perhaps a long way past it. It would also take us into a political world which, despite some continuities, was significantly different from that in which party politics first developed, came to fruition, and reached a climax under the later Stuarts.

REFERENCES

1.   Plumb, *The Growth of Political Stability in England 1675–1725*, p. 172.
2.   See in particular: Colley, *In Defiance of Oligarchy: The Tory Party 1714–60*. A useful overview of the current debate over the survival of party under the early Hanoverians can be found in J. V. Beckett, 'Stability in Politics and Society, 1680–1750', in Jones (ed.), *Britain in the First Age of Party, 1680–1750: Essays Presented to Geoffrey Holmes*, pp. 1–18.
3.   Kenyon, *Revolution Principles: The Politics of Party 1689–1720*, ch. 10.
4.   Holmes, 'Achievement of Stability'.

Bibliography

PRIMARY SOURCES

This book has employed a wide variety of primary sources, both printed and manuscript, and full references are given in the notes. In particular, I have drawn heavily on contemporary pamphlet material. Wherever possible, I have given references to the original edition of pamphlets, rather than to a subsequent compilation in which the source appears. Because many of the titles in the seventeenth-century Short Title Catalogue have been microfilmed and are widely available in University libraries, it is often easier for interested scholars to check references against the original on microfilm, than it is to find the tract in a compilation, such as the *Somers Tracts*, which fewer libraries might possess. Anyone wishing to familiarise oneself with the political pamphlets of the late-seventeenth and early-eighteenth century, however, would find the following collected editions indispensable: *State Tracts: Being a Collection of Several Treatises Relating to the Government* (1689); *State Tracts: Being a Farther Collection of Several Choice Treatises Relating to the Government* (1692); *A Collection of State Tracts Published on Occasion of the Late Revolution in 1688 and during the Reign of King William III* (3 vols, 1705–7); *Somers Tracts*, Walter Scott (ed.) (13 vols, 1809–15). Useful modern collections of sources include: Andrew Browning (ed.), *English Historical Documents, 1660–1714* (1953); J. P. Kenyon, *The Stuart Constitution 1603–1688* (Cambridge, 1966); Joan Thirsk (ed.), *The Restoration* (1976); Geoffrey Holmes and W. A. Speck, *The Divided Society: Parties and Politics in England 1694–1716*

(1967). The best bibliography covering the whole period is M. F. Keeler, *Bibliography of British History: Stuart Period, 1603–1714* (Oxford, 1970). This can be updated by reference to *Royal Historical Society: Annual Bibliography of British and Irish History.*

SELECTED SECONDARY SOURCES

Ashcraft, Richard, *Revolutionary Politics and Locke's 'Two Treatises of Government'* (Princeton, 1986)

Beddard, Robert, *A Kingdom Without a King: The Journal of the Provisional Government in the Revolution of 1688* (Oxford, 1988)

Beddard, Robert, *The Revolutions of 1688* (Oxford, 1991)

Behrens, B., 'The Whig Theory of the Constitution in the Reign of Charles II', *Cambridge Historical Journal*, **7** (1941)

Bennett, G. V., 'English Jacobitism, 1710–1715: Myth and Reality', *Transactions of the Royal Historical Society*, 5th series, **32** (1982)

Bennett, G. V., 'King William III and the Episcopate', in G. V. Bennett and J. D. Walsh (eds), *Essays in Modern English Church History* (1966)

Bennett, G. V., *The Tory Crisis in Church and State, 1688–1730: The Career of Francis Atterbury, Bishop of Rochester* (Oxford, 1975)

Bosher, R. S., *The Making of the Restoration Settlement: The Influence of the Laudians, 1649–1662* (1951)

Brewer, John, *Party Ideology and Popular Politics at the Accession of George III* (Cambridge, 1976)

Brewer, John, *The Sinews of Power: War, Money and the English State, 1688–1783* (1989)

Briggs, J. H. Y., 'The Burning of the Meeting House, July 1715: Dissent and Faction in Late Stuart Newcastle', *North Staffordshire Journal of Field Studies*, **14** (1974)

Browning, Andrew, 'Parties and Party Organization in the Reign of Charles II', *Transactions of the Royal Historical Society*, 4th series, **30** (1948)

Browning, Andrew and D. J. Milne, 'An Exclusion Bill Division List', *Bulletin of the Institute of Historical Research*, **23** (1950)

Browning, Andrew, *Thomas Osborne, Earl of Danby and Duke of Leeds, 1632–1712* (3 vols, Glasgow, 1951)

Burton, I. F., P. W. J. Riley and E. Rowlands, *Political Parties in the Reigns of William and Anne: The Evidence of Division Lists*, (*Bulletin of the Institute of Historical Research*, Special Supplement 7, 1968)

Cannon, John (ed.), *The Whig Ascendancy: Colloquies on Hanoverian England* (1981)

Chandaman, C. D., *The English Public Revenue, 1660–1688* (Oxford, 1975)

Clark, J. C. D., *English Society 1688–1832* (Cambridge, 1985)

Clark, J. C. D. 'A General Theory of Party, Opposition and Government, 1688–1832', *Historical Journal,* **23** (1980)

Clark, R., 'Why was the Re-establishment of the Church of England in 1662 Possible? Derbyshire: A Provincial Perspective', *Midland History,* **8** (1983)

Clifton, Robin, *The Last Popular Rebellion: The Western Rising of 1685* (1984)

Coleby, Andrew, *Central Government and the Localities: Hampshire 1649–1689* (Cambridge, 1987)

Colley, Linda, *In Defiance of Oligarchy: The Tory Party 1714–60* (Cambridge, 1982)

Cruickshanks, Eveline (ed.), *By Force or By Default? The Revolution of 1688–1689* (Edinburgh, 1989)

Cruickshanks, Eveline (ed.), *Ideology and Conspiracy: Aspects of Jacobitism, 1689–1759* (Edinburgh, 1982)

Cruickshanks, Eveline, *Political Untouchables: The Tories and the '45* (1979)

Cruickshanks, Eveline and Jeremy Black (eds), *The Jacobite Challenge* (Edinburgh, 1988)

De Beer, E. S., 'Members of the Court Party in the House of Commons 1670–1678', *Bulletin of the Institute of Historical Research,* **11** (1934)

De Krey, Gary S., *A Fractured Society: The Politics of London in the First Age of Party, 1688–1715* (Oxford, 1985)

De Krey, Gary S., 'The London Whigs and the Exclusion Crisis Reconsidered', in Lee Beier, David Cannadine and James Rosenheim (eds), *The First Modern Society: Essays in English History in Honour of Lawrence Stone* (Cambridge, 1989)

De Krey, Gary S., 'Political Radicalism in London after the Glorious Revolution', *Journal of Modern History,* **55** (1983)

Dickinson, H. T., *Liberty and Property: Political Ideology in Eighteenth-Century Britain* (1977)

Dickinson, H. T., 'The Poor Palatines and the Parties', *English Historical Review,* **82** (1967)

Dickson, P. G. M., *The Financial Revolution in England, 1688–1756: A Study in the Development of Public Credit* (1967)

Downie, J. A., 'The Commission of Public Accounts and the Formation of the Country Party', *English Historical Review,* **91** (1976)

Downie, J. A., *Robert Harley and the Press: Propaganda and Public Opinion in the Age of Swift and Defoe* (Cambridge, 1979)

Evans, John T., *Seventeenth-Century Norwich: Politics, Religion and Government, 1620–1690* (Oxford, 1979)

Feiling, Keith, *A History of the Tory Party, 1640–1714* (Oxford, 1924)

Ferguson, William, *Scotland 1689 to the Present* (1968)

Finlayson, Michael G., *Historians, Puritanism and the English Revolution: The Religious Factor in English Politics Before and After the Interregnum* (Toronto, 1983)

Fitts, J. L., 'Newcastle's Mob', *Albion*, **5** (1973)

Fletcher, A. J., 'The Enforcement of the Conventicle Acts 1664–1679', in W. J. Sheils (ed.), *Studies in Church History. 21. Persecution and Toleration* (Oxford, 1984)

Furley, O. W., 'The Whig Exclusionists: Pamphlet Literature in the Exclusion Campaign', *Cambridge Historical Journal*, **13** (1957)

George, M. D., 'Elections and Electioneering, 1678–81', *English Historical Review*, **45** (1930)

Glassey, L., *Politics and the Appointment of Justices of the Peace, 1675–1720* (Oxford, 1979)

Goldie, Mark, 'Edmund Bohun and *Ius Gentium* in the Revolution Debate, 1689–1693', *Historical Journal*, **20** (1977)

Goldie, Mark, 'John Locke and Anglican Royalism', *Political Studies*, **31** (1983)

Goldie, Mark, 'The Revolution of 1689 and the Structure of Political Argument', *Bulletin of Research in the Humanities*, **83** (1980)

Goldie, Mark, 'The Roots of True Whiggism 1688–94', *History of Political Thought*, **1** (1980)

Greaves, Richard L., *Deliver Us from Evil: The Radical Underground in Britain, 1660–1663* (Oxford, 1986)

Greaves, Richard L., *Enemies under his Feet: Radicals and Nonconformists in Britain, 1664–1677* (Stanford, 1990)

Green, I. M., *The Re-establishment of the Church of England 1660–1663* (Oxford, 1978)

Gregg, Edward, *Queen Anne* (1980)

Gregg, Edward, 'Was Queen Anne a Jacobite', *History*, **57** (1972)

Grell, Ole Peter, Jonathan I. Israel and Nicholas Tyacke (eds), *From Persecution to Toleration: The Glorious Revolution and Religion in England* (Oxford, 1991)

Haley, K. H. D., *The First Earl of Shaftesbury* (Oxford, 1968)

Haley, K. H. D., ' "No Popery" in the Reign of Charles II', in J. S. Bromley and E. H. Kossman (eds), *Britain and the Netherlands*, **V** (The Hague, 1975)

Haley, K. H. D., 'Shaftesbury's Lists of the Lay Peers and Members of the Commons, 1677–8', *Bulletin of the Institute of Historical Research*, **43** (1970)

Haley, K. H. D., *William of Orange and the English Opposition 1672–4* (Oxford, 1953)

Halliday, James, 'The Club and the Revolution in Scotland 1689–90', *Scottish Historical Review*, **45** (1966)

Harris, Tim, *London Crowds in the Reign of Charles II: Propaganda and Politics from the Restoration until the Exclusion Crisis* (Cambridge, 1987)

Harris, Tim, 'Was the Tory Reaction Popular?: Attitudes of Londoners towards the Persecution of Dissent, 1681–6', *London Journal*, **13** (1988)

Harris, Tim, Paul Seaward and Mark Goldie (eds), *The Politics of Religion in Restoration England* (Oxford, 1990)

Hayton, David, 'The Country Party in the House of Commons 1698–1699: A Forecast of the Opposition to a Standing Army', *Parliamentary History*, **6** (1987)

Hayton, David, 'Moral Reform and Country Politics in the Late Seventeenth-Century House of Commons', *Past and Present*, **128** (1990)

Henning, Basil Duke (ed.), *The House of Commons, 1660–1690* (The History of Parliament Trust, 3 vols, 1983)

Hill, B. W., *The Growth of Parliamentary Parties, 1689–1742* (1976)

Hill, B. W., *Robert Harley: Speaker, Secretary of State, and Premier Minister* (1988)

Holmes, Geoffrey (ed.) *Britain after the Glorious Revolution, 1689–1714* (1969)

Holmes, Geoffrey, *British Politics in the Age of Anne* (1967, revised edn 1987)

Holmes, Geoffrey, *The Electorate and the National Will in the First Age of Party* (Lancaster, 1976)

Holmes, Geoffrey, *Religion and Party in Late Stuart England* (1975)

Holmes, Geoffrey, 'The Sacheverell Riots: The Crowd and the Church in Early Eighteenth-Century London', in Paul Slack (ed.), *Rebellion, Popular Protest and the Social Order in Early Modern England* (Cambridge, 1984)

Holmes, Geoffrey, *The Trial of Doctor Sacheverell* (1973)

Hopkins, Paul, *Glencoe and the End of the Highland War* (Edinburgh, 1986)

Horwitz, Henry, 'The General Election of 1690', *Journal of British Studies*, **11** (1971)

Horwitz, Henry, *Parliament, Policy and Politics in the Reign of William III* (Manchester, 1977)

Horwitz, Henry, 'Protestant Reconciliation in the Exclusion Crisis', *Journal of Ecclesiastical History*, **15** (1964)

Horwitz, Henry, *Revolution Politicks: The Career of Daniel Finch, Second Earl of Nottingham* (Cambridge, 1968)

Hosford, David H., *Nottingham, Nobles and the North: Aspects of the Revolution of 1688* (Hamden, Conn., 1976)

Hutton, Ronald, *Charles II, King of England, Scotland, and Ireland* (Oxford, 1989)

Hutton, Ronald, *The Restoration: A Political and Religious History of England and Wales, 1658–1667* (Oxford, 1985)

Israel, Jonathan I., *The Anglo-Dutch Moment: Essays on the Glorious Revolution and its World Impact* (Cambridge, 1991)

Jenkins, Geraint H., *The Foundations of Modern Wales: Wales 1642–1780* (Oxford, 1987)

Jenkins, Philip, *The Making of a Ruling Class: The Glamorgan Gentry 1640–1790* (Cambridge, 1983)

Jones, Clyve (ed.), *Britain in the First Age of Party, 1680–1750: Essays Presented to Geoffrey Holmes* (1987)

Jones, Clyve, 'The Parliamentary Organization of the Whig Junto in the Reign of Queen Anne: The Evidence of Lord Ossulston's Diary', *Parliamentary History*, **10** (1991)

Jones, Clyve (ed.), *Party and Management in Parliament, 1660–1784* (Leicester, 1984)

Jones, Clyve and David Lewis Jones (eds), *Peers, Politics and Power: The House of Lords, 1603–1911* (1986)

Jones, G. H., *The Main Stream of Jacobitism* (Cambridge, Massachusetts, 1954)

Jones, J. R., *Charles II: Royal Politician* (1987)

Jones, J. R., *Country and Court: England, 1658–1714* (1978)

Jones, J. R., 'Court Dependents in 1664', *Bulletin of the Institute of Historical Research*, **34** (1961)

Jones, J. R., *The First Whigs: The Politics of the Exclusion Crisis, 1678–83* (Oxford, 1961)

Jones, J. R., 'James II's Whig Collaborators', *Historical Journal*, **3** (1960)

Jones, J. R. (ed.), *The Restored Monarchy 1660–1688* (1979)

Jones, J. R., *The Revolution of 1688 in England* (1972)

Kenyon, J. P., *The Nobility in the Revolution of 1688* (Hull, 1963)

Kenyon, J. P., *Revolution Principles: The Politics of Party 1689–1720* (Cambridge, 1977)

Kenyon, J. P., *Robert Spencer, Earl of Sunderland* (1958)

Kishlansky, Mark A., *Parliamentary Selection: Social and Political Change in Early Modern England* (Cambridge, 1986)

Lacey, Douglas R., *Dissent and Parliamentary Politics in England, 1661–1689* (New Brunswick, 1969)

Landau, Norma, 'Independence, Deference and Voter Participation: The Behaviour of the Electorate in Early Eighteenth-Century Kent', *Historical Journal*, **22** (1979)

Landau, Norma, *The Justices of the Peace, 1679–1760* (Berkeley, 1984)

Lee, Maurice, *The Cabal* (Urbana, 1965)

Lenman, Bruce, *The Jacobite Risings in Britain 1689–1746* (1980)

McInnes, Angus, *Robert Harley: Puritan Politician* (1970)

McLynn, Frank, *The Jacobites* (1985)

Miller, John, *James II: A Study in Kingship* (1978, 2nd edn 1989)

Miller, John, *Popery and Politics in England, 1660–1688* (Cambridge, 1973)

Mitchison, Rosalind, *A History of Scotland* (2nd edn, 1982)

Monod, Paul, 'Jacobitism and Country Principles in the Reign of William III', *Historical Journal*, **30** (1987)

Monod, Paul, *Jacobitism and the English People, 1688–1788* (Cambridge, 1989)

Nenner, Howard, *By Colour of Law: Legal Culture and Constitutional Politics in England, 1660–1689* (Chicago, 1977)

Newman, Aubrey (ed.), *The Parliamentary Lists of the Early Eighteenth Century: Their Compilation and Use* (1973)

Norrey, P. J., 'The Restoration Regime in Action: The Relationship between Central and Local Government in Dorset, Somerset and Wiltshire', *Historical Journal*, **31** (1988)

Plumb, J. H., 'The Growth of the Electorate in England from 1600 to 1715', *Past and Present*, **45** (1969)

Plumb, J. H., *The Growth of Political Stability in England 1675–1725* (1967)

Pocock, J. G. A., *The Ancient Constitution and the Feudal Law: A Study of English Historical Thought in the Seventeenth Century* (Cambridge, 1957, reissue with a retrospect, 1987)

Pocock, J. G. A., *The Machiavellian Moment: Florentine Political Thought and the Atlantic Republic Tradition* (Princeton, 1975)

Reitan, E. A., 'From Revenue to Civil List, 1689–1702: The Revolution Settlement and the "Mixed and Balanced" Constitution', *Historical Journal*, **13** (1970)

Richards, James O., *Party Propaganda Under Queen Anne: The General Elections of 1702–1713* (Athens, Georgia, 1972)

Riley, P. W. J., *King William and the Scottish Politicians* (Edinburgh, 1979)

Riley, P. W. J., *The Union of England and Scotland: A Study in Anglo-Scottish Politics of the Eighteenth Century* (Manchester, 1978)

Roberts, Clayton, 'The Constitutional Significance of the Financial Settlement of 1690', *Historical Journal*, **20** (1977)

Rogers, Nicholas, 'Popular Protest in Early Hanoverian London', in Paul Slack (ed.), *Rebellion, Popular Protest and the Social Order in Early Modern England* (Cambridge, 1984)

Rogers, Nicholas, *Whigs and Cities: Popular Politics in the Age of Walpole and Pitt* (Oxford, 1990)

Rubini, Denis, *Court and Country, 1688–1702* (1967)

Sachse, William L., 'The Mob and the Revolution of 1688', *Journal of British Studies*, **4** (1964)

Schwoerer, Lois G., *The Declaration of Rights, 1689* (Baltimore, 1981)

Schwoerer, Lois G., *'No Standing Armies!': The Anti-Army Ideology in Seventeenth-Century England* (Baltimore, 1974)

Scott, Jonathan, *Algernon Sidney and the English Republic, 1623–1677* (Cambridge, 1988)

Scott, Jonathan, *Algernon Sidney and the Restoration Crisis, 1677–1683* (Cambridge, 1991)

Seaward, Paul, *The Cavalier Parliament and the Reconstruction of the Old Regime, 1661–1667* (Cambridge, 1989)

Seaward, Paul, *The Restoration 1660–1688* (1991)

Slack, Paul (ed.), *Rebellion, Popular Protest and the Social Order in Early Modern England* (Cambridge, 1984)

Smout, T. C., 'The Anglo-Scottish Union of 1707', *Economic History Review*, **16** (1964)

Snyder, Henry L., 'Party Configurations in the Early Eighteenth-Century House of Commons', *Bulletin of the Institute of Historical Research*, **45** (1972)

Speck, W. A., 'The General Election of 1715', *English Historical Review*, **90** (1975)

Speck, W. A., *Reluctant Revolutionaries: Englishmen and the Revolution of 1688* (Oxford, 1988)

Speck, W. A., *Tory and Whig: The Struggle in the Constituencies, 1701–1715* (1970)

Speck, W. A. and W. A. Gray, 'Computer Analysis of Poll Books: An Interim Report', *Bulletin of the Institute of Historical Research*, **43** (1970)

Speck, W. A., W. A. Gray and R. Hopkinson, 'Computer Analysis of Poll Books: A Further Report', *Bulletin of the Institute of Historical Research*, **48** (1975)

Spurr, John, 'The Church of England, Comprehension, and the 1689 Toleration Act', *English Historical Review*, **104** (1989)

Spurr, John, ' "Latitudinarianism" and the Restoration Church', *Historical Journal*, **31** (1988)

Straka, Gerald M., *Anglican Reaction to the Revolution of 1688* (Madison, Wisconsin, 1962)

Swatland, Andrew, 'The Role of the Privy Councillors in the House of Lords, 1660–1681', in Clyve Jones (ed.), *A Pillar of the Constitution: The House of Lords in British Politics, 1640–1784* (1989)

Szechi, Daniel, *Jacobitism and Tory Politics 1710–14* (Edinburgh, 1984)

Townend, G. M., 'Religious Radicalism and Conservatism in the Whig Party under George I: The Repeal of the Occasional Conformity and Schism Acts', *Parliamentary History*, **7** (1988)

Walcott, Robert, *English Politics in the Early Eighteenth Century* (Oxford, 1956)

Watts, Michael R., *The Dissenters: From the Reformation to the French Revolution* (Oxford, 1978)

Western, J. R., *Monarchy and Revolution: The English State in the 1680s* (1972)

Weston, C. C., and J. R. Greenberg, *Subjects and Sovereigns: The Grand Controversy over Legal Sovereignty in Stuart England* (Cambridge, 1981)

Whatley, C. A., 'Salt, Coal and the Union of 1707: A Revision Article', *Scottish Historical Review*, **66** (1987)

Willman, Robert, 'The Origins of "Whig" and "Tory" in English Political Language', *Historical Journal*, **17** (1974)

Witcombe, Denis, *Charles II and the Cavalier House of Commons, 1663–1674* (Manchester, 1966)

Index